# Assist Our Song

*Music Ministries in the Local Church*

Douglas Galbraith

SAINT ANDREW PRESS
Edinburgh

First published in 2021 by
SAINT ANDREW PRESS
121 George Street
Edinburgh EH2 4YN

Copyright © Douglas Galbraith 2021

ISBN 978 1 80083 010 3

Unless otherwise indicated, scripture quotations taken from the New
Revised Standard Version Bible: Anglicized Edition, copyright © 1989,
1995 National Council of the Churches of Christ in the United States
of America. Used by permission. All rights reserved worldwide.
Other versions used are
The Revised English Bible, copyright © Cambridge University Press
and Oxford University Press 1989. All rights reserved.
Bible extracts are from the Authorized Version of the Bible
(The King James Bible), the rights in which are vested in the
Crown, are reproduced by permission of the Crown's Patentee,
Cambridge University Press.

British Library Cataloguing in Publication Data

A catalogue record for this book is available from the British Library.

It is the publisher's policy to only use papers that are natural and
recyclable and that have been manufactured from timber grown
in renewable, properly managed forests. All of the manufacturing
processes of the papers are expected to conform to the environmental
regulations of the country of origin.

Typeset by Regent Typesetting
Printed and bound in the United Kingdom by
CPI Group (UK) Ltd

# Contents

## Skills

## Related Issues

Ye holy angels bright
who wait at God's right hand,
or through the realms of light
fly at your Lord's command,
assist our song,
or else the theme
too high doth seem
for mortal tongue.

*Richard Baxter (1615–91) and*
*John Hampden Gurney (1802–62)*

# Acknowledgements

This book has been years in the making and many people have contributed. I am particularly grateful to those who have represented different denominations in giving advice or in reading chapters: Peter Moger, formerly of the Church of England Liturgical Commission and Canon Precentor of York Minster, now Rector of the Scottish Episcopal congregations on the Isle of Lewis; Sally Harper, Welsh musicologist, honorary research fellow of Bangor University, chaplain to St Asaph Cathedral, and a spiritual director; Laurence Wareing of the Methodist music website, Singing the Faith Plus, who was a conduit into the practice of the Methodist Church throughout the UK; Michael Ferguson, who discussed with me his doctoral thesis on the Roman Catholic Church in Scotland and beyond, and other colleagues and friends in that Church; John P. Kitchen MBE (Edinburgh City Organist; director of music at Old St Paul's Episcopal Church, Edinburgh; President of the Incorporated Association of Organists) who acted as mentor to the chapters on organ skills; and Alan Buchan (organ adviser, Scottish Federation of Organists, and archivist, Scottish Historic Organs Trust) for his help in the chapter about the organ as instrument.

Others have allowed me to build on their work: Suzanne Butler (working with praise bands and instrumental groups), Brigitte Harris (organist, choir director, and teacher of organ), Ian McCrorie MBE, d. 2019 (choral director, Scottish Festival Singers and other leading choirs), Marion Dodd (minister, choral director and leader of workshops with congregations), Walter Blair BEM (organist of Holy Trinity Church, St Andrews, on practising and preparing organ music), and Graham Maule

(d. 2019), artist, hymn writer, and member of the Wild Goose Resource Group (using technology in worship).

Others have shared their expertise and provided me with information: Duncan Sneddon (Gaelic psalm books), Michael Harris (St Giles' Cathedral, Edinburgh), Phill Mellstrom (contemporary worship music), Anne Harrison (resources), Iain McLarty (resources), Nigel Uden (former Moderator of the United Reformed Church General Assembly), and Nicola Lawrence (organist and member of the RSCM Scotland Committee) who made suggestions as to content. These I thank, along with others who at various times have shared information or offered views and encouragement.

I am also most grateful to John Harper who, as professor in the School of Music and director of the International Centre for Sacred Music Studies, Bangor University (North Wales), supported and supervised the studies I undertook there, of which the results surface from time to time in these pages.

I am particularly indebted to my wife, Daphne Audsley, who closely read several drafts and made perceptive comments and suggestions for both content and presentation.

# Preface

We are in the early stages of a profound church renewal.[1]

This rather unexpected claim, when many prefer to talk of managing decline, appears in the opening pages of a book for those whose ministry is the leading of worship. *Assist our Song* is for those others whose ministry is leading and making the music in the local church, but the remark is equally apt.

For the music-makers, this is also a time of renewal, adjusting to fewer resources but seeking new strategies to meet greater opportunities. There can be bewilderment about the volume of new writing, frequently found online, and the need to navigate a good deal of hurt and resistance when changes are proposed. There is a revaluing of the traditional, but some unease about how the old and the new may marry.

The author of the book quoted observes that in a time of church renewal, questions begin at a fairly superficial and manageable level, and then almost imperceptibly each problem and question invites us deeper and deeper into the heart of the church where all roots are intertwined. The solution, he suggested, does not come from clever techniques and new programmes; nothing less than conversion and total commitment is required.

Worship and its music is one of the strongest roots upon whose nourishment Christian people draw. The church which looks to its roots in our day needs to find an increased commitment from its music-makers, new skills, fresh energy, a deeper understanding of worship, more imagination, greater risk-taking, especially in the local parishes throughout the land who are nearest to the challenges to existing patterns of church life and worship which arise from changes in public life: in how people communicate, how they understand belonging, and the multifarious ways they approach matters of inner health and the life of the spirit.

*Assist our Song* explores the ministries carried out by directors of music and their associates, and the ministry of choirs and other groups of singers and players. It is less obvious that the congregation have a music ministry, or that the clergy also have ministerial duties and responsibilities of a musical nature. Yet these two categories are included also, and what they have to offer is of high importance at this particular time.

The book from which the opening quotation comes is arrestingly titled *Strong, Loving, and Wise* and is by Robert Hovda, who was an American Roman Catholic priest. Yet in spite of the denominational divide, this particular representative of a Reformed branch of the church had the uncanny feeling of meeting someone who knows us better than we know ourselves. This should not be a surprise. It is in the areas of worship, liturgy and music that the churches come nearest to experiencing the unity for which Jesus prayed (John 17:21), and the present book has drawn from the experience of all denominations and seeks to share the results with all.

If this book has an inspiration, it was a volume published by the Church of Scotland in 1932, *Manual of Church Praise* – which must have been widely used if the fact that no fewer than six copies have accumulated on the writer's shelves nearly a century later is any indication. As the title suggests, it was intended as a practical guide, including necessary background, for the music-makers of the church, with the congregation firmly included. It is hoped that the present volume will also be of practical use to their successors in any branch of the church.

*Douglas Galbraith*

### Note

1 Hovda, Robert, 1981, *Strong, Loving, and Wise: Presiding in Liturgy*, Collegeville, MN: The Liturgical Press.

# Worship and Music

# Word, Water, Wine and Bread

## *Understanding Worship*

The church bell has fallen silent, the last worshippers have clattered into their place, the beadle hoists the Bible on to the lectern, the minister climbs to the pulpit, the organ voluntary reaches its final cadence. There is a hush of expectation ...

(*or perhaps*) ...

In the ancient cathedral, the organ swells and the congregation rises to sing an opening hymn as the procession of choir and clergy weave their way to the chancel and settle in their stalls, and a collect harvests the diverse thoughts of the people present ...

In the sanctuary of the modern, multi-purpose church centre, a praise band strikes up as the people assemble, excitement builds through songs and choruses until, at a signal from the worship leader, the sound of praise gradually sinks to a prayerfully reiterated refrain ...

In a west Highland glen, the soberly dressed elders and congregation face down the path as the minister approaches, greets them, and leads the way as they shuffle in silence into the church ...

On the village green, a handful of people slip through the slanted dawn light to their seats in a side chapel for early Communion, kneel and bow their heads in prayer ...

Round a table in a café, the news and the greetings over, a Bible is put in the midst, and a discussion begins which becomes thoughtful, and then prayerful ...

At Messy Church, after time spent exploring a Bible story through different crafts, chairs scrape as children and adults converge for a time of story, prayer and song ...

In a Zambian village, one choir after another engages the gathering people in waves of song until it is sensed that the time has come to begin ...

*... so many approaches to worship. The curtain has risen. What now?*

In a broadcast essay late one night on Radio 3, theatre director Bartlett Sher was revealing the secrets of his trade.[1] When people visit a gallery or go to a concert or the theatre, what they are doing, he said, is not just seeking entertainment but looking for something additional in their lives, something *more*. They want to be set free, they want to break through into another world, they want – and he used the word – to *transcend*. As directors rehearse with a cast they wrestle to unveil what he called, in a phrase from the poet Edmund Spenser, the 'inward sound' of each person in the audience. A well-made play has rhythms and movement which keep us on the edge of our seats, and the director works with these rhythms, getting exactly the right tempo so that they touch into and overlap with the rhythms of those in the audience. The hope is that, with their own inward sound released, people will find themselves pulled into a new rhythm, one that is beyond the clamorous and dissonant rhythms of multi-layered contemporary existence.

Could this describe our expectations of worship? We may come seeking sanctuary, a place of peacefulness amid the pressures, but also the possibility of peace and reconciliation in human society which is declared and enacted in worship; we may be uncomfortably aware how much store we place on things that are expendable and peripheral and come to church to rediscover and embrace the essentials; we worry about the masks we are so often forced to wear to cope with the range of relationships which must be kept up; we feel shame for how disconnected our private lives can become from the issues affecting the public life of the world and its need; we are exercised about the rise of extremism, the dangers of social media, the climate emergency, poverty, and the seeming impossibility of ending conflict and oppression. So we seek an experience of things falling into place, where sense is made, where hope is found. No – more than that. We hope, gathered together in God's name, that God will be in the midst, that we will be in God's company, that we will encounter God, that God will be with us here and when we go to live our faith in the world.

## Worship's palette

How might this come about? How is the inward sound generated that finds an answering echo within us? We think of worship as the one thing that is fixed and unchanging. In fact it has proved itself one of the most resilient of phenomena, adapting to enfold every era and every human experience. It has no equal in its ability to reach and embrace the whole human being, body and soul. To this end, over the centuries worship has accumulated an unusually generous palette. It is too easily assumed, as we examine denominational service books and authorised liturgies, and indeed as we listen from week to week, that worship is spoken text – that, like some hymn books, it is 'words only', or at least 'words mainly'. Worship is written and then spoken. This would be to overlook the rubrics ('red' type or italics) telling us, 'do this', 'go there') that scatter the pages. It would also be failing to notice what is actually going on as we worship, not just around us but through our senses. It requires a whole range of 'media' to shape an act of worship.

There is the *visual*, the impact of our surroundings, the curve of a roofbeam, the beauty of embroidered pulpit fall or table frontal; the well-crafted furnishings and how they symbolise stages and events in the course of worship; the colours that

spill on the ground from intricate window glass; clergy vestments and people's Sunday best which dignify the moment. In
some traditions there are icons – paintings which are frozen
prayer and which, when contemplated, draw out the people's
own prayer; statues which bring to mind stories from Scripture and the saints, which put our own attempts at prayer and
service in a strengthening mould.

There is *movement*, at the entry of the choir, the presentation
of the offering, the going forward to the table at Communion
or assembling at the font, processing on Palm Sunday or at
thanksgiving for harvest; *gesture* in the raised hand for benediction or the clasping of hands in petition, the sign of the
cross, or simply as we greet fellow worshippers; *posture* as we
stand to sing, kneel or bow in prayer; *touch* as we exchange the
Peace, receive the bread from a neighbour or take the wafer on
the tongue. There are *olfactory* experiences, the homely smell
of the loaf, the tang of wine, the wafting incense, even the
musty odour of sanctity that for so many defines the church.
And of course there is the important place given to the *hearing*
as the Word of God is read, directly from Scripture but also
married with our own experiences and situations in sermon or
homily.

This palette, like the painter's, is not the picture itself. Worship
does not consist of these things; rather they are only the surface
of a deep running flow whose current is the God who reaches
out to creation, and we respond – perhaps, like the leaping
salmon, making something of great beauty. The various media
and artefacts that give worship form must be designed to open
both sides of the dialogue. The language must be such that lies
between speaking in tongues and mystical silence and must partake of both. Put another way, to be capable of such two-way
traffic, a certain transparency is desirable in what we say and
do, unclogged by other agendas – the selfish sounds of a desire
to impress or win acclaim – or by off-the-peg forms and phrases
with other messages still clinging to them. This is not the same
as arguing for more silence in worship, albeit very necessary,
but rather to craft the media of worship in such a way that
there is space and silence within them and through them.

Through these varied media which carry our adoration and petition we hear in return the divine voice. The line of a hymn suddenly strikes us with a truth, or a gesture warms us as we feel loved and accepted, or a striking stained glass window uncovers for us beauty in ourselves that we have suppressed, or a memory of another act of worship is awakened in well-known prayer words or musical cadence and re-sets our wavering discipleship – each a whisper of God. The idea that God speaks through the media of our worship suggests that we are not mere observers but in divine company. As the church reflected on the experience of being renewed by its worship age after age, it raided the limits of understanding, interrogated Scripture, struggled in prayer and strove in debate (the birth of a doctrine is rarely casual but occurs out of a driven need to capture, nurture, and share a precious truth), and uncovered the insight that in our prayer we were echoing the intercessions of Jesus Christ, our great High Priest, at the throne of grace. That our lips should move in time with Christ's suggests a presence with us – Christ with us intimately as two or three gather.

Having grown up with a more distant God, many find it difficult to comprehend such an intimacy. That this has been the church's belief from earliest times is illustrated by a helpful definition of hierarchy from a Lutheran liturgiologist.[2] In our mind, he says, we spell it *higher-archy*. But the word means in Greek 'having a sacred origin', and rather than the congregation being distanced from God, say, by a layer of ordained clergy, it actually suggests the most intimate connectedness possible. Dionysius, the sixth-century Syrian writer who coined the phrase, said hierarchy was to enable human beings to be as like God as possible and to be one with God. A modern writer puts it: 'The church in her liturgy partakes of the life of the divine society of the three persons in God'.[3] Is this perhaps what is meant in that puzzling passage in John 17:20–23 where Jesus prays that his disciples 'may ... also be in us', as the Father is in him, and he in the Father, embraced within the blessed Trinity?

## When we cannot worship

Yet these factors in themselves do not guarantee a full experience of worship. One obstacle is identified in another theatrical parallel. Recently the Church Service Society[4] held a consultation whose main speaker was Icelandic theatre director and playwright, Kolbrún Björt Sigfúsdóttir, who asked participants what they hoped for when they went to the theatre. We all gave our answers, but her own answer was different still: that we go to the theatre to *recognise ourselves*, to find our experiences and feelings represented in the action of the play. How well do we enable people to recognise themselves in worship?

People worship first of all not with liturgies but with who they are. Worship fails for anyone if they have to say: I might as well not have been there, I did not recognise myself. This may happen when the forms worship takes become hardened and squeeze people out. They may have come to lack the flexibility that can stretch to encompass a person's whole experience of life (including the life of the spirit). Inclusiveness in worship is not just a matter of language. The culprit is often not the orders for worship themselves but the idiom of church life: how we greet each other, the social smiles, the sort of conversation topics which are allowed to be broached, the level at which we permit involvement with each other. There is often a self-satisfaction in our life together that limits the reach of our worship, which is threatened by those 'not like us', or who are tainted with misfortune, or whose style and experience of life is different, often because circumstances compel them to live this way. Pharisees and Publicans alike may not feel welcome![5]

Even regular churchgoers may feel 'excluded' at times. You slip into your usual pew but this week you avoid the eyes of your neighbour. Something has happened to cause you pain and grief: the loss of a job, injury to someone close to you, betrayal by someone you love, news that you have a serious health problem. You may be angry with those who are the cause – even angry with God that it should happen to you. But this is church and you put a brave face on it. You leave at the end feeling your anger and sorrow have not been addressed. Or you greet your fellow churchgoers as normal but, yet again, you wonder why they should be so friendly to you. Your feelings of inadequacy, even shame, never really go away: the unshakeable belief that you are socially awkward, unintelligent and unattractive. You may even have absorbed a prevailing disapproval or discomfort with the social group or cultural background you come from. There may be a real cause for shame: you feel you have put off facing a difficulty, or that you have let someone down, or carried out a task incompetently.

Our liturgies provide for the whole gamut, from deep penitence to glad thanksgiving, but in practice we often feel at one remove: a list of sins not quite ours; intercession for situations which feel as remote from us after as before the prayer; thanksgiving for the more obvious blessings; benedictions which brush our foreheads without healing our souls. This is particularly so in congregational gatherings where the style of worship is relentlessly upbeat. There is surely truth in the belief that our proper stance in worship is joy and humble acceptance before the sovereignty and providence of God, but the psalmists also show the honesty that acknowledges one's anger, bewilderment and doubt.

Another possible obstacle is that changing circumstances mean that we are trying to pack too much into the Sunday service. In a paper to the Church Service Society, Michael Perham (later, bishop of Gloucester) suggested that many congregations now try to incorporate all that was formerly spread across seven days into one hour on Sunday morning – worship, education, outreach, the creation of fellowship. (We may observe how today it is becoming more common to begin worship with a focus on the human community gathered in worship as The Welcome takes pride of place, our 'good mornings' establishing who we are before whose we are, and it is often difficult to move from this warmth of togetherness to an awe in God's presence – however glad we are to have recovered this sense of fellowship.) A similar analysis is offered from a Catholic perspective by North American liturgical scholar John Baldovin SJ, who suggests that, given the frenetic pace of life in post-industrial society, the main weekend service will most likely be the only time that most Christians come into formal contact with the church, and so the opportunity is taken of getting everything in. The problem is, he suggests, that once liturgy becomes an instrument to achieve other ends it loses its fundamental *raison d'être*. Former Uniting Church in Australia president D'Arcy Wood notes that this trend may be behind disagreements and dilemmas about music. These different aspects of church life potentially drew on a variety of idioms of music and of song collections, and we often find ourselves trying to compress this spread of sounds into that one hour whether suitable or not. In our attempt to incorporate 'a variety of desirable things', he concludes, we can forget that 'worship is attentiveness, waiting, listening, meditating, seeking to hear what God says to us'.[6]

Another factor which can contribute to a lack of engagement is also a result of social change. It relates to how worship is approached. Today, we can jump in a car and be in our pew within ten minutes. In times past, the transition from life to worship was literal in that people had to cross long distances on foot. The effort involved in getting to the place where worship was to take place would give it a special profile. People today particularly value the worship when they have travelled to a shrine or sacred destination: Taizé, Walsingham, Lourdes, Iona or other centres, or indeed events like Greenbelt and Spring Harvest or an international ecumenical assembly. They find that worship takes on new layers of meaning because of the journey and on the expectation of arrival, not to mention the companions on the way. The fast-increasing number of pilgrim routes in our day may recover this dimension for many more people.

In some contexts the liturgy of life merges with the liturgy of worship, as in the monastic communities. In Iona Abbey today, worship takes place consciously in the context of the day's work. George MacLeod, founder of the Iona Community, in bringing together young ministers and stonemasons to live in community and rebuild the historic Abbey, designed the day so that work and worship were one single weave. As one of the young ministers, I knew the power of moving straight from morning worship to stone and cement-mixers and the co-operation and camaraderie of the day, and the gratitude and relief in entering the cool of the Abbey Church in the evening after work was ended. You don't need to belong to a religious community to find in your work, your duties and responsibilities a context, resource and launch-pad for worship, but it may need weekday focus in, say, a pattern of prayer and reading.

Over the centuries other rituals and practices have grown, themselves small liturgies, which have helped make the transition from the midst of life to the heart of worship: a period of fasting, a visit to the confessional the evening before, daily devotions or the daily office, a weekday Bible study or prayer group, studying the lectionary in advance. And for many still, on the morning itself, the self-imposed discipline that from first rising seeks a quietness of demeanour which continues through to the time and place of worship, taking one's place without gossip or noise.

There are also the rituals that lead directly into the actual event. In some traditions there is the reverencing of the holy table or host when entering and leaving the sanctuary. Robing clergy may recite prayers over each item of dress. There are prayers with the choir, prayer with the preacher or presiding minister. And there are the bells! – in these days often common ground between churchgoers and those who have ceased to attend but whose enthusiasm and skills continue to serve the church. Bells can begin the final approach to worship, not least when a peal of bells intensify their pattern as the time approaches. St Salvator's, the university church of St Andrews, possessed two ancient bells, Katherine (first cast 1460) and Elizabeth (1520) (four more have now been added). The two would ring together, but shortly before the service began one fell silent leaving the other to continue alone. In my time as the university's chaplain, waiting in the quadrangle to preside at the weekly university service, this moment was palpable, almost ominous, a reminder of one of the chants from medieval liturgies for the consecration of a church, *Terribilis est locus iste* ('Fearsome is this place'). We can enter church too casually, treating it as any other human space and forgetting that to prepare to meet a God who is Judge as well as Shepherd is not only momentous but risky: we might be called to account, or led out on to a new way.

These examples suggest that worship is not so much an activity, more a disposition, a readiness, a state of mind, a habit of soul, which nevertheless finds its highest expression when we gather with others in worship, but already begun before a word is said or a note is struck.

## Word, water, wine and bread

The shape of worship which is common to most mainstream churches has two 'arcs', one culminating in the preaching of the Word, the other in the sacrament of Holy Communion. (We might say also that there is a third arc that begins with the Dismissal and curves out and over into the life of the world.) Both have this in common, that in their different ways they 'make Christ present'. The sermon sets out to make vivid the Christ of the Gospels, filled out by the Old Testament backdrop and the aftermath of the Acts and the Epistles, all the while playing a light on the world we inhabit and the life we live. It is sometimes thought that different church traditions 'major' on one or the other, sermon or sacrament. Now, however, it is widely accepted across the church that these two pinnacles of worship work together to enable us to recognise the presence of Christ with us. As Karl Barth wrote: 'Preaching is a commentary on and an interpretation of the sacraments',[7] while John Calvin observed that 'the sacraments have the same office as the Word of God: to offer and to set forth Christ to us, and in him the treasures of heavenly grace.'[8]

It is remarkable how simply the momentous event of Holy Communion is experienced compared with the complexities that too often burden the church. With a beauty we do not often expect in reports to synods and assemblies, the Committee of Forty, one of the commissions to have tackled the need for change in the Church of Scotland, wrote that the difficulties being experienced in our time were:

not a disaster for the church but ... a God-given opportunity to discard the inessentials and concentrate on the vital things by which alone any church really lives: the power of the Risen Christ bringing life out of death and, in material terms, the water, the bread, the wine and the book, which cost us little and give us everything we need.[9]

These symbols, buttressed with word and ritual, make for a powerful combination that appeals both to the understanding and the senses, powerful enough to incorporate us into long-ago events and a future hope which otherwise would be beyond our grasp, and help us enter into a holy mystery. Robert Bruce, an early Reformation minister of Edinburgh's High Kirk, now St Giles' Cathedral, expressed this memorably by saying how in these symbols you get 'a better grip of Christ'. Central in the rich Communion prayer is the key word, 'remembering', not here meaning call to mind but more like renewing in our experience. The name for this section is *anamnesis* when the great act of redemption is recalled and replayed in the contemporary setting and we are placed within this reality, no longer a distant memory.

What is perhaps less familiar to us is the idea that this Eucharist (a term now being shared across the church with its meaning of thanksgiving) is not just to build up the church but is an agent of transformation for society at large. At first sight, it is difficult to see how this act behind closed doors consisting of words and rituals has any reference beyond the walls. Sister Mary McGann is an American liturgical scholar who, over a period closely observing an Afro-American worshipping community, noted a correlation between what was done on Sunday and how the group lived with and through each other from day to day. Elders and children, women and men, young adults, all were accepted in an 'order' that did not flow from patterns of wider society but from valuing the gifts and visions of each member. In this, she said, they modelled the 'redemptive re-ordering of relationships' which is one of the characteristics of the Kingdom of God and this in turn empowered people to work for re-ordered relationships in wider society.[10]

This comes about because of the rituals in worship. Ritual is an unhelpful word to some, but what it means is a group of words and actions which fit together to fill out meaning or intention – like the water of baptism with which words are combined as part of the action. McGann explains how we used to understand the power of rituals as something constant and repeated (indeed 'vain repetition' used to be the charge against them) but have now realised that the real effect comes from the way we adapt and *perform* them. In our performing we are *trans*formed, in the way a new habit can make us a different person. Whether it's sharing the peace, or passing the wine, or gathering the children, or helping the elderly to their place, or reverently processing with the Bible, we are at the same time modelling our conduct outwith the liturgy.

Just as our engagement in the rituals of worship offer to transform us, and then, through us, the human society beyond, so it is with the symbols at its heart, the bread and wine. David Grumett invites us to approach these elements not just symbolically but aware of the realities that have shaped the symbols.[11] He finds in the traditions of the church much recorded reflection not just on the finished work but arising from the processes by which bread and wine come about; in the case of the bread, for example: sowing, winnowing, crushing and grinding into flour, moistening and blending, leaven, oil, the energy of the baker and her intimate contact with the materials, the transforming fire of the oven – documenting how all of these have been seen by earlier theologians as commentary in some way on the redemption in Christ of the matter of creation. Within this are raised issues relating to our living in community, social justice, the care of the earth and its people.

## Doxology

When the New Testament wants to capture the essence of the church as it takes shape, it uses the word *koinonia* and its derivatives, which means community or communion. This has been a starting point for many of the ecumenical dialogues in recent decades and in one landmark conversation between Anglicans and Roman Catholics has resulted in a memorable and much-quoted description of the church as the 'sign, instrument, and foretaste' of the promised reconciled community, the Kingdom of God.[12] Of this culmination, the church, as it proclaims in its speech and life what are the characteristics of the new community, is a *sign*; through its outward movement in mission and service it is an *instrument*; showing in its life together an outcrop of the Kingdom in the present age, and in pointing to other manifestations, it is a *foretaste*. Yet the mystery of the Kingdom of God, here now but still to come, is a concept so far beyond our imagining and grasp that Scripture can only express it as song, the song of angels round the throne of God singing 'Holy, holy, holy', 'Praise and honour', 'Blessing and glory and wisdom', songs now captured in our worship as the recurring doxology (in such words as 'Glory be to the Father ...'). It is doxology, 'words of glory', which is at the heart of worship, the praise given by creation to its Creator. It is doxology also which is at the heart of the Christian life. To live with thanksgiving colours one's life and opens our hearts both to others and to the Holy Spirit in our midst. When the church gathers to worship, the whole of creation is giving praise to its Creator. In the giving of thanks (Eucharist), and in living thankful lives, is revealed the transformation that a perspective of gratitude brings to life together.

## Notes

1 BBC Radio 3, 10 July 2013.

2 Fagerberg, David W., 2016, 'Liturgical theology', in Alcuin Reid (ed.), *T&T Clark Companion to Liturgy*, London: Bloomsbury T&T Clark, pp. 10f.

3 Michel, Virgil, OSB, quoted David Fagerberg, 'Liturgical theology', p. 11.

4 A society founded in Scotland in 1865 for the study and renewal of worship.

5 Luke 18:9–14 (Authorized or King James Version). In modern versions, this is translated as the parable of the Pharisee and the Tax Collector.

6 Wood, D'Arcy, 'Sunday worship can suffer from overload'. Report of address given to the National Consultation on Worship, Adelaide, January 1982, in the Queensland Synod of the Uniting Church in Australia newspaper, *Life and Times*, n.d.

7 Barth, Karl, 1965, *Prayer and Preaching*, London: SCM Press, p. 75.

8 Calvin, John, 1961, *Institutes of the Christian Religion*, Book IV, xiv, 17, London: SCM Press, p. 1292.

9 *Reports to the General Assembly of the Church of Scotland*, 1975, p. 511.

10 McGann, Mary E., 2002, *Exploring Music as Worship and Theology: Research in Liturgical Practice*, Collegeville, MN: The Liturgical Press, pp. 38–9.

11 Grumett, David, 2016, *Material Eucharist*, Oxford: Oxford University Press. The same kind of analysis has been applied to the wine of the Eucharist by a theologian from a family of vintners: Gisela H. Kreglinger, 2016, *The Spirituality of Wine*, Grand Rapids, MI: Eerdmans.

12 Anglican-Roman Catholic Dialogue, 'Church as Communion', in Gregory Gros, Harding Meyer, and William G. Rusch (eds), 2000, *Growth in Agreement II*, Geneva: WCC Publications and Grand Rapids, MI: Eerdmans, p. 334, para. 24.

# 2

# 'Get Me a Musician!'

## *How Music Relates to Worship*

A moment remembered in 2 Kings chapter 3 is the incident in which Jehoram, king of Israel, facing an acute water shortage for his army and animals, calls on the prophet Elisha to give him guidance from God. Elisha's first step is to issue the order: 'Get me a musician!' The account continues: 'And then, while the musician was playing, the power of the LORD came on him' (v. 15). Was this a trick of the trade, a diversion while the prophet got his act together? Or was it intended to defuse the situation and restore a sense of proportion through a cooling-off period of mutual meditation? Perhaps a bit of both, but the narrative claims more for the music than that. In the end it was neither manipulative nor therapeutic but resulted in the power of the Lord entering the situation. For prophet, king and his nervous advisers, the music reached deep into the soul, renewing and empowering body and mind, touching the place where humanity encounters the mystery of its origin, its existence and its destination, the common ground where divine and human dance together.

In the previous chapter, we reflected on the way the media of worship gave into a space in which the assembled people might hear as well as tell. Perhaps more than any other medium, music possesses this quality. This high calling of music was acknowledged in *Sacrosanctum Concilium*, one of the documents emanating from the Second Vatican Council, when in its chapter on Sacred Music it describes the music of the church as a treasure greater even than any other art.[1] What is it about music that wins it this high place?

One characteristic is that music has grown with Christian worship as it has taken shape from the beginning. Music is not there to embellish or decorate, or to add something otherwise lacking. You might say that language and ritual carry within them their own music, that there is music in worship before a note is heard. Words polished by long use sound in our souls like a melody. In a spoken dialogue between presiding minister and gathered people the alternating sounds contrast in cadence. In our movements and gestures, dance is not far below the surface. Even the silence holds music, because music comes from silence and leads to silence, and itself is a mix of sound and silence. Therefore, you could say that music is not something to be added but one of the many registers in which worship comes to expression. To discuss church music is also to discuss worship.

This is reflected in the strand of music which later became known as the *jubilus*. It is perhaps no surprise to learn that in the history of church music there have been times when clergy and councils have tried to bring musicians into line! The musicians were more than a match, creating music where they could get away with it. Most notable was the 'tail' of the Alleluia, the chant which greeted the Gospel, where the last syllable was extended into sheer joyous melody. Fr Joseph Gelineau, well known for his innovative psalm settings which have captured something of the original Hebrew rhythms for modern worshippers, once devised a diagram to show the gradation as words and music merge into each other – ordinary speech, moving through proclamation, meditation (psalmody), chant, hymn, acclamation (a musical shout), finally becoming the *jubilus*, pure vocalisation (like singing in tongues).[2] Sometimes words dominate, as musical sound 'heightens and formalises speech', while at the other end of the spectrum text melts into music. Somewhere in the middle is the setting of words. But here too, text and music do not remain distinct from each other; the act of singing 'enlarges both' so that there is a new, single unity.[3] Usually, the process is that the composer listens to the words and 'releases' their music. The Alleluia-extensions are an example of the opposite, where music has birthed the words. For to help singers remember these new melodies, which were in extended phrases and not easy to remember, words were written, one syllable to a note, giving rise to the popular form of the sequence, like 'Stabat Mater', 'Veni Sancte Spiritus', and 'Dies irae'. There, music came first and the words followed as music spilled over from the liturgy.

The second source of music's unique contribution comes from its being an integral part of being human. Augustine asked, 'What does singing in jubilation signify?' and answered: 'to realise that words cannot communicate the song of the heart', an inner song which is more intuitive than intellectual.[4] An eighteenth-century commentator saw this form of pure music as having its counterpart in the call/song of the agricultural worker alone in the fields. Nearer our time, the wordless and non-rhythmical 'holler' of the enslaved African-American cotton worker, expressing both pain and hope, was thought to have meshed with the metrical hymn to produce the free, improvisatory form of music we know as jazz.

Music is made as human beings face the mystery of existence, who we are, why we are here, our fear, our complaint, our hope, and our love also. Music is perhaps an earlier version of language than speech, expressing feelings or giving signals. Some suggest that music originates in each person as the infant picks up the prosody of the words in a parent's voice. Primitive peoples have expressed musically the narrative of their origins, like the indigenous Australians described by Bruce Chatwin in *The Songlines* as 'singing up the landscape' and the creator-beings who peopled it in the time of Dreaming – making in effect a musical map. Music also accompanied and regulated human tasks: sea shanties to keep a pulling rhythm when hoisting a sail, or the waulking songs of the Outer Hebrides where the dunt of the rhythm enabled the women round the table to work the tweed. Our whole experience of being conscious and relating to our fellow human beings has a musical quality. So music wells up both from the worship and from the worshipper. What are the ways in which musical sounds point to the mystery within?

## 1 Music creates a listening community

It does seem that human beings don't just like to sing but *need* to sing. (Perhaps it is this that compels people to risk their reputations and their peace of mind by taking part in television talent shows.) Singing marks us as creatures in community. As we sing we search for other voices to sound with; singing carries within it a desire for connectedness. In the fourth century, Basil the Great wrote enthusiastically about the 'harmonious melodies of the Psalms', celebrating their role in calling together the worshipping assembly:

> a psalm forms friendships, unites the divided, mediates between enemies; a psalm, a musical word is the voice of the church. The singing of psalms brings love, the greatest of good things ... uniting the people in the symphony of a single choir.[5]

Basil was drawing on an understanding of music that we do not now share, that the integrity of the universe derived from a mixture of maths and music, and this heavenly harmony affected life on earth, but this in no way discredits his observation.

The musicologist Walter Ong builds on a more contemporary scientific basis in his explanation as to how music 'unites groups of living beings as nothing else does'.[6] When people enter a church building (or indeed a train or other space where people gather), they will leave room between themselves and the next person. Only when it becomes necessary will they move closer, but even then there is a limit, a tolerance beyond which people are uncomfortable. John Bell, addressing singing in church, proposes an intriguing rule of thumb that 'if you sit more than three feet (91.44 centimetres) away from someone you'll not sing in case they hear you. If you sit closer than three feet you will sing because you hear them.'[7] From Ong we learn why we are willing to sing in close proximity with others whom we might not know well, if at all. He notes that distance tolerated in terms of sound is very different from touch. Sound allows access to an individual's inner self

without physical invasion, since it binds 'interiors' together.[8]
Sound doesn't jostle or threaten. You can sing with people
before you can talk to them. People can therefore explore in
song issues and feelings they would be embarrassed or afraid
to talk about. Folk song, say, allows someone to express loss
or sorrow, or the tenderness of a loving relationship, to lament
or to celebrate, to mention the unmentionable, to taste the
laughter you dare not risk. We need others so that we may
find ourselves. For before the Christian faith is personal it is
communal. 'We, who are many, are one body in Christ, and
individually we are members one of another' (Rom. 12:4–5).
We do not seek out Christ but are rather brought by Christ
himself into relationship with him. The gifts of the Spirit are
channelled through members to the whole body. Music is such
a gift, embracing all the gathered people as one.

Characteristic of this body is that it is a *listening community*,
one which combines to reach into an encounter with the divine
with a resonance that is not usually available to an individual.
Do we not have to listen to others to keep in time, to keep on
the right pitch, to start and finish together? The necessity for
listening is even sharper with styles of music which depend
on more than one unit for their texture. Antiphonal music,
where singers on one side of a church answer those on the
other, has returned to the worship of all denominations today
in the form of call-and-response music from other cultures; the
return of hymns or songs in a carol or folk style with a refrain
following each verse; the modern psalm settings of the Roman
Catholic church shared between the cantor's verse and congregation's antiphon; the spontaneous harmonising in song from
parts of the world church; the combining of melodic lines to
make harmonies in canons and rounds; the music of the Taizé
Community with its several units that blend into a musical
architecture; unaccompanied psalm singing with a precentor:
all depend on the alertness of each to what the other is doing.

Choirs know that in singing together listening is paramount
– so that the pitch is true, so that no voice stands out, so
that rhythm is exact – and that in the work they do together
they become more aware of *who* they are singing with. On a

larger scale, a congregation should also be aware not only of the different voices others are gifted with but that also they have come to worship from their varied backgrounds and diverse approaches to their common listening for absolution, for peace, for new direction. The quality of the interaction in a congregation or assembly, whether spiritual, intellectual, physical or musical, is contributory to the readiness to listen together, a quality which can happen naturally but also needs to be sought and nurtured. Music is both cause and result of such interaction. Ethnomusicologist Christopher Small notes that human relationships are 'enormously complex, too complex, often, to be expressed in words ... but ... not too complex for our minds to encompass ... [Music and ritual] provide us with a language by which we can understand and articulate these relationships.'[9]

## 2 Music enhances meaning in movement and ritual

Even in word-based cerebral worship, there are movements and rituals, the scaffolding of the liturgy, and music helps to release their significance. Making music is physical. Medical observation indicates that singing involves virtually every muscular system, which makes each of us a potential musical instrument. Singing brings the whole human being into play. It has been noted that in moving from speech to singing, the voice tends to become richer, clearer, more sonorous. Behind music is dance, a very physical movement, involving the whole person. These movements and rituals include the opening voluntary or processional hymn where minister and choir enter, the bringing forward of the offering, carrying in the Communion elements, singing a blessing (which is an action) upon someone who has been baptised, joining in a hymn as the preacher ascends the pulpit. Music adds dignity and meaning, enabling us to share in what others are doing. Music can do this, musicologist Viktor Zuckerkandl explains, because as music-makers we are not units over against the world making personal artistic or spiritual responses, but rather our inner and that outer world 'meet in melody' and 'penetrate each other'. So our music is not ethereally 'going up' but materially 'going across', horizontal not vertical, so that we are moving in the music with the movers.[10]

## 3 Music makes us creators

The physicality of song, in connecting us with each other and locking us into the bodily dimension of worship, requires that we make choices: to sing softly or loudly, where to breathe, how to make a succession of pitches sound like a coherent melody, how to shape the music to bring out the meaning, the casting of the voice to express the conviction we feel, the appreciation of the skill of the accompanist or instruments or the inspiration of the composer, and how we respond and combine so that we sing (and pray) in concert. In so doing, we are calling on our own creativity and offering it to the Creator. The hymn writer Thomas Troeger says this marks us off as part of God's creation. 'We do not just think theological thoughts about creation, we actualize the doctrine as we fill our lungs with air and send it through the larynx and against the soft and hard structures of the mouth into the air.' This of course applies also to those who play in a band or accompany on the organ, where the physical effort involved is more visible and the creative component more audible. Hildegard of Bingen (d. 1179), herself a composer of church music, did not see music as something merely experienced passively. She believed that a Christian person engaged in the process of creating was by this taken into the presence of God.

Many members of a congregation may not recognise themselves as being creative in this way, either because they do not consciously aim for these things, or they feel themselves 'unmusical'. A local church at worship, even, can come to believe that they are 'not a singing congregation'. We may feel a chasm lies between us and the professional artist or musician or the talented amateur. Yet what we have in common with them is much greater than we realise. If this weren't the case,

their work would go over our heads. They may have honed
their skills, dedicated themselves to their art just as all do in
their own sphere of life, but it is our creativity that recognises
theirs. Coleridge remarked: we know a poet because he makes
us poets. In one of the great south windows by Louis Davis in
the Choir of Dunblane Cathedral is a depiction of the visionary
poet William Blake, who writes in 'Pentecost':

> Unless the eye catch fire,
> the God will not be seen.
> Unless the ear catch fire,
> the God will not be heard.
> Unless the tongue catch fire,
> the God will not be named.
> Unless the heart catch fire,
> the God will not be loved.
> Unless the mind catch fire,
> the God will not be known.

Another way of talking about the creativity within persons
is to speak of their uniqueness. What distinguishes one from
another is what we make of the gifts we have been given and
the circumstances of life we have been dealt (think the parable
of the talents). As music director of a community arts festival
in a city housing area lacking in facilities and resources, I never
ceased to find it remarkable how young people who had had
few advantages in life would discover, as they took to the
stage, something they didn't know about themselves, a talent
they hadn't known they possessed, and thereby found a worth
in the eyes of others as they realised they had something the
community needed from them. There were also many in that
community who brought creativity to the daily demands of
carving out a life against the odds. If we remain uncomfortable
at being included among the creative, perhaps we should recall
the Anglo-Saxon word 'scop', a practical word meaning both
'shaper' and 'poet', which Caedmon, protégé of St Hilda of
Whitby, uses to speak of God creating the world. Similar was
the old word for poet in Scots, 'makar'. The joint meaning of

poet and maker (and the title given to God, Maker) seem to bring together the practical and the imaginative, the down to earth with the inspired, producing something 'workable'. As we makars together bring the best of our praise, then God will be (in Blake's words) 'seen ... heard ...named ... known'.

## Music brings back memories

Music unites the church of the past with the church of the present and the future. Church musicians sometimes feel despair at congregations' default mode of preferring the old favourites. Lists of the top twenty hymns or similar invariably contain a high proportion of hymns and songs that have been in the repertoire for some time. But this desire to revisit the tuneful and well-worn melodies of past eras (notwithstanding that 'new favourites' are just waiting to be embraced) reveals part of the power of church music. A melody has the ability to, almost instantly, recall and restore the memory of earlier experiences of worship or a previous strength of conviction, a hinterland of teaching, preaching, relationships within church and family. A gathering for worship always starts at a disadvantage – that the problems and frustrations of that week, or that morning, do not immediately translate into the right mood for worship. Some may in addition feel strange in that place, whether visitors or irregular attenders. Others may have experienced changes in their circumstances, health or family matters. All need to take their place in the great sweep of Christian worship and be reminded of all that has brought them to this day, without having laboriously to construct it *de novo*. Music has an immediacy that carries us into the communion of saints, recalls our nurture, confirms that we have been 'called by name' (Isa. 43:1). A hymn, old favourite or not, can bring back feelings, memories, precious ideas and encounters, and put us in touch again with who we are, and whom we serve.

It is not just that we remember old hymns and through this renew contact with all that has formed us as Christians; there is something about the music itself which allows one time zone to enter another. We sometimes find in listening to music that time stood still; we do not notice how long the music is taking. The stillness of a concert audience, the person with earphones on a train who does not just seek entertainment but another time world that shortens the commute, the folk song that embraces the reality of lives of sorrow and loss but also affirms there is a future and leaves one warm with hope. The church exists in time but also out of time; its present is contemporary with the saints of old but it also recognises the Kingdom of God begun in its midst. We may not know how long a piece lasts but we have experienced some kind of quality within it which cannot be measured in minutes and seconds. Theologian Jeremy Begbie notes that a melody or a movement of a symphony is made up of shorter phrases or waves which do not quite end (for example, halfway through a hymn melody), leaving an expectation that there will be continuation. Taken together the 'partial fulfilments' of the single phrases, sounding within longer and longer sections until the end of a melody or longer work, heighten the expectation of a future climax somewhere beyond, as creation 'waits with eager longing' for fulfilment (Rom. 8:19)[11] but also finds it swimming into focus in the smaller kingdom cadences of life in society, new surges of joy, love, service, reconciliation.

## Music uncovers the beauty at the heart of worship

Beauty is a concept that has to be rescued, in many Christian traditions, from partial and sometimes damaging interpretations. On the one hand, it is often used to describe the decorative, attractive, appealing; on the other it is seen as a risk, as dangerous – 'Handsome is as handsome does!' In some traditions, including the Reformed, there has been a distrust of the visual, seen as distracting people from the true nature of religious belief and worship. In a searching critique of music written for the church, Erik Routley warns against aiming for beauty in its own right (which he saw as a fault of much nineteenth-century church composition), suggesting that the result is too often mere pretentiousness.[12] David Fergusson asks whether in our picture of God we have missed some cues in Scripture and overemphasised the moral and the intellectual – upright lives and right doctrines – at the expense of a third attribute, namely God's *beauty*, as captured, for example, in Psalm 27:4:

> One thing I asked of the LORD, that will I seek after:
> to live in the house of the LORD all the days of my life,
> to behold the beauty of the LORD and to inquire in his temple.

Music is sometimes also seen as lure, as (say) in seeking appealing music to attract more people to come to church. St Basil in the fourth century seemed to concur with this interpretation:

> For when the Holy Spirit saw that humankind was ill-inclined toward virtue and that we were heedless of the righteous life because of our inclination to pleasure, what did he do? He blended the delight of melody with doctrines in order that through the pleasantness and softness of the sound we might unawares receive what was useful in the words, according to the practice of wise physicians, who, when they give the more bitter draughts to the sick, often smear the rim of the cup with honey.[13]

Basil, however, does not see music as mere decoration but as a powerful partner in the proclamation of the faith. His view was that people are formed as Christians as they sing, 'educating their souls'. It is music which takes us through the curtain of the doctrines to the Being whose attributes they can only struggle to articulate. Music is a channel into the presence of a beautiful God.

Pope Benedict XVI helps to take the argument further. In 2007, he issued an Apostolic Exhortation, *Sacramentum Caritatis*, which, although it primarily concerned the Eucharist, contained some reference to music. He speaks of a 'liturgical category of beauty', which is 'no mere aestheticism, but the concrete way in which the truth of God's love in Christ encounters us, attracts us and delights us'.[14]

Our exploration of the nature and effect of beauty in music is helped by looking at a parallel form of art. Icons, those colourful depictions of Christ, of Mary, of disciple, of saint, of core incident in the gospel narrative, seen in profusion in Orthodox churches throughout the Christian East, are a form as old as the fourth century. To appreciate icons we have to put aside some of our assumptions about how to look at paintings. These are not mere decorations on the screen of an Orthodox church, nor aides-memoire of gospel stories, but liturgical events, to be approached as we would approach the actions of Holy Communion. Icons are not illustrative of the faith, they are *part of* the faith. Each is, and this is the word used, a little epiphany in itself. One writer explains: what the word says, the image shows us silently; what we have heard, we now see. An early church council, when the art and practice of the icon was being established, declared: 'What the gospel says to us in words, the icon announces to us in colours and *makes it present* to us' (my italics).[15]

A report from the Doctrine Committee of the Scottish Episcopal Church takes this to its conclusion:

> The Christian vision of beauty is not like that of Plato, nor that of the Scottish Enlightenment philosopher David Hume, for it does not lie in the contemplation of the eternal forms nor through the training of the inner eye of the mind. Rather, Christians come to know true beauty through their encounter with the Incarnate God ... In Christian history, and also in the history of much Western art, the very possibility of artistic endeavour takes its rise from the real presence of Christ and the enactment of that real presence in the liturgies and the lives of the early churches. As the cultural critic George Steiner suggests, the liturgical re-enactment of this real presence in sacramental worship is, to a large degree, the cultural root of the extraordinary creativity and richness of European art and music from the twelfth to the eighteenth centuries.[16]

This exploration has required us to visit again what we mean by beauty, and various ways have been offered of defining the concept. Could it be that the beauty in anything is not just in the outcome that you see but is just as much in the process that created it? The artist wrestles with language, sounds, paint, movement, emotion, to show what she sees. If there is beauty, it is the result of engagement, struggle, on the part of those who write, create and compose – and not only the artist but any one of us who brings creativity to the tasks of life and of faith. Beauty may be said, therefore, to do with people and their gifts. It comes into focus when people reach deep and offer the most, as they show costly love, as they strive in putting their own resources to the test in their search for meaning, for significance, for God. Thus a 'new thing'[17] is created, not merely an object of abstract beauty but the effort of arriving at this point, including others' receiving of it with attention and engagement. Don Saliers was making a similar point when he remarked that beauty is the heart at full stretch,[18] which he also identifies as 'prayer in its fullness'. Music, he said, is 'sung prayer'. Beauty may therefore be said to be a spiritual as well as an aesthetic quality, the result of our offering of ourselves for our remaking in the image of God the Makar, who in Christ struggled to reach and reconcile humanity and creation.

## Notes

1 https://www.vatican.va/archive/hist_councils/ii_vatican_council/documents/vat-ii_const_19631204_sacrosanctum-concilium_en.html (accessed 17.5.21), chapter 6, 'Sacred Music', paragraph 112.

2 Jones, Cheslyn, Geoffrey Wainwright and Edward Yarnold (eds), 1978, corrected 1980, revised with additional editor Paul Bradshaw, 1992, *The Study of Liturgy*, London: SPCK, p. 504.

3 Duchesnau, Claude and Michel Veuthey, trans. Paul Inwood, 1992, *Music and Liturgy: The Universa Laus Document and Commentary*, Washington: The Pastoral Press, section 5.5, p. 20.

4 Blackwell, Albert, 1999, *The Sacred in Music*, Cambridge: The Lutterworth Press, p. 16.

5 St Basil, *Homily on Psalm 1*.

6 Foley, Edward, 1984, *Music in Ritual: A Pre-Theological Investigation*, Washington: The Pastoral Press, p. 16.

7 Bell, John L., 2007, *The Singing Thing Too*, Glasgow: Wild Goose Publications, p. 22.

8 Foley, *Music in Ritual*, pp. 16–17.

9 Quoted in McGann, Mary E., 2002, *Exploring Music as Worship and Theology: Research in Liturgical Practice*, Collegeville, MN: The Liturgical Press, pp. 38f.

10 Zuckerkandl, Victor, trans. Willard R. Trask, 1956, *Sound and Symbol: Music and the External World*, London: Routledge & Kegan Paul, pp. 4, 368.

11 Begbie, Jeremy, 2000, *Theology, Music and Time*, Cambridge: Cambridge University Press, p. 99.

12 Routley, Erik, 1980, *Church Music and the Christian Faith*, London: Collins Liturgical Publications, p. 32.

13 Strunk, Oliver (ed.), 1981, *Source Readings in Music History*, London and Boston: Faber & Faber, Vol. I, p. 65.

14 www.vatican.va/holy.father/benedict_xvi/apost.exhort ations/documents/hf_ben_xvi_exh_20070222_sacramentum-caritatis_ en.html, para. 35.

15 Evdokimov, Paul, trans. Steven Bigham, 1990, *The Art of the Icon: A Theology of Beauty*, Redondo Beach, CA: Oakwood Publications, p. 178.

16 Scottish Episcopal Church Doctrine Committee, Second Grosvenor Essay, *Theology and the Power of the Image*, Scottish Episcopal Church, pp. 6–7.

17 2 Corinthians 5:17.

18 Saliers, Don E., 2005, 'Sounding the symbols of faith: exploring the nonverbal languages of Christian worship', in Charlotte Kroeker (ed.), *Music in Christian Worship*, Collegeville, MN: The Liturgical Press, p. 20.

# The Music

# 3

# Psalms, Hymns and Spiritual Songs

There are two virtually identical references in the New Testament, one in Ephesians 5:19, the other in Colossians 3:16, where Paul encourages his readers: 'with gratitude in your hearts sing psalms, hymns, and spiritual songs to God.' There has been much conjecture as to what is being described here and it may be that these are not the clearly defined categories they seem but an inclusive phrase which reflects a variety of forms and the indistinctness of boundaries between them.

'How shall I sing that majesty?' John Mason's hymn puts the question that is to be explored in these next three chapters. What are the musical forms that have emerged as humanity strains to echo the alleluias of the heavenly choirs which sound through this hymn? What is their nature? How did they come to be? What can they offer? That particular hymn, for all its psalmic overtones, is one of the earliest compositions that can truly be called a hymn rather than a metrical psalm version, and reminds us that before we can talk about the hymn, for many worshippers their staple diet, we have to trace its origin back to the metrical psalm.

## Psalms

There is no older church song than the psalms. It is clear from the number of times psalm verses are quoted in Gospel and Epistle that the psalms were very much part of the new church's life, but it is not known for certain if and how they featured in its worship.[1] As the centuries unfolded, Christian communities became more structured and patterns of worship were formalised. The Old Testament psalms were in the forefront, not just to carry the praise and adoration of the faithful, as in the daily monastic offices, but also to shape a disciplined life of prayer in religious communities by private recitation and meditation. In abbeys and local churches, a sinuous, unmeasured and haunting style of singing, later to be known as plainchant, emerged[2] and gradually became standard across Europe. The complexity and variety of the settings, coupled with the fact that they were in Latin, meant that they had to be learned by rote in song school or made familiar by long exposure before full participation could be achieved.

What was to make the psalms suitable for ordinary people to sing, and to sing together, was that they were put into metre (measured) so that lines fitted into a verse and all the verses were identical, enabling them to be sung to the same simple melody. The story of how this new form evolved is remarkable, if somewhat unexpected. When the Dutch Catholic reformer Desiderius Erasmus (d. 1536) created his famous word picture of the ploughman at the furrow, the watchful weaver at the loom, the captain wrestling with the tiller, the wife patient at her distaff – all singing 'the mystical psalms in their own mother tongue' – his hope was that the psalms, rescued from the Latin and made into the cadences of popular song, would replace the trivial, the frivolous and the bawdy, and redirect their thoughts in a more worthy direction.[3]

Others took him up on it. Two remarkable pre-Reformation publications, Miles Coverdale's *Goostly psalmes and spirituall songes* and, in Scotland, the *Gude and Godlie Ballatis*,[4] contained metrical psalms in English and Scots with tunes, the latter containing additional *contrafacta* (new texts for old tunes) by which popular melodies like 'Johne cum kis me now' and 'Go from my windo' were made vehicles to popularise the (so-called) new Reformed doctrines. This use of popular melody already had a long pedigree. In the Irish Franciscan *Red Book of Ossory* (earlier 1300s), Latin religious lyrics are substituted for the words of such ditties as 'The maid that on the moor lay', so that monks would be spared from 'polluting their throats with lascivious songs' and dwell on a more exemplary maiden. The purpose of these *contrafacta* was didactic, to teach the faith, to increase piety. Similarly Coverdale's preface commended the book as 'meet to be used by all sorts of people privately for their solace and comfort, laying apart all ungodly songs and ballads, which tend only to the nourishing of vice and corrupting of youth', while the *Ballatis* were 'changed out of profane songs into godly songs for the avoiding of sin and harlotry'.

Neither of these snappily titled works made it into the bestseller list (in fact Coverdale's was banned) and it took Thomas Sternhold (d. 1549), groom of the King's bedchamber at the courts of Henry VIII and Edward VI, to start the landslide of psalm versions that continued for the next two centuries or so. Sternhold made use of a version of the fourteener, the metre of the popular ballad (two breathless lines per verse) but in a four-line form which we now know as common metre (CM in our hymn books) – two pairs of lines, the first of the pair eight syllables, the second six. The author is said to have sung these as he went about his duties and, given his proximity to the king's person, Edward also picked them up and they became something of a court craze, doubtless displacing – or at least making a dent in – the frivolous and the bawdy, as was the intention. Not a great deal is known about the tunes originally used, but cameos from Shakespeare some decades later may offer clues: in *The Winter's Tale*, the Clown talks of the singing shearers among whom is a puritan 'who sings psalms to horn-pipes' (IV, iii), while in *The Merry Wives of Windsor*, Falstaff's words and deeds are said to 'no more adhere and keep pace together than the Hundredth Psalme to the tune of Green Sleeves'.

Apart from Coverdale (who shared royal duties with him), Sternhold is likely to have been influenced or encouraged by his exact opposite number (coincidentally) at the court of the French king, Clément Marot (d. 1544), who also doubled as court poet. Marot had become known for his psalm versions, and perhaps these were carried to England by exiled French Protestants. From Antwerp too there might have come *Souterliedekens* (psalter-songs, 1540), metrical rhyming psalms set to folk songs

35

mainly from the Low Countries. However, neither Sternhold nor Marot had any inkling that their work would become the staple of the new worship. It was sufficient that they have private devotional use, in preparation for religious festival or in helping people cope with their daily lives. It was to take the exile of Protestant sympathisers,[5] fleeing the regime of (Catholic) Queen Mary in England, who had succeeded Edward VI, and a similar exodus of would-be reformers from Scotland, gathering at places like Frankfurt and Geneva, to seize on these early experiments as a godsend for their worship. The English exiles would have brought with them the latest printing of Sternhold's psalms (added to by John Hopkins, although not yet up to the full 150). With revision and addition by various writers this became (with the liturgies attached) the *Forme of Prayer*, as used by the Anglo-Scottish community in Geneva. It is noteworthy that, either before leaving England or subsequently, the ballad-style tunes had given way to music seen as more suitable for worship. When it became possible to return, the psalter, tried and tested and approaching completion, was repatriated, one version to England, a later version to Scotland.

The driving force that propelled the metrical psalm to the heart of worship was as much due to cultural change as worship reform. It was a time of greater social equality, of the opening up of ideas assisted by the invention of printing, of the spread of educational opportunity. In church and university the new techniques of scholarship were brought to bear on the Bible, causing a review of some treasured doctrines but also meaning many more people had their own access to Scripture rather than it being filtered through the clergy. The Reformers found by the relocation of song from the choir to the whole congregation their chief expression of the priesthood of all believers, the conviction that all have equal voice and value before God.

The story of the development of psalm singing differs in each of the three nations. In Scotland, the 1564 psalter (bound with service book) had 105 tunes to the psalms, employing over 30 different metres, compared with 63 tunes and 12 metres in the English equivalent.[6] These tunes were soon harmonised by leading Scottish composers under the editorship of Thomas Wode (pronounced Wood) and circulated independently, many surfacing in the most famous of all the psalters, that of 1635, which was set entirely in harmony, with also the striking form of 'psalms in reports' (imitation, either at the beginning but sometimes during, as in *Bon Accord*, still in use). The Wode Psalter has in recent years been reconstructed from scattered part books in a project by the University of Edinburgh (2008–11).[7]

As the sixteenth century gave way to the seventeenth, calls were being made for a revision of the Psalter. There was no progress until the Assembly of Divines, convened by the English Parliament in 1643 and with Scottish representation, sought among other things to approve a revised psalter to be used throughout the two kingdoms. The Scots were slow to give approval and by the time it had gone through many revisions, latterly in Scotland, before being adopted in 1650 by the General Assembly, the finished version had become known as the *Scottish Psalter* (by now the intention of a joint psalter had faded). This has been the official psalter until the present day, notwithstanding the awkwardnesses of language necessary to ensure that the psalms were an accurate representation of their scriptural originals. If the demands of metre sometimes challenged sense, nevertheless the language, in Sir Walter Scott's words, 'though homely, is plain, forcible, and intelligible, and very often possesses a rude sort of majesty'.[8]

In England, the first complete Sternhold and Hopkins psalter was published by John Day in 1562 as *The Whole Booke of Psalmes*, which is said to have been the most popular music book of sixteenth and seventeenth century England.[9] Although it would be replaced by Tate and Brady's New Version in the eighteenth century, it would continue to appear in print until 1828. Within that time, fresh editions and compilations were continually being produced by a variety of editors and composers to keep up with the appetite for metrical psalms, which penetrated deeply into the life of the people – worship, work, in the home, education (both for their content and for teaching music), and leisure (from early on, four-part versions were available, and used both for voices and instruments), not to mention the incidents and turning points in both private and national life in which psalms featured. Their transmission was mainly aural, people then being much quicker at picking up and remembering both words and tunes than most are today.

In Wales, by 1621 there had appeared Edwmnd Prys's *Llyfr y Psalmau*, all 150 texts along with 12 tunes, which went through several reprints up to 1770 when it was reproduced with a larger selection of tunes. Six of these, at least, are still in use, for example in *Emynau'r Llan* (*Hymns of the Church*) (Church in Wales, 1997), widely used for Welsh-language services. The Roman Catholic hymn book in Welsh, *Emynau Catholig* (2006), includes four of Prys's metrical psalms.

First recorded in England was the practice of lining out, when a precentor read or intoned each line in turn. It had the disadvantage both of disrupting the fluency of the content and the speed of singing. In addition, as people 'took up the tune' there was considerable distortion as people tried to capture the melody, and the custom developed of individual decoration, causing a rather dense and often cacophonous texture. Robert Bremner in his *Rudiments of Music* of 1756 speaks of 'nonsensical graces', and tells of the Scottish precentor who insisted that the first note of the tune *Elgin* must have no fewer than eight quavers. This practice lingers still in the singing of psalms in the Gaelic-speaking areas of the West Highlands and Islands, creating a sound of unearthly beauty, whose strangeness still leads a few to claim exotic origins. Gaelic versions of the metrical psalms began to appear from 1658 and a full Gaelic Psalter was published in 1694 by the Synod of Argyll. No radical revisions have since appeared apart from orthographical updating.

Whereas the psalters from the Reformation onwards contained music, in Scotland the 1650 one did not, perhaps because of the political upheavals of the time. This, however, had its effect in that the repertoire of tunes dipped disastrously and a barren period persisted until revival in singing took place in the eighteenth century. Nevertheless, throughout the intervening period there was growing discomfort at the restrictiveness of the psalms as the sole diet, because 'the solemn praises of a New Testament Church are too much limited when confined entirely to ... Old Testament composures', to quote a minute of the Presbytery of Paisley from 1747. Part of the answer was already on the way, namely the provision by the General Assembly of the *Scottish Paraphrases* (1781), a unique group of 67 portions of Scripture, of which 35 were from the New Testament. These were luminous biblical passages which had music in them and demanded to be sung. They were very much like the psalms in sound and shared the same tunes, but at least you could now sing of the Resurrection. Some of these became well travelled, such as 'O God of Bethel', 'Come let us to the Lord our God with contrite hearts return' and 'The Saviour died and rose again'. Yet these too were limited by the fact that the texts were already given, with the versifiers having no leeway in terms of vocabulary and content. In the *Paraphrases* Scotland had got halfway to hymns. Even so, it was to be almost another century before the Presbyterian churches officially sanctioned hymn collections.

## Hymns

Hymns belong to a nation's culture as well as to the worship of the church. When, in April 2019, the iconic twelfth-century cathedral of Notre Dame de Paris was badly damaged by fire, a *Church Times* reporter wrote: 'But it was the sight of hundreds of people in their teens, twenties, and thirties gathering on the Left Bank to sing hymns which they clearly knew by heart and certainly didn't learn at school which was a puzzle to many. After all, France has been a secular state since 1905.'[10] There is evidence also of a similar attachment to hymns in the wide audiences for the *Songs of Praise* programme on BBC television or the broadcasts of carols at Christmas. Hymn parodies rise from the stands at football matches, while 'Abide with me' is still sung at cup finals. References to hymns are found in the titles of novels, and some phrases have become proverbial –

the trivial round, the common task; change and decay; time like an ever-rolling stream; hold the fort; the garish day. As J. R. Watson remarks, 'Hymns can be of great value in crossing the divide between the Church and the secular world, and in their human appeal they may be said to belong to all men and women who love them, believers, half-believers, and non-believers ... all those who feel the stirrings of some religious sense, of some deeper and more poignant emotion, or some half-felt or half-understood apprehension of the spiritual.'[11]

Hymns are a strange alchemy. They are not only words ('texts' is the usual parlance) but words and music together. However, they are not texts that have found tunes or tunes that have acquired lyrics, but something else again. In a hymn, words and music 'complete' each other. Often, alternative tunes can bring out different nuances. A tune can be 'for life', even when in the case of 'Abide with me' or 'For all the saints' it is a second marriage. The tune causes a ripple in the text that uncovers feelings, sharpens coherence of thought, stirs the soul. Its mixture of steps and leaps, long notes and short, its balances of rise and fall, movement and rest, alert the mind, engage the body, uncover a trail of memories that reawaken faith, and bind us to each other.

Hymns are often described as the people's part but this is to suggest that the rest of worship calls for a lower level of participation. The derivation of the word 'liturgy' (people-work) already suggests the involvement of a body of people,[12] which is expressed not just when they give voice but as they offer their mind and body with all its senses. Hymns are as much part of the dialogue of worship, in which we both hear and respond, as any other part. They also belong to the lives of faith that continue on from that act of worship.

There is nothing casual about creating a hymn. While committees argue strategies, preachers deliver eloquent sermons, marchers take to the streets, new community projects are launched and individual Christians undertake costly acts of service, some people are already writing hymns. That is *their* response. They are responding to the church's own searching, of which they are a part. Therefore, as new situations develop and fresh challenges open up, the church *grows* the hymns it needs.

However, there is another very important part of this dynamic. As well as growing hymns, the church *grows into* the hymns that result. For hymn writers do not just record what they have heard. As persons of prayer, compassion and insight, and with an open Bible, these writers are creating new statements of faith and praise that invite the church to take a step forward in faith and witness, to pray with more urgency, serve more single-mindedly, be ready to cross boundaries and overstep margins, to embrace the unloved, to move heaven and earth. The hymn accompanies the church as it stumbles into each new landscape. Telling phrases, burnished by repetition, lodge themselves in the consciousness of the people of God, deepening understanding and alerting them to new areas and forms of witness, service, fellowship and praise. It is often said that congregations sing because of what they believe, and believe because of what they sing.

It is with the worship of the church that hymns are most associated, but they may be used differently across the various parts of the church. In some, they are bedded in the liturgy, 'office hymns', marking a stage in the service, the commemoration of a saint, the time of day, the stage reached in the Christian Year. For others, hymns *are* their liturgy, expressing their participation just as others might make vocal responses in prayer or use gestures such as kneeling or making the sign of the cross. In truth, there is overlap in these functions. Office hymns most certainly engage the worshippers fully and actively, while hymns are often chosen to help shape the course of the worship and enhance its meaning as it progresses.

Hymns contribute to the variety of texture and of mode in an act of worship: song as against speech, voicing in the midst of listening, the expression of feelings over against the understanding of the mind, physical movement to complement attentive rest. They also enable further insight on Scripture heard and preached, the declaration of belief, reflection on living life in accord with the gospel.[13] Further, familiar phrases and well-loved melodies bring back to mind one's whole history of faith, so that we are not dependent on this day's worship alone but our whole nurture. Above all, they help us feel our identity as a church as we combine our voices with others'.

There may be another quality about the hymns we use, namely that, created as individual utterances, they have become a body of hymnody by use and wont, but also because a branch of the church has considered the issues facing the people of the day, the newest thinking about faith and doctrine, and the needs of the church on the ground, and brought a particular range of hymns together in a denominational collection. There is thus a unifying, rallying and focusing quality in the hymns we sing that shapes that particular denomination, contributes to the growth to maturity it needs, cements its partnership with other branches of the church and identifies the nature of its mission and service, all along with the quality of worship that these factors demand.

## From psalm to hymn

It is usually acknowledged that it was largely in the work of Isaac Watts (1674–1748) that the transition from metrical psalm to hymn took place. Watts worked at first from within the psalms, making versions which were faithful to the originals. However, as well as versifying other scriptural passages (some of which became the starting point for the *Scottish Paraphrases*), he began to rewrite the psalms 'imitated in the language of the New Testament'. At one end of the psalm–hymn spectrum there was 'Jesus shall reign where'er the sun', which is pure psalm (72), and at the other, 'When I survey the wondrous Cross', which is pure gospel, and considered one of the greatest of hymns in the English language. What Watts brought to the task, as well as being a poet in his own right, was a breadth of learning and a deep knowledge of the philosophical and scientific discoveries of the age (his book on *Logic* continued to be used in universities a hundred years after its publication). He wrote some 750 hymns, of which as many as 50 could be said still to be in active circulation.

This is not the place to attempt a history of hymnody[14] but it would be difficult not to mention Charles Wesley (1707–78), who might be said to have completed the transformation from psalm to hymn as well as set the bar for all subsequent writers. First, his hymns are a tapestry of texts, where allusions, quotations and biblical images enrich and illuminate each other (no fewer than eleven such references are found in the first verse alone of 'Love divine, all loves excelling') so that the truths of Christian doctrine are brought into focus. Second, this is no intellectual pursuit but arises from conviction passionately expressed as his hymns (over 6,000 were written) tell of his own conversion and all that spilled out of that as the writer grew in spiritual maturity. Finally, what enables the personal utterance to become universal is the poetic grace with which he writes, which does not crowd us with his enthusiasm but places it between us with room for our own distinctive response to be made. 'Love divine, all loves excelling', for example, is modelled on 'Fairest isle, all isles excelling' from the popular opera *King Arthur* (John Dryden, music by Purcell). This chemistry of Scripture, passion and poetry has defined what is meant by a hymn ever since.

Since that time, several waves of hymn writing have occurred, all of which have contributed to the current repertoire. One wave that must be mentioned is the translation of older hymnic writings – from those quoted in the New Testament[15] and the writers of the first millennium, from the office hymns of Ambrose, through Prudentius, Fortunatus and Columba, to the fine eucharistic hymns of Aquinas (d. 1274) – as scholar-writers such as John Mason Neale and Edward Caswall captured their work and that of many other anonymous earlier authors into English and into the metrical forms of today. It is noteworthy that some of our established hymn writers are now making new versions of these and others for our own day.

Yet the 'new song' never reaches its final cadence. It is remarkable how, in a time of seemingly reduced religious observance, the provision of fresh hymns seems to be at the flood, and also how the hymn form continues to be renewed. Two examples will suffice. Fr James Quinn frequently abandons rhyme, seeking more freedom, believing that this will not matter provided that there are compensating cadences. To this is added a limpidity and directness of language where Scripture speaks seemingly without art, yet with words set down with such precision that you are taken inside their meaning, and where repetition and grammatical structure place an idea where you cannot look past it:

> You did not choose me: I chose you,
> appointed you, and chose you all,
> each one to go and bear much fruit,
> fruit that will last beyond all time.[16]

His work is also a reminder that the hymn writer's true medium is not the writing but the life of devotion.

Second, I was privileged to be present at what was nothing less than a coup staged in 2008 by the United Reformed Church when at its Assembly, that year held in Edinburgh, three of their established hymn writers were brought together – Brian Wren, Alan Gaunt and Fred Kaan (not long before the latter's death). Asked what they saw as most important in a good hymn, they agreed, rather surprisingly, that the first quality was precision of language. We know and have sung so often the big picture, but it is when a hymn illuminates a small corner of faith or practice or captures a specific but typical moment – of longing, of possibility, or glimpse of Bible story – that it arrests and engages us, and enables us to carry our faith into yet another of life's cracks and crevices.

Because of the importance of familiarity in appreciating a hymn, it is always tempting to pilot a meandering way back to the hymns we know. Those, however, who check the dates at the foot of hymns and seek out ones by contemporary authors will find great riches and may be led into new paths of discipleship.

## Singing hymns

It is not necessarily the case that a hymn has to be sung by all together. To orchestrate a hymn in terms of using groups of voices in different ways can encourage people to be more alert to each other as they sing and perhaps, too, more likely to pay attention to the content of the lyrics. It can also add a variety of texture to our usual congregational sound. For example, one of the inner verses may be sung by a solo voice, or as a duet, or even the choir – desirable in the latter case especially where the harmonies are particularly arresting and would not be heard and savoured when the whole assembly is giving voice. There could be treble voices for one verse contrasting with deeper voices for another (but check the content first; there was a fashion for a while for 'treble voices only' – which in most congregations effectively meant the women – to sing v. 3 of 'Praise, my soul, the King of heaven', which contains the line, 'well our feeble frame he knows').

In one of his books, John Bell offers interesting suggestions for performing some well-known hymns.[17] For example, 'Come, Holy Ghost, our souls inspire', which is set to *Veni, Creator Spiritus* (its original plainsong melody from the ninth century or earlier) could be sung unaccompanied, as the chant would have been. He suggests that the first verse be sung in Latin (which he provides) by a solo male voice 'positioned not at the front of the church, but at the back or in a gallery, as this song is more of a prayer than a proclamation'. Unison male choir voices enter at v. 2, with the whole assembly singing subsequent verses, in English. Another example illustrates how an alternative arrangement can bring out the true nature and power of a melody. He suggests that for *Slane* ('Be thou my vision' and other texts) all the men on one side be asked to sing the Eb below middle C and the men on the other the Bb below that (if the tune is played in the key of Eb). This is held as a drone while the treble voices sing v. 1; for v. 2 the roles are reversed. It is worth studying the hymn list for an upcoming service, paying attention to the nature of the melody and the content of the text, and asking: Is there one thing we could do to heighten the interest in singing one of the hymns today?

Aside from their place in worship, other creative approaches to hymn singing can be explored: a *Songs of Praise* format, with interviews as in the television programme; a sequence of psalms, either based on variety of theme or mood, from adoration to lament, or on the variety of types of musical setting; a hymn sequence which celebrates an author, or explores a historical era, or highlights the part of the Calendar reached, or a part of the world; a workshop might be built round a hymn, with discussion, creative work with children, the writing of prayers.[18]

## Songs

When St Paul writes of 'psalms, hymns, and spiritual songs', 'song' is translated from the Greek word that gives us 'ode'. In 1 Corinthians 14:26 there is another rare reference to song. Here it is usually translated 'hymn', but is actually the Greek *psalmos*, reinforcing the possibility that the three categories represent a mix of musical idiom. In that passage, the writer asks that some order be introduced in forms of worship which were developing: 'When you come together, each one has a hymn, a lesson, a revelation, a tongue, or an interpretation. Let all things be done for building up.' His anxiety was that a chaos of sound was preventing the emergence of an attitude of worship and reverence, but also that there was a danger of people grandstanding, using their particular talent to build a reputation. Yet Paul does not wish to stifle this spontaneity. The forms of song we consider in this section contain in different ways that spontaneous element: where participation grows in the singing; where a choir practice is not required to learn them; which draw in the body's rhythms; and which create community. They also have a variety in their idiom, in this way mirroring what experts tell us was the 'sound' of early Christian worship, deriving from synagogue origins: a wide spectrum from the spoken to the sung in which there would be shouts, acclamations, responses and chants, and improvisatory incantation.

## Short songs and chants[19]

In the most contemporary hymn collections, these usually have their own section. For example, *Ancient and Modern* (2013) has a final section of Short Chants, *Church Hymnary 4* of Short Songs, and *Singing the Faith* of Liturgical Settings. In all these cases there are other similar items in their appropriate thematic section. This ready availability of such material is a signal that even those churches whose only music has consisted of hymns and metrical psalms are becoming interested in singing at other points in a service. Short chants and songs bring three charisms to worship.

### 1 They open the way to increased spontaneity

They accompany actions and events within worship, allow us to respond to what has just occurred, and enable us to express immediately and spontaneously what we feel, without the encumbrance of announcement from the leader of worship, or the need to look up hymn books to find appropriate words, or to heave ourselves to our feet.

### 2 They offer more fluency in worship

Sometimes an act of worship can seem episodic, one item following another. It may also feel too full of announcements. A song like 'Listen now for the gospel', the opening call from a cantor with the people responding, can prepare our minds to hear the readings from Scripture. 'Know that God is good' or 'Goodness is stronger than evil' are affirmations that could greet the readings or the sermon, again introduced by a solo voice with the people joining in as the verse becomes established.

## 3 *They can contribute to a deeper engagement*

It can be difficult for us to lose ourselves in the service, to be swept along and caught up in it. Some traditions find responsive prayers more involving than those spoken by a single voice. Many people who are quite unused to responding verbally in services, and feel awkward, may be willing to sing. Chants to punctuate a time of prayer, like 'Stay with me' (Taizé), 'Lord, hear our cry' (Iona), 'O Lord, listen to my prayer' (Rizza) or 'Mayenziwe' (South Africa) add the people's voice to the leader's on an equal basis.

## 4 *They bring out the significance of actions and gestures*

As it anticipates, accompanies or affirms an action that is taking place, a short song or chant helps us to savour and expand a moment, allowing it to transform us. For example, the Peace may be prefaced or followed by 'The peace of the earth be with you' (Guatemala) or 'Calm me, O Lord' (Adam), the Offering accompanied by 'Take, O take me as I am' (Iona) or 'Here am I, Lord' (Northumbria), the Dismissal by 'May the God of peace go with us' (Jamieson), 'We will walk with God' (Swaziland), 'Send me, Lord' (South Africa), 'Now go in peace' (Caribbean).

### Taizé chant

In any collection of short songs and chants, the music of Taizé features largely, but it is given separate notice here, not so much because of the size of the repertoire or, being early on the scene, its trail-blazing character but because of the avenues it opens up of more adventurous musical opportunities involving congregations, choral groups, soloists and instruments.

Music from the ecumenical Taizé Community, based in the hills of Burgundy in the eastern part of France, is now embedded in the repertoire of the whole church. It makes use of short repetitive units of which the melodies and words are easily memorised. They may be a single line, or in two or more parts. These units may stand alone or provide the foundation for more complex music as (one or more of) choir, cantor, descants, keyboard or guitar accompaniments, individual or groups of instruments, are added to the texture. The music can be extended in different ways. Some are canons, the voices coming in at intervals and continuing as long as is wished. These set a variety of types of text: meditative biblical verses, traditional worship and eucharistic texts, chants within prayer, acclamations, psalm settings, a continuous musical context for spoken prayer, appropriate verses for feasts and festivals.

In this music, long-standing forms are recovered and made contemporary. Its repetitive nature, its simplicity and a musical style deeply embedded in tradition, enables a relaxed and prayerful experience of worship and a deepening of devotion, which is the reason why in many places groups gather for Taizé worship, valued for the different atmosphere it can create. An interesting feature is that, given the spread of languages spoken by visitors and pilgrims to Taizé, to avoid prioritising any one culture, extensive use is made of Latin, a 'dead' language and thus common to all, but one that is quite easy to pick up and has been proven through the centuries as satisfying to sing.

## Songs from the world church

For centuries, missionaries had carried their hymns to 'Afric's sunny fountains' and 'India's coral strand'[20] but now the Western church is welcoming back a returning upsurge of song from the global church. Sometimes the West finds its own songs returned but made new. 'Night has fallen', now a popular choice for ending evening meetings and services, was originally a setting of words written by a Scottish missionary in 1885. The melody had been collected from boatmen on the Zambezi river, but this in turn is believed to be the remnant of a song about the Virgin Mary introduced by Jesuits some two or three centuries earlier. Full circle was when another missionary, Tom Colvin, brought it in translation to Scotland in the 1970s.[21]

These songs may bear other gifts. They can remind us that we ourselves have a far more varied musical tradition than some of our recent habits suggest. Take the exuberant rhythm of 'Singing, we gladly worship'. It reminds us that in an earlier guise the chorale tunes (*Ein' Feste Burg, Lobe den Herren* and the like) displayed in jig-like melodies their roots in folk music and dance. Or take the full-throated unaccompanied renditions of the Zimbabwean 'Come, all you people', with its different layers of voices weaving and clashing. What better reminder of our unaccompanied heritage of psalm singing – not to mention the clever Reformation arrangements where the people's melody was descanted above and supported below, or where as many as seven voices launched out one after the other 'in reports'. Or a Pakistani melody like 'Prabhoo Lay Lay', helping us recall that before our music was straitjacketed into being major or minor, there were other shapes of scale, the ecclesiastical modes which brought heaven to earth for our ancestors. Probe below the surface of these melodies and you find that behind the different voices is the one voice of the people of God, now and in all ages.

However, world church songs are not to be enjoyed as something different, to make our worship brighter and more appealing. We do not just add to our repertoire, but a dimension to our prayer. We may with our own voices be taking up the song of people who live under oppressive regimes, who struggle for water, who daily clear up the debris of the previous night's raids. We could be receiving fresh light from the gospel refracted through congregations who live the faith in places where other faiths are dominant or where poverty or political tensions threaten to stifle hope. Even as they express the hurts or hopes of another people, these songs are offering us the healing and hope of the gospel in our own disappointments and dilemmas. And even as they exuberantly mirror the movement of the Holy Spirit under another sun, they invite us to release ourselves to the spontaneous movement of the Spirit in our own time and place.[22]

## Notes

1 See further Foley, Edward, 1992, *Foundations of Christian Music: The Music of pre-Constantinian Christianity*, Alcuin/GROW Liturgical Study 22–23, Nottingham: Grove Books.

2 See Chapter 4.

3 Duguid, Timothy, 2014, *Metrical Psalmody in Print and Practice*, Farnham: Ashgate, p. 1.

4 MacDonald, Alasdair A., (ed.), 2015, *The Gude and Godlie Ballatis*, The Scottish Text Society, Woodbridge: Boydell & Brewer.

5 The break between England and the papacy came in 1534, a Bible in English in 1536, the dissolution of the monasteries in 1536 and 1539, and the first Book of Common Prayer (in the English language) in 1549.

6 Duguid, *Metrical Psalmody*, p. 89.

7 Downloadable from www.churchservicesociety.org.

8 Quoted in Patrick, Millar, 1949, *Four Centuries of Scottish Psalmody*, Oxford: Oxford University Press, p. 213.

9 Duguid, *Metrical Psalmody*, p. 50.

10 Ashworth, Pat, 2019, *Church Times*, 29 November.

11 Watson, J. R., 1999, *The English Hymn: A Critical and Historical Study*, Oxford: Oxford University Press, p. 17.

12 The frequent definition of liturgy as 'a work of the people' is not quite right; the reference is to a single donor's generous public endowment in favour of, to benefit, the common people, which took place in a classical Greek context.

13 Watson, *The English Hymn*, p. 8.

14 Watson, *The English Hymn*.

15 Leith Fisher's 'Christ, of God unseen the image', based on Colossians 1:15–20, is one example.

16 The hymn begins, 'This is my will, my new command'.

17 Bell, John L., 2007, *The Singing Thing Too*, Glasgow: Wild Goose Publications, pp. 81ff.

18 It is common for hymn books to provide an index of hymns suitable for children and adults to sing together.

19 All titles in this section are listed with sources in the Appendix.

20 From the hymn 'From Greenland's icy mountains' by Reginald Heber.

21 Published by the Iona Community in *Free to Serve* (music editor Peter McLean) and *Leap my Soul* (music editor Douglas Galbraith).

22 This examination of 'psalms, hymns, and spiritual songs' has not included contemporary 'praise and worship songs', whose nature and content, and their accompaniment, is separately explored in Chapters 5 and 15.

# 4

# Service Music

## Introduction

It is a common view that you can tell which branch of the church you are in by the music you hear. Roman Catholics intone the Mass, Anglicans chant tastefully articulated four-part psalms, Methodists sing enthusiastic hymns, Presbyterians render sombre psalms, while Charismatic gatherings sway to praise and worship songs. Caricatures, yes, but these signatures in sound define 'who we are' – at least in terms of who we are not! – to the extent that there is resistance to forms of music that seem alien and, it is assumed, difficult. These cartoon-like depictions conceal the fact that there is considerable overlap between denominations in respect of these musical categories – both historically and in recent emerging practice. Many in the Church of Scotland, for example, are surprised to learn that, in the latter part of the nineteenth century and into the twentieth, all three main Presbyterian denominations published their books of prose psalms and canticles pointed and set to Anglican chant. As recently as 1927 a minute of the General Assembly's Psalmody Committee called for the repertoire for Choir Festivals to contain canticles from the *Revised Church Hymnary* 'to secure a place for chanting in the programme', while a minute from the following year records that work on the revision of the Prose Psalter is in progress. The main purpose of this chapter is to continue to examine the variety of musical genres past and present, but it also contains an implicit invitation to consider whether there are any of these, as yet unfamiliar, which might add to the depth or beauty of our own worship.

Under the term 'service music' are here gathered together uses of music other than the psalms, hymns and songs already examined. Sometimes called liturgical settings, the term does not suggest that hymns and songs are not 'liturgical'. What is explored in this chapter are those parts of worship where the liturgical text has been born in music or has subsequently become wedded to musical settings, where the music is written to flow in and out of the spoken word.

## Mass settings and the Communion service

Traditionally, the highest point of Christian worship is Holy Communion – or the Mass, Eucharist or Lord's Supper. Its importance has been acknowledged both by its frequency (daily or weekly) as well as by its infrequency, an example of the latter being the Scottish Communion season when maybe twice a year a whole weekend would be set aside for preaching and the several 'tables' (sittings) required, and when neighbouring ministers were in attendance to assist. The traditional Latin Mass has attracted music from the beginning, first in plainsong settings, then from the fourteenth century in polyphony, the earliest extant complete version being Guillaume de Machaut's striking *Messe de Notre Dame*. At first, composers were writing music purely for use in church celebrations, but for choral composers of later centuries the Mass was also a libretto of choice for more elaborate settings, influenced by developments like opera, employing soloists and instruments, and finding their audiences outside worship. This dual purposing, for church and concert hall, has continued into the present century, acting as a bridge between the sacred and the secular. Being often written in response to a particular context (cultural, conflict, notable events), and the traditional text sometimes interleaved with other material, these Masses speak just as powerfully to contemporary concert audiences as to worshippers.

There are two types of text in the Mass: the Ordinary, which never varies, and the Proper, which changes in accord with the particular time of year or the circumstance of a celebration. It was the text of the Ordinary that composers were required to set: Kyrie eleison (Lord, have mercy), Gloria in excelsis Deo (Glory to God in the highest), the Credo (I believe), the Sanctus and Benedictus (Holy, holy, holy ... Blessed is he who comes), and the Agnus Dei (Lamb of God, you take away the sins of the world). (Those who do not use sung settings will recognise most of these as said by the minister or spoken in dialogue.) These five items originate in the period from the second to the fifth centuries and found themselves fused together in the Ordinary through various pathways: for example, it was an early custom for the central act of Communion to be prefaced by other readings and songs, which included the Kyrie and the Gloria, and these in time became part of the whole. The Gloria and the Creed were not only longer but contained ideas that appeal to composers, which meant that a mass setting could be longer than was comfortable for normal worship. As well, therefore, as the full and extended setting there was the *missa brevis* where composers were more economical with the music and found ways of reducing its length, typically by excluding the Gloria and the Creed.

While the texts for the Ordinary remain the most prominent, those of the Proper are no less important in our modern cele-brations, and open the door for other music. These are the *introit* (the opening procession), the *gradual* (the reference is to the steps or *gradus* – that is, where the Gospel was brought so that it would be read in the midst of the congregation), the *alleluia* (the responses to hearing Scripture read), the *tract* (a more sober setting replacing the alleluia in Lent), the *sequence* (thought to have originated from the florid endings of the alleluia to help remember the words, more song-like in character and relating to particular seasons or festivals or particular occasions), the *offertory* (the bringing and preparation of the Communion ele-ments), and the *communion* (the procession of the faithful to partake of the bread and wine).

Most of these traditionally were a combination of antiphons and psalm verses, the former focusing a theme related to psalm and season. Thus one of the Lenten introits begins with an antiphon which sets Isaiah 66:10, 'Rejoice with Jerusalem, and be glad for her', the original Latin 'Laetare Jerusalem' giving the name to this fourth Sunday, halfway through the rigours of Lent – Laetare Sunday (or Refreshment Sunday), marking a relaxation of the penitential mood, an oasis in the wilderness. The second Sunday of Easter, Low Sunday, is another example; the antiphon begins 'Quasi modo geniti infantes'. It comes from the passage in 1 Peter 2:2 which speaks of longing for the pure milk of growing in the faith, giving a name to the day on which those who had been baptised on Easter Day now laid aside their white garments to launch on their spiritual journey. It was from his being found on the steps of Notre Dame on that Sunday that gave Victor Hugo's famous character Quasimodo his name.

One of the great blessings of living in the times we do is that we have before us centuries of magnificent settings of this, the kernel and heart of human praise and thanksgiving. Navigating the richness of the choice depends on the nature of the congregation as much as the musical resources available. Some are able to use whole settings by well-known composers. Anywhere would have done – but I picked out two congregations in the city of Edinburgh whose entrances practically face each other across the Royal Mile. In both, Communion is celebrated weekly. St Giles' Cathedral (Church of Scotland) draws on a repertoire of some 44 Communion settings, from Mozart to Matthias, Lassus to Leighton, Byrd to Berkeley. Old St Paul's (Scottish Episcopal Church) has an equally comprehensive list: from the composers of the Renaissance onwards, English and continental, up to the standard settings from the Anglican tradition such as Stainer, Stanford, Parry, Howells, and from living composers such as James MacMillan (the Mass for Westminster Cathedral from 2000). In both cases, the music is bedded into the action of the liturgy, although, due to time constraints or the desire for congregational involvement, not all movements are necessarily used on all occasions.[1]

There are also settings in which the congregation can participate, employing music which is easy to remember and where there is a thematic unity. It is not uncommon for a cantor to sing a line, which is then repeated by the people. Style and idiom varies greatly, both for choral or participative settings: simple-traditional, jazz, folk song and other styles with a popular accent. Some hymn books now incorporate individual movements, or a sequence of movements from a particular congregational setting. There are also metrical (hymn) versions: among these, the Gloria (Timothy Dudley-Smith, Barbara Rusbridge, Christopher Idle), the Creed (Timothy Dudley-Smith) and the Sanctus (Nathan Fellingham).[2] Visiting the RSCM Music Direct website where it lists Holy Communion settings is to see in one place the wide variety of setting and idiom available.[3]

For Roman Catholics, patterns of singing during the Mass have been twice interrupted since the middle of last century, and in some ways Catholic parishes are still struggling to find an equilibrium. After the Second Vatican Council (1962–65), when fresh emphasis was thrown on to those who gathered for worship, whose 'full and active participation' was to be ensured, there was immediate experiment in more accessible forms of music which would be easy for congregations to sing. There had also been an acknowledgement of the variety of the cultural background of those who gathered, and this was further interpreted as indicating acceptance of musical styles many would feel most at home with, such as folk and popular idioms. The second interruption was the withdrawal of the first English version of the Mass (1998), whose translation had followed the principle of dynamic equivalence (natural usage prioritised over strict accuracy) and the provision of a new one (2011) where formal equivalence guided the translator. It is taking time for the required new settings to appear and to become established. It is true that the 2011 translation was furnished with chants at key points, but as we shall see in discussing plainchant (below), this is not always taken up. A practice across many Catholic parishes is to substitute hymns: at the entrance of Mass, the offertory, the communion and the recessional. However, in many parishes parts of the Ordinary are sung, especially the Sanctus and, less frequently, the Agnus Dei.[4]

In the Church of England, still to be found is the setting by John Merbecke, first published following the First Prayer Book of Edward VI (1549). This used melodies akin to plainchant but part-rhythmical to encourage participation from the congregation, and intended to be sung unaccompanied. Dormant for some time, it was revived at the time of the Oxford Movement. A version appears in the *New English Hymnal* where the melodies are freed to respond better to the rhythms of speech, and an accompaniment is provided which encourages a fluent tempo.

Here also *short songs and chants* come into their own. Those who would not usually participate by speaking or singing in the wording of the Communion service may find through these an acceptable way of joining in, assisted by their brevity and simplicity. They do not only provide ways of joining in the Kyrie, the Gloria and other key moments but also offer musical participation in other parts of the service, including those which traditionally were called the Propers – adaptable to theme, time and season.

Something of this variety of Communion setting, as well as canticles and psalm versions (both discussed below), is captured in the very comprehensive collection, *Music for Common Worship: Music for Sunday Services*, edited by John Harper (RSCM 2000), which comprises music for Holy Communion, and settings of prayers, dialogues, psalms and canticles, varied in idiom from plainchant and Anglican chant to contemporary metrical versions. These are designed so that they can be sung by congregations. A second volume is provided for presiding clergy.

## Canticles

The word comes from the Latin *canticulum*, a small song. Canticles traditionally were used to enable one passage of Scripture to reflect on another. To some worship traditions, the name canticle sounds remote and formal. Yet the examples which are the most used today tend to have been spontaneous and emotional utterances in response to cataclysmic events or expressing visions too large to capture in mere words. Canticles are passages in the Bible that cry out to be sung. They scatter music as they go and very often were actual songs in their own right. The most commonly heard are the Lucan canticles (from their appearance in the Gospel of Luke). One captures Mary's wonder at hearing the angel's news (the Magnificat); there is Zechariah finding his voice after the longed-for son, to become known as John the Baptist, is born (the *Benedictus*); and Simeon about to retire after a relatively uneventful life as a temple official recognises a boy visitor as the Messiah who will change the world (the Song of Simeon or the Nunc dimittis). Equally common is the Benedicite, the Song of the Three Holy Children in the Apocrypha, 'Bless the Lord all you works of the Lord'. These verses 'resound with unheard music'[5] and inspire new settings in every age.

Others are poems inspired by but not taken directly from the Bible, including the *psalmi idiotici* (private psalms), an example of which is the Te Deum. Today, worship books and hymn books identify other passages from Scripture as canticles, often to be read responsively rather than sung. The Church of England Franciscan office, *Celebrating Common Prayer*, includes as canticles even passages composed up to the last century.[6] The first psalm books of the Reformation in England and Scotland contained canticles in metrical form to be sung to psalm tunes. Canticles are generally sung during the morning and evening services of the daily office. They have attracted various musical styles, including Anglican chant. Since the 1960s new metrical versions of canticles have appeared, such as Timothy Dudley-Smith's 'Tell out my soul' (the Magnificat) or Christopher Idle's 'God, we praise you' (the Te Deum).[7]

## The anthem

At Matins and Evensong in the Anglican Book of Common Prayer of 1662, after the Third Collect it is famously stated, 'In Quires and Places where they sing here followeth the Anthem'. This corresponded to the 1559 prayer book's requirement of 'an hymn, or such-like song, to the praise of Almighty God, in the best sort of melody and music that may be conveniently devised' and re-opened the way for serious composers after the Reformation to make a contribution to the church's worship. This suggests that, like the hymn later, the anthem was related in form and function to the metrical psalm, and in fact the vast majority of post-Reformation anthems used psalm texts. By the end of the sixteenth century more elaborate polyphonic music was being composed, by such as Weelkes and Tomkins, surprisingly enough encouraged by the arrival of the Italian madrigal with its word-painting and expressiveness.[8] A development was the verse anthem, when solo and choir alternated, Gibbons being a prime exponent. Particularly through the Chapel Royal, and in the hands of such as Purcell and Blow, the form developed, enriched by new styles from the continent. Later exponents included Handel. There was something of a lull thereafter until the recovery of the form in the work of Samuel Sebastian Wesley.

The anthem as it developed from that point, apart from making space for well-crafted music for worship in the styles of the time, was understood (in the words of the *Scottish Anthem Book* of 1892) to be a 'spiritual song by which we may "speak to ourselves" or "teach and admonish one another"', teaching in the same way that Scripture lessons and sermon teach. That the anthem should relate to the season, shape and theme of worship is underlined by the stipulation that 'the Minister should arrange that it be in tone or subject appropriate to the rest of the service'. Its successor, the *Church Anthem Book* of 1933 shows the variety and quality of the form over the intervening centuries and has only relatively recently been superseded by the *New Church Anthem Book* (ed. Lionel Dakers) and other related publications. In parts of the church, there was still a discomfiture about choirs being 'given the floor' and congregations were supplied with small books which gave all the words of the anthems in the collection used. These may have been intended to encourage singing along with the choir; at least they enabled better silent participation by being able to follow the texts.

None of the three categories we have here discussed (communion settings, canticles, anthems) has come with its own unique musical packaging. There are, however, three musical idioms or forms which have developed along with them and have been found not simply to set words but to contribute something distinctive or characteristic to the experience of worship. These are now described.

## Psalm settings, the responsorial psalm, and the role of the cantor

Dean Inge famously remarked, referring to psalms in which two groups sang in dialogue style, that it was like a 'conversation between two deaf men'.[9] Yet such interaction contributes to making worship not a sequence of events but a drama which compels participation. Today's responsorial psalm contributes to this interactivity, but it also enables the psalms to be performed with a sense and fluency that the metrical psalm often lacked. Anglican chant certainly preserved the flexibility of the original poetry, but during last century and this, new forms have sought to release the psalms still further while also allowing fuller participation from the congregation.

This new valuing of the psalms has been accompanied by much analysis and writing on the part of scholars, and an awareness of the way they run the gamut of human experience, from praise and adoration to loss and lament. It is now generally recognised that worship needs to touch all bases, not only giving feelings and emotions a place but also making room for the honesty with which the psalmists spoke before God.

Apart from the form we are examining, this renewed interest has given rise to a variety of approaches: the settings of Gelineau which seek to capture the nature of the Hebrew originals; the settings from Taizé where a single voice or group sings against an ostinato; the verse and refrain style of Bernadette Farrell – measured yet flexible; the prose versions pointed to fit a five-note melody which can also be sung in four-part harmony; verses spoken by a reader with an antiphon sung by the people against a pattern of moving triads; those read antiphonally by the congregation; the recovered fluency of plainchant; and various new metrications – to jazz settings, folk melodies, Latin

American dance rhythms and newly written tunes.[10] In Wales, *Salmau Cân Newydd (New Psalms for Singing)* by Gwynn ap Gwilym, priest and poet (d. 2016), a new and complete metrical version of the psalms with suggested tunes, was published in 2008. It is based on the 1988 Welsh translation of the Bible, and also includes new metrical settings of the main canticles and a Credo.

In the responsorial psalm, a simple antiphon enables the congregation to respond to a cantor's, or small choir's, verses, sung in prose form. The antiphon is a melody easily sung by a congregation once they have heard it (generally introduced by the cantor, then sung by the choir, after which the congregation joins in), who thereafter punctuate the intonation of each verse with their response. The melody of the antiphon, usually a flowing or rhythmic melody in a variety of styles, with words or ideas derived from the psalm in question, contrasts with the chant-like treatment of the verses.

The dependence of the responsorial psalm on a cantor brings a new valuing of an old role in the making of music. Some denominations may feel uncomfortable about another leader in worship, especially where previously the musician has been much heard but almost never seen. That the title is in Latin makes it worse! Yet all denominations somewhere in their family tree have cantors or something like them lurking. The cantor is not unlike the contemporary worship leader in another musical idiom, who enables praise and worship songs. The cantor demonstrates melodies as well as giving the cues for the people's entries and setting the pace for the song. Some carols and a few hymns also may alternate between solo and chorus, while world church songs often rely on the interplay between leader and people.

## Plainchant

In 2008, some Cistercian Monks from Austria recorded an album of Gregorian chant called *Music for Paradise* which not only topped the classical music charts in several countries but reached number seven in the top twenty in the UK. It was an indication, perhaps, that where this music is approached without suspicion or prejudice it has a broad appeal. The new release had followed, at a stately monastic pace, a similar success twelve years previously by the Benedictines of Santo Domingo de Silos, called simply *Chant*, which had sold around six million copies. Although the marketing accompanying these recordings emphasised their therapeutic potential, many must surely have found themselves more than simply soothed by these simple, soaring melodies. The music critic of the *Scotsman*, seeking a reason for their popularity, wrote: 'What plainchant has, it seems, is mystery, an ability to recreate the presence and power of time long past; and it has a quality that reaffirms that, beneath all our clatter and sophistication, our spirit is still willing.'[11] Those whose experience of worship includes the hearing or singing of plainsong would testify to its quality of *otherness*, its ability to bring them closer to the 'beyond in the midst'. When Pope Benedict XVI visited that Cistercian monastery, which has been occupied by monks continuously for 875 years, he found their singing 'a little bit of heaven becoming present on earth'.

The term 'chant' (also known as 'Gregorian chant') derives from a Latin description, *cantus planus*, which is much more recent than the form itself. By the thirteenth century, more complex music had begun to emerge and 'the song that is level, clear, or plain' contrasted with this, being single-voiced, unmeasured, and unaccompanied. Of all church music, this is a living link with the earliest church, whose music is thought to have been a kind of song-speak. As the church was given public status during the reign of Constantine (d. 337 CE), and worship moved from rooms in houses to larger buildings, it is not unlikely that the spoken would be intoned so that it might carry.

Those unfamiliar with plainchant might define it in terms of what seems to be missing. At its simplest, the melody relates to its text syllable for syllable; occasionally a single syllable will be spread over a number of notes in a sinuous melisma. Its single line of melody lacks any harmony or suggestion of harmony. Modern musicians who have to accompany plainsong today find it a demanding skill where the usual rules don't apply. Unlike the later hymn or psalm tune, it seems to have no shape or form or rhythm which would help lodge it in the memory. There are no regular bar lines, or repeated motifs, or shapes that stay in the mind. It's not catchy. It does not have feeling content, at least compared with a hymn tune which can directly arouse emotions with its harmonic tensions and evocative melodies. Its careful movements and its reciting notes, where the verse of a psalm is intoned unmoving on one pitch, makes for lack of momentum. To overindulged modern ears, it lacks a fullness.

Yet this reckons without a number of factors. At first it would have been sung by a solo voice to which may have been added a response from others present, at intervals or at the end. Then in mid-fourth-century Antioch antiphonal singing (shared between two groups) became popular. Both for the singers and those listening in a large building, the music coming from two places or two forces, together with the effect of the acoustic, could add clashings and excitement to the sound. More than that, however, this so-called plain music had developed an internal structure which was only made manifest in the eighth and ninth centuries when Charlemagne (d. 814) of the Franks wished to bring his kingdom into unity of practice with Rome. Without existing manuscripts, scholars worked on the oral tradition to extract guidelines to ensure uniformity and aid learning, in the bygoing unearthing a structure of eight ecclesiastical modes that make for a rich variety of sound and colour.

These modes, given names deriving from musical theory of ancient Greece, can be recreated by us if we play eight-note scales only on the white notes of a modern keyboard, four beginning on D, E, F or G and the remaining four (the plagal modes) beginning in each case on the fourth below. Modes do not define the pitch but refer to the particular arrangements of tones and semitones that characterise the mode, which can be sung at any pitch. Each mode has its own *tenor* (the 'held' note), where a singer may recite the words at a single pitch, and a *final*, on which the melody ends. There is a twist to this tale. As if to stop us getting too set in our ways, there is a ninth mode, called Tonus Peregrinus (a tone is a mode applied to psalm singing). Its peculiarity is that it breaks the rule of having a constant and secure reciting note; instead it has two – that is, the note is a 'wandering' one (Latin: *peregrinus*).

If this still seems alien, these sounds may be closer than we realise, for its seems that folk music uses a similar variety of scales. Francis Collinson in his *The Traditional and National Music of Scotland* shows[12] how Scottish and Gaelic folk music on closer inspection may be found to be based on the same ecclesiastical modes, including the bagpipe scale. He finds examples for each one, even the very strange and haunting Lydian mode.[13] Like the church modes, such traditional song is at home being unaccompanied. Denominations which do not use plainchant often draw on hymn tunes which have originated in plainchant, like *Veni Creator* ('Come, Holy Ghost, our souls inspire') or *Verbum supernum* ('Come, gracious Spirit, heavenly Dove').

Although plainchant has never gone away, it has seen something of a revival recently through the work of Dr Mary Berry (aka Sister Thomas More). Since the Second Vatican Council, the place of plainchant in worship has been hotly debated within the Roman Catholic Church. One interpretation of the call for 'full, conscious and active participation' has been to step back from plainchant and polyphony, seen as necessitating skilled singers for their execution. Statements both before and after the Council, however, have been unequivocal that 'Gregorian chant has pride of place'.[14]

For those new to it, plainchant sounds daunting to learn but in fact it is not difficult when shown how, and people are often surprised as to how much they like it. However, one might say that this is music that is more to be absorbed than taught. One of the monks on the Cistercian CD remarked: 'In Gregorian chant, listening to others is more important than opening one's own mouth.' Those who become familiar with the idiom may find themselves in agreement with Pope John XXII in a decree of 1325,[15] feeling its 'modest risings and temperate descents' as leaving space for the soul to breathe. They may sense something truly iconic in the way the lack of flourish or undue embellishment in its melodies, the open-endedness of its cadences, and the resting places in its contours, offer a space into which one might gaze and from which one may feel gazed upon. Some say, simply, that it is prayer twice; the music and text are fused, a double devotion.[16]

## Anglican chant

This is another of those distinctive styles that we noted above that have become characteristic of certain forms of worship. It is put in context in one of Angela Tilby's regular columns in the *Church Times*[17] where she is commenting on news that attendance at weekday cathedral services is on the rise. Prominent among these is Evensong, whose congregations, Tilby suggests, are boosted by representatives of a large constituency who have given up on other forms of church life. She suggests that people's appreciation of this unique form goes beyond the music alone. 'The music is important, of course, but so is what the rhythm of speech and music does for them: that slowing of the heart rate and breathing, the quietening of the mind, the sense of space and mystery and presence.' She quotes with approval the Twitter message she received, and forwarded – 'Evensong should be available on prescription.'

Central to Evensong is the chanting of psalms prior to the Old Testament reading. What we call Anglican chant was originally derived from the harmonised embellishment of plainsong psalm-tones (faburden) but it was some time before the form as we know it today emerged. This embellishment, which lasted from the early fifteenth century to the Reformation, was improvised, although according to an accepted procedure. The psalm tone itself was the middle voice; a second voice sang the chant a fourth higher, while a third sang a third below, except when a fifth would help strengthen a cadence, halfway through and at the end. The effect would have been like a sequence of six-four chords except at closures, where there could also be strengthening by slight ornamentation.[18]

The Anglican chant is generally in four-part harmony and can be single (one verse of the psalm) or double (two verses).

Basically, Old Testament psalms are arranged in pairs of lines (one verse), albeit with some flexibility. In the chant, each line is typically set to a reciting note and a three-note (first line) or five-note (second line) closing phrase. In the single chant, the first line ends in a half close, the second on a full; in a double chant, the half close comes after the second line, the full close at the fourth. The longer chant gives more scope for harmonic variety. Vertical lines in the text show how the text corresponds to the bar lines in the music, and where it is not obvious how to arrange words in accord with the melody (for example, where there are three syllables for two notes), a dot shows where the words are divided (a signage known as pointing). The words are sung as they would be spoken naturally. In a long psalm it is the custom to move to a second or third chant. This form, with its built-in flexibility, enables the singing of the psalms in their original prose form, with all the beauty and power that this allows.

That said, the form continues to evolve. Rigid adherence to Coverdale's verse divisions and (described above) the two-halves structure has compromised intelligibility and some newer psalters have taken a more creative approach to versification. In the Psalter for York Minster, for example, there is a setting of Psalm 66 in triple chant, to accommodate the fact that at some points the sense is spread over three verses. Here, a central section is added which is continuous with the existing music, but which can be omitted at points where a double chant only is needed without disturbing the flow of the music.[19]

When well sung there is a simplicity and spareness, even humility, before the text, as the music fits itself to the words. Each chant is a minimalist composition in its own right and has its full quota of harmonic incident, yet it does not entirely rely on this for its interest. The cadence may be performed very lightly, leaving the memory with the reciting note and the text it sets. A skilful accompanist can enhance this by bringing out the import of the words by imaginative registration. Although it may be repeated many times, it is never the same twice, since every verse is a different length. This is music that does not draw attention to itself but is bedded in the act of worship.

## Conclusion

This chapter has carried a hidden invitation to open our doors to each other's music – to respect it, even to embrace it. In music a denomination makes its nearest approach to Christian unity. At the Edinburgh 2010 missionary conference I was playing host to an Orthodox Patriarch who was to preach at morning worship. Some local children had come to the conference centre to participate, move among the people, and help to lead worship. The congregation were led in song by Fischy Music.[20] They were exuberant and upbeat and we were all invited to dance. On my right, in the rather conspicuous front row, was a young Caribbean woman for whom dance was second nature, who moved beautifully and freely to the music. On my left was the Patriarch, who moved not a muscle – possibly, I thought, in disapproval. I felt duty bound to relate in some way to them both. I think my right side may have jerked a little to the music, my left respectfully kept more or less an ecclesiastical dignity. The result must have been of someone with a strange persistent itch! I need not have worried. The Patriarch in his homily warmly mentioned the children as his fellow ministers in that act of worship. But it is how he ended his sermon that has remained with me ever since. It spoke to those who seek the unity of the church, and who may often at this time feel stranded in a Lent that never ends, where it seems that some things are non-negotiable, some church systems too closed, too complete in themselves, to hear from each other of their future and that of the world in a deeper, united praise.

> When we look up, we now see brothers and sisters from other Christian communities offering us gifts that are the fruits of grace. Painfully, often too slowly, we have acknowledged how much already unites us through our baptism into Christ and the faith we profess ... There is no turning back now. This road leads to the fullness of communion with one another and with the Blessed Trinity. Let us encourage one another to persevere in this search for full visible unity among Christians.[21]

## Notes

1 I am grateful to Michael Harris, Organist and Master of the Music at St Giles' Cathedral and Dr John P. Kitchen, Director of Music at Old St Paul's for this information.

2 The hymn collections listed in Appendix 1 have examples of those mentioned.

3 www.rscmshop.com, communion settings.

4 Ferguson, Michael, 2015, *Understanding the tensions in liturgical music-making in the Roman Catholic Church in Contemporary Scotland*, PhD thesis, University of Edinburgh. This contains a survey of practice in local Catholic parishes in Scotland and makes reference to wider practice in the United Kingdom.

5 Bloxam, M. Jennifer, 2019, 'Cum angelis et archangelis', in Teresa Berger (ed.), *Full of Your Glory: Liturgy, Cosmos, Creation*, Collegeville, MN: Liturgical Press Academic, p. 211. These are the papers from the 5th Yale Institute of Sacred Music Conference in June 2018.

6 Jeanes, Gordon, 2002, 'Canticles', in Paul F. Bradshaw (ed.), *The New SCM Dictionary of Liturgy and Worship*, London: SCM Press, p. 95.

7 These first appeared in *Psalm Praise*, London: Falcon Books, 1973.

8 Arnold, Denis, 1983, 'Anthem', in Denis Arnold (ed.), *New Oxford Companion of Music*, Oxford: Oxford University Press, p. 88.

9 Routley, Erik, 1968, *Words, Music, and the Church*, London: Herbert Jenkins, p. 140.

10 Examples of all of these can be seen in the opening (psalm) section of *Church Hymnary 4*.

11 Miller, Mary, *Scotsman* newspaper, 1994, n.d.

12 Collinson, Francis, 1966, *The Traditional and National Music of Scotland*, London: Routledge & Kegan Paul.

13 *Common Ground: A Hymnbook for all the Churches*, Edinburgh: St Andrew Press, 1998, no. 55.

14 There is further discussion on the debate in the Roman Catholic Church in Chapter 18.

15 Blackwell, Albert, 1999, *The Sacred in Music*, Cambridge: The Lutterworth Press, p. 224.

16 Miller, *Scotsman*.

17 Tilby, Angela, 2018, *Church Times*, 2 November.

18 Gant, Andrew, 2016, *O Sing unto the Lord*, London: Profile Books, p. 40.

19 The composer is Robert Ashfield.

20 Edinburgh-based Fischy Music is a charity that works with children, usually through schools, approaching matters of health and well-being through songs written by the group, as well as support-

ing those who work with children. The focus is on helping children, regardless of outlook or religious belief, make sense of emotions and of day-to-day life and the difficulties that can be encountered. Based within the Christian faith, the group works also in churches.

21 Metropolitan Professor Dr Nifon of Targoviste, 2011, in Kirsteen Kim and Andrew Anderson, *Edinburgh 2010: Mission Today and Tomorrow*, Oxford: Regnum Books, pp. 23–5.

# 5

# Contemporary Worship Music

I can still remember the frisson, the sense of doing something forbidden, when at morning worship at the Student Christian Movement (SCM) Bristol Congress at the beginning of January 1963 we rose to sing new words to a tune from the hit parade. The instrumental 'Telstar' by the Tornados was the bestselling British single of 1962, and had reached no. 1 in America. It celebrated the recently launched communications satellite of that name which symbolised the new world in which was to be heard 'Christ's call to service now', the theme of the gathering.

A few years earlier, Anglican priest and Cambridge college chaplain Geoffrey Beaumont, later of the Community of the Resurrection, had published his *20ʰ Century Folk Mass* (1957), drawing on the styles of the cinema and the Broadway musical. It was a response to the new, distinctive youth culture of the 1950s, a culture which seemed to adults to have become alienated from mainstream society and religion – and expressed in a rock and roll music whose history was one of alienation. (Predictably, the *Musical Times* found the new Mass more suited to the 'fetid atmosphere of a nightclub' than a church.) Not long after came the rock and roll Passion play (1960) *A Man Dies*, written, with actor Ewan Hooper, by the Revd Ernest Marvin, a member of the Iona Community, for his youth club in the post-war housing area of Lockleaze, Bristol. Two rock bands who frequented the club set the lyrics to music and the cast were club members. Both reached large audiences through the medium of television. In Scotland soon after came *Sing!* (1965), mixing material from the re-emerging charismatic renewal movement and song texts from Iona Community members and others to existing hit tunes and original melodies in a rock-music style.[1]

However, what started contemporary worship music (CWM) on its 50-year trajectory to become 'the most widely sung Christian repertory in the world'[2] was a confluence of coffee-bar evangelism undertaken within the English evangelical community and the Jesus Movement which was emerging within the 1960s charismatic revival in the mainstream churches in the USA. Musical Gospel Outreach (MGO) and its magazine *Buzz* became the umbrella both for the new bands and for those who were writing lyrics to popular songs as well as original hymns and tunes in a more accessible, and more rhythmic, style. Somewhere in the mix was the Fountain Trust (founded 1964), whose purpose was to promote charismatic renewal in the mainstream churches in the UK. Large gatherings such as the Festival of Light (its music headlined by Cliff Richard and Graham Kendrick) in the early 1970s, Spring Harvest (from 1979), and Soul Survivor and New Wine (1989), contributed to the spread of the songs as well as of charismatic styles of worship. Influential publications at this time included *Youth Praise* (1966), *Sound of Living Waters* (1974), and *Songs of Fellowship* (1981).

This movement has now a history of half a century and there has been much variation in style in that period, mirroring changing idioms in popular music. This has created a repertoire of which a great deal is still in use. To safeguard the composers, not least with the growing use of screens to display words, the Christian Copyright Licensing Scheme was established in 1985, and now continues as Christian Copyright Licensing International (CCLI). Of the (by now) different licence-granting bodies,[3] CCLI is the one most used by churches where worship songs are sung. It publishes a running list of the one hundred top titles recorded as being used at any one time, along with downloadable (for a subscription) sheet music (in the key you want) or, separately, lyrics, chords (for guitar/keyboard) etc. One way of exploring this body of Christian song is to examine the top ten in any one week. What follows comes from a week chosen at random but subsequent checks have suggested that the mix has been similar in other weeks (at least over a period of months). The titles are not in order but grouped for purposes of comment. What should be noted is that, unlike in lists of bestselling books, an item does not necessarily rise to the top and then gradually fade; a title may return to top place several times over a longer period. All those cited here may be found on YouTube.

## The songs

No. 9 on the list reminds us of the older generation of the worship song, reaching back to the mission hall and evangelistic rally. *How great thou art* ('O Lord my God! when I in awesome wonder') became popular following the 1950s Billy Graham crusades (the Swedish original dating back to 1885) and was once voted the United Kingdom's favourite hymn by BBC television's *Songs of Praise* programme.

*Cornerstone* (7) represents a growing category of worship song, the reworking of traditional material, usually called 'retuned hymns'. This example takes a well-known nineteenth-century hymn by Baptist pastor Edward Mote, beginning 'My hope is built on nothing less'. In place of the original refrain ('On Christ, the solid rock, I stand ...') is an impassioned new chorus, 'Christ alone, Cornerstone', drawing on the full power of the band. It is listed as being translated into 15 other languages. Another in this category is 'Just as I am – I come broken', where an entirely new second section, words and music, is added to the traditional words by Charlotte Elliott and tune by William Bradbury. The new material contrasts with the devotional mood of the original in its urgency, at a higher register, calling again on the forces of the whole instrumental ensemble.

The largest category consists of a group of five songs which have a family resemblance in form, idiom and content.

*This is amazing grace* (6) is by Phil Wickham from California, a prolific writer and recording artist. It is an energetic song with words in the style of a psalm of praise to the Creator but celebrating also the atoning sacrifice of Jesus Christ, expressing wonder 'that you would take my place, that you would bear my cross'. It has been taken up by the leading megachurches (including Hillsong and Bethel), although the writer himself is not directly associated with any one church base.

*O praise the name*, or Anastasis (Resurrection) (3), comes from the Hillsong group of churches. It is a hymn with verses on Calvary, the empty tomb and the second coming of Christ. It is more regular in structure than the other four in this category. In performance it contains several features which heighten the drama, both visual and musical, including in some performances leading to several minutes of spontaneous response with singing in tongues.

*What a beautiful name* (4), again from Hillsong, engenders and expresses adoration for the Name of Jesus ('Our sin – your love is greater', 'you have no rival, you have no equal'). It is ecstatic in style with a repetitive text in a setting based round a simple musical phrase. The chorus is not the same length each time and there is a long bridge passage, part of which is repeated after the last chorus, which leads to a tag to finish the song.

*Build my life* (10) is by Brett Younker, who is associated with another of the influential platforms for CWM, the Passion Conferences. The song acclaims Jesus as 'worthy of every song we could ever sing' and declares 'Holy, there is no-one like you'. Then comes a promise that 'I will build my life upon your love'. This material is repeated several times through the song, interspersed with instrumental interludes. It builds towards the end, reiterating the promise over and over, when in a semi-improvisatory section, Bible verses are spoken ('Put not your trust in princes ...' etc.) which are recognised and acclaimed by the audience/congregation, and then the song continues repeating the promise, quietening to a stillness.

*How great is our God* (5) is by one of the best known of contemporary 'worship artists', Texan Chris Tomlin, who like the previous writer is associated with the Passion Conferences. It consists mainly of groups of psalmic phrases ('the splendour of the king ... clothed in majesty ... darkness trembles ... worthy of all praise') intersected with a refrain 'How great (is) our God' returning in the manner of a rondo throughout.

The three remaining songs in the top ten are by British song-writers (albeit well known on the global circuit). *In Christ alone* (2), by Keith Getty and Stuart Townend, is written in double long metre (8 lines of 8 syllables). The attractive melody has the feel of an Irish folk song (Getty, a Durham music graduate, comes from Northern Ireland). It charts the life, death and resurrection of Jesus Christ, and is a statement of believing faith of some subtlety. There has been criticism of the inter-pretation that in the death of Christ 'the wrath of God was satisfied', causing it to be rejected by the committee preparing the new Presbyterian Church USA hymnal as perpetuating 'the view that the cross is primarily about God's need to assuage God's anger'.[4] It was sung at the enthronement of Justin Welby as Archbishop of Canterbury in 2013.

*How deep the Father's love* (8) is also by Stuart Townend and, again, is in a regular hymn metre, 8787D. It is a hymn of the Cross and humankind's salvation from sin. It also has a Celtic-flavoured melody.

*10,000 reasons* (to bless the Lord) (1) is by English song-writer Matt Redman in collaboration with Jonas Myrin, both now resident in California. Quoting Psalms 103 and 86, it has a verse and refrain structure. Its moving theme is of a song of worship sung at morning but also at the end of life as strength fails. Like the previous two, this also is proof of the current popularity of Celtic cadences.

It is possible that the weighting towards the music of the megachurches in the top ten gives too narrow a picture of the repertoire in actual use. In the remaining ninety songs in CCLI's hundred best, there are many which have originated at different stages in the past half century and which are now staple in local congregations in the UK – songs like: 'Be still, for the presence of the Lord'; 'Here I am, Lord' ('I, the Lord of sea and sky'); 'He is Lord'; 'Make me a channel'; 'There is a Redeemer'; 'Spirit of the living God'; 'Seek ye first'; 'Brother, sister, let me serve you'. Many of these are now found in denominational hymn books and are sung in the Sunday wor-ship of mainstream denominations, along with traditional hymns and psalms.

## The worship song in context

The group of five songs in the middle of our list originate from a small group of charismatic-independent megachurches originating in the USA and Australia but with plantings in other parts of the world, as well as from associated conferences and stadium-style concerts. These are supported by sophisticated marketing operations directly associated with these 'brands'. This includes websites where, as songs are written, scores and other helps are made available. Perhaps more influential are the videos on YouTube, often uploaded independently by enthusiasts, which enable potential users to mimic the ideal performance as well as allow worshippers to become familiar with the content of the songs and with the style of the worship.

The videos, usually made at actual worship events, show a common scenario. Lighting (quite often the worshippers are in semi-darkness) highlights the artists on stage. Flexible sound systems enable the singers to use the whole expressive range of their voices from breathless awe to ecstatic shout. A range of instruments, intricately balanced and blended, help to create moods and orchestrate feelings, from the typically unassuming simple, often chordal, quasi-improvised openings, through periods of pent-up stillness to high excitement. Often there are quite extensive periods of a controlled ecstasy when improvised words, familiar texts or speaking in tongues are heard over the music, before the song is picked up again. Bodily gesture is important. The participation of the worshippers may be in raised hands, swaying or dancing, upturned faces, all modelled by those on stage, and singing to the words on the screens. There are other uses of screens, visual media, which, changing continuously, show words, symbols, colours, scenes. (It has been suggested that screens are the stained glass and icons for the electronic media age.[5])

The people follow rather than make the song, one reason being that this type of writing and performance is not regular as would be a metrical hymn. There are many obstacles in the music to be negotiated: tempo variations, instrumental interludes, lines of lyrics of varied length, bridge passages, repetitions, tags, and – a characteristic – much improvisatory rendering on the part of the musicians. They can be quite difficult for a congregation to sing and demanding for local bands to accompany.

It has always been an issue in worship song that there can be too much focus on performance. I was present at a weekend gathering of Christian bands at the St Ninian's Centre in Crieff led by Graham Kendrick in the 1970s. One theme that he continually stressed, in working with these enthusiastic young performers, was the importance of the congregation as an active force in music-making and the place of the band as serving this. Matt Redman, similarly, believes that the proper role of the singer is 'to lead strongly so that people follow but not so strongly that we ourselves become the focus'. The best worship leaders, in his view, end up fading into the background and point the people to God. Redman prefers the description 'lead worshipper ... The real worship leader is the Holy Spirit.'[6]

That said, it is not out of place by any means to listen to someone else enhancing your engagement in worship by bringing what you yourself could not. The Anglican service of Evensong, which speaks both within and beyond the church, involves a high listening component. We listen to anthems, which depend on the skills of a choir. Nor is it a problem to have a solo voice leading a song; think of how cantors are now emerging today to engage worshippers in musical dialogue.

## CWM and the local church

Many local churches have recognised in this music a quality that they feel is lacking in their own gatherings. They may also fear that younger people will leave to look for a more congenial environment and the rock-concert thrill to be found in media-savvy religious gatherings. How well does it transplant? Pete Ward[7] believes that charismatic worship is now the default setting in most evangelical churches in Britain. While CWM may broaden the repertoire and widen the demographic reach of the congregation, Ward sees a downside in that it can alter the shape and style of local worship without that being a deliberate choice. It also may remove congregations from their accountability to their denomination and the contact which nurtures and strengthens it. He further suggests that our theologies are being changed by the songs – how the church understands itself in relation to the world, the importance of diversity in the local fellowship, and the thrust of its service and outreach.

If this seems far-fetched, we have to consider that in the neo-charismatic context the song *is* the worship. A 'time of worship' frequently refers to a twenty- to forty-minute segment during which the band leads the singing of a sequence of songs. Matt Redman describes this progression as: call to worship, engagement (connecting with God and each other), exaltation, adoration (bringing love songs before the throne of God), culminating in a time of intimacy when the worshipper experiences a visitation from God.[8] In this reading, where a traditional order would move through the hearing and preaching of the Word to prayer and offering, followed by sending out or the sharing in the sacrament of Holy Communion, here the final section of 'visitation from God' might be seen as corresponding, in other contexts, to the deep sharing in the body of Christ as the elements of the bread and wine are offered and received in an act of thanksgiving.

Graham Kendrick wrote his earliest songs as a result of his belief that 'traditional hymns can be too dense' for young people nourished by contemporary popular music. 'Popular rhythms speak to the body, to the feelings, before we analyse the words.' That does not mean that he is not critical of how things have developed since the early years. Indeed, most of the constructive criticism in the area of CWM comes from those involved directly in the movement. One matter being addressed is the danger of there being a feelgood factor about the music, the media and the moment, when the realities of life are suspended for a period in the intensity of the experience. Kendrick has not been alone in fearing that, for some, this form of worship can become an end in itself. He has warned that we should avoid getting trapped into one style of worship. It is also good to worship alongside other diverse people.[9] It was precisely this that the organisers of Soul Survivor in the 1990s, suspecting that worshippers were becoming connoisseurs of worship rather than participants, made radical alterations to the way in which worship experiences were designed.[10]

## Song content

The songs themselves have come under scrutiny. Keith Getty, co-author of *In Christ alone*, is concerned that too many contemporary songs do not have the content and quality that will carry people through life. Contemporary worship seems to be more about an immediate emotional connection with no particular theological depth or long-term approach. He suggests that 'shallow songs' may last for three years, and breed shallow believers who last for a just as long.[11] It is true that many have found their own life journey to be more complex, more ambiguous, than the songs allow. The focus on images of the greatness of God can leave questions unanswered, while an 'optimistic jollity'[12] holds no echo for those who are experiencing grief, loss, failure or fear. Stuart Townend urges that we should try to encompass as broad a range of emotion as the psalms.[13] Now songs are being written in response, such as 'Blessed be your name' (Matt and Beth Redman), to 'encourage us to worship God through the storms of life'.[14]

There is also the matter of Scripture content. Since the songs are the takeaway from worship, there needs to be about them a strength and a resilience so that they can unpack to give support in the daily dilemmas of work, family and society. A song should not simply express the faith of the writer but also of the church, where Scripture and doctrine shape Christian belief and conduct. There is no question about contemporary song not being scriptural and doctrinal. With the most frequent focus on Calvary, and on the power and might of God, both central to the faith, the question is rather whether the songs contain *enough* doctrine or theology and a sufficient breadth of the witness of Scripture. While it might be argued that a strong focus on the atonement is to be found in the hymns of Charles Wesley, this is accompanied by the scouring of Scripture and an uncovering of all its nourishing imagery, so that one gets a sense of the 'breadth and length and height and depth' of the love of God so as to be 'filled with all the fullness of God' (Eph. 3:18–19). The God of praise and worship songs, however, can seem one-dimensional, with little sign of the 'God of many names'.[15] The eventful life of Jesus, his encounters, stories, signs and sayings, and his resurrection appearances along the weary road, in the upper room and on the beach with fishermen after the night shift, all help make sense of the Cross and contribute to the shaping of the life of faith. If we don't have this, how will we be able to recognise the presence of Christ in the mundane? It is also pointed out that texts with an individualist bias need to be balanced with others which recognise the corporate nature of the worshipping community.

Related to this is the absence of reference to issues of the day and the society in which we live, areas where at-one-ment and reconciliation are so badly needed (this is not to overlook the outreach work engaged in by megachurches and conferences in their local communities and on behalf of people overseas). There are welcome exceptions, of which Kendrick's 'O Lord, the clouds are gathering' is one. Monique Ingalls wonders if that same restricted neo-Calvinist theology is a factor in this, which says human beings are ultimately depraved and therefore powerless to do good on their own. Only God can be the active agent, and all we can do is have faith.[16] Ingalls also worries, from her attendance at conferences in the USA, when sessions were set aside to work on overseas-related projects, whether there is a hint of the powerful being generous to the poor, the target group interpreted as victims needing charity with no sense of dialogue with them to right wrongs, and where there is no encouragement to question our Western lifestyle as contributing to the imbalance of resources or the misuse of power. (She makes an exception for Urbana, a conference sponsored by the InterVarsity Christian Fellowship, noting also that their leadership of the worship and the music is more racially diverse.)[17] It is noteworthy that quite recently there has been an emergence of a number of individuals and collectives seeking to expand the boundaries of the worship song to engage with real-time matters of faith and experience and with peace and justice issues such as the climate emergency, one example being Resound Worship.[18]

There is also the matter of what is not being sung. Several song composers have gone on record as suggesting that contemporary worship song needs to pay more attention to the church's tradition of song-making. Here is Matt Redman: 'I'm deeply concerned that the beautiful heritage of singing beautiful hymns, and teaching our children and grandchildren, is being lost in an empty, commercially driven façade.' Kendrick would agree, challenging writers always to submit their compositions to the standard of Scripture. Both he and Redman warn that it is important in a generation where so many people write off the past that we value our heritage in the church. Redman has gone even further back and made a version of the third-century Christian hymn *Phos Hilaron* (cheering light),[19] sung at the lighting of the evening lamp. Are people who grow up on worship songs missing out on the rich theology and poetry of traditional hymnody?[20] In similar vein, Townend's advice to modern writers is that they should 'gather together all the scripture you can find on the subject you feel inspired to write about, and read other books around the subject so you get a real understanding and sense of revelation about what the scripture is saying'.

What makes a song potentially shallow is not just verbal content but music, and there is criticism of the quality of the music of many worship songs. It is true that when you remove the special effects and the presentation of the songs, one might question the strength of some of the underlying music. The melodies can seem casual, plucked out of the air, and to the same palette of chords. However, it is a fact of life that each new age produces far more ephemeral songs and texts than those of lasting value. It is often difficult to tell, amid a welter of composition, what has the freshness that will last, until it does. Nevertheless, this music is nourishing this generation and it is legitimate to try to judge whether particular music is strong enough to support a witness and worship sufficiently robust for our day.[21]

These reservations make clear what a huge responsibility rests upon those who lead worship. Students preparing for ordination would have had the opportunity to reflect and learn about these matters but this may not be the case for worship leaders. Doug Gay of the University of Glasgow sees an urgency in the present situation:

> Contemporary Christian Music is here to stay and it is going to form a major part of the worship diet of many of our churches, probably most of them – and almost certainly most of the growing ones. So we need to get better at it. We have contracted out the lyrical/verbal content of much of our worship to young men and women who have minimal theological education and less liturgical awareness, who have mostly not done a creative writing class – and who never get edited! There is a lack of critical friends, a preciousness about 'anointed' texts, a lack of understanding of why a skilled editor might be a gift of grace, a charism.[22]

Jeremy Perigo, the director of worship and music programmes at the London School of Theology, takes a similar view. He is aware that people who lead sung worship now enjoy 'a lot of influence ... They are involved in the faith formation of an entire community, by songs, by prayers ... They need to be contextually, culturally aware, both critically and constructively, and theologically astute, in addition to being able to sing and play the guitar well.' In addition, he says, it is important that future leaders be exposed to a variety of liturgical traditions, and important to understand how these can contribute to supporting people through 'the long haul – why praying the Lord's prayer is important, why confession [is important]'. He predicts that, in the future, worship music will be 'both more global and more local' – the latter quality resulting from churches putting more emphasis on 'thinking about their own theology, their own contribution, their own gift and talents within the church, instead of just grasping the dominant styles that work well in California or Australia'.[23]

## Conclusions

Notwithstanding these critiques and appraisals, CWM carries challenges to the worship and song of the mainstream churches. One relates to the body and feelings. The word 'feelings' is deliberately chosen in preference to 'emotions'. Charles Davis distinguished between them in saying that the former are balanced by insight, by intellect. 'Where feelings differ from emotions ... is in their being spiritual and rational in their animating core.'[24] It is clear that the multitudes who attend the conferences, concerts and acts of worship which feature CWM find there an excitement that is not always present in the local church, where worship can often feel flat, verbose and over-intellectualised. Yet need this be so? Doug Gay suggests otherwise:

> I have become fascinated by a phrase which is used in the Westminster Directory of Public Worship – that the minister is to lead prayer in such a way that it will 'stir up suitable affections'. That's our job. If you are trusted with the privilege of leading public prayer, you'd better learn how to stir up suitable affections! Too often I worry that people in Presbyterian worship services just don't feel very much – neither beautiful nor intense ... it doesn't touch the deeps in us ... it's not immersive.[25]

An example he gives is prayer that is lacking the element of praise and adoration: 'This is where some of the charismatic evangelical churches put the rest of us to shame, but in my experience recently ministers seem to find it very hard to stay in the mode of praise to God – praise and thanksgiving and adoration.'[26] Affective experience, from adoration to the intimacy of presence that worshippers are led towards in song, is something that is also the hope of worshippers in mainstream churches, where worship is understood ultimately as encounter with God, and all that this means. Perhaps there is need to cultivate spontaneity, the point when things can go either way, when the unexpected is possible. Some call it 'breaking the image' – where a crack appears that allows access behind the rites and rituals. Again, this is not a quality that is taboo in the local church but it is certainly true that history and habit can conspire to prevent it. Spontaneity is not brought about by trickery or special effects. In long-standing liturgies it is endemic, in the music and other worship media as well, and it is there to be released in how well we choose words, accompany a hymn, move within the building, behave towards each other, decorate the space. Spontaneity – the word in Latin means 'of one's free will' – is when something fresh and unexpected opens up. In fact it is the creative component of a musical composition, what makes a particular melody a 'new song' and not a tired imitation.

The church, however, has to avoid the danger of thinking that a particular type of music will automatically solve a problem – here, the lack of younger people. What may attract them is more likely to be the whole package and the buzz of being in an amenable and hospitable community. The challenge to the local church is to develop an environment and quality of interaction that embraces all comers. That is, it is not just about music. In any case, as Maggi Dawn observes, it is odd to think that all young people like the same kind of music.[27] The assumption that popular music will 'bring in the young' can often exclude younger people whose preferred musical genre is what is often called classical. It is not uncommon to find in our churches younger people who are studying music, including developing their skills in instrumental playing, who find themselves having to play in a praise band where the only attraction is the physical act of playing and the music does not nourish them. There is something here about the need for a greater variety of opportunity locally, such as the employment of instruments over a wider musical spectrum – to accompany hymns or provide the equivalent of organ voluntaries or reflective music during worship.

What the local church has often done, of course, is to have more than one style of worship at different times which can attract different congregations. There is always the opportunity for people to migrate between them and there may be the occasional festive coming together. We should also be alert to one of the groups being infected by the other. Spending a month with an Adelaide (South Australia) church, it was made clear to me at the outset that I was only to work with the early service (all-age, lively, buoyant) but to keep away from the second, more formal congregation – a condition that this church made in agreeing to the project. Not long into the process, the second congregation became curious and asked to be introduced to some of the songs, which then became part of their repertoire.

The qualities of spontaneity, intimacy, community and the engagement of body and senses is found also in other styles of church music now being embraced by both young people and by mixed gatherings. The music from the Taizé Community attracts and engages large numbers of young people with its intimate, prayerful nature, the warmth of its harmonies and the excitement of the musical processes and instrumental arrangements. There are the songs from the world church, giving common cause with Christians living the faith in very different and often threatening contexts, rich in their harmonies, growing with repetition, and enthusiastic in performance, with, in the case of the Latin American contribution, the dance-like nature of the melodies. Nearer home there is the music of the Iona Community, which opens out congregational song in another direction from the worship song, with music in a fresh style and lyrics which make full acknowledgement of issues of life and faith.

There are also many inventive new ways of celebrating Holy Communion and many experiments under the heading of alternative worship which draw on tradition, technology and the arts, capable of deep engagement on the part of the worshipper. There is evidence, in a study from an evangelical seminary in Kentucky, of a new interest in traditional patterns of liturgy on the part of young people. The attraction, it is suggested, is that these offer to embrace all aspects: mind, body and soul; that they offer depth and mystery rather than pragmatic consumerism; that they provide an anchor for faith and instil habits leading to formation and growth – as well as other reasons.[28]

There is some evidence of a more eclectic approach to worship and music, with different styles and idioms rubbing shoulders. In the UK, this note is also being struck. Graham Hunter, who has studied charismatic approaches to the eucharist, writes with the intention of persuading charismatics 'that there is real value in the liturgical tradition' and those from a more formal and liturgical expression of worship 'that it is possible to make space to integrate Charismatic approaches to worship in our services'.[29]

To combine different musical genres in a single service of worship is no more difficult than constructing a concert of music from different centuries, and which might even include the premier of a new work. Many churches are now exploring such an integrated approach. One report is of a Huddersfield Church of England congregation in which services regularly include plainsong, Orthodox harmonised chant, responsorial psalms, world music, traditional hymns and contemporary worship music.[30] As Hugh Morris, the director of the Royal School of Church Music, points out, contemporary Christian music is 'not necessarily something that has to replace what has gone before, but something that adds to the breadth of it'. The integrated approach, however, is not a question of just throwing different things together. There is real skill involved, both musical and liturgical, so that the result is not just 'a log-jam of styles'.[31]

Matt Redman, some of whose perceptive comments on the contemporary worship music scene we have quoted, has a song reminiscent of Amos chapter 5 and Micah chapter 6, whose strictures call to account all our song in whatever idiom, and all our worship, however creatively crafted:

I'll bring you more than a song,
for a song in itself
is not what you have required.
You search much deeper within,
through the way things appear,
you're looking into my heart.

I'm coming back to the heart of worship
and it's all about you,
it's all about you, Jesus.
I'm sorry, Lord, for the thing I've made it
when it's all about you,
it's all about you, Jesus
… all about you.[32]


## Notes

1 Galbraith, Douglas and Ronald Beasley (eds), 1965, *Sing!* Church of Scotland Youth Department. This was an early attempt to bring together renewal music with the mainstream church repertoire.

2 Ingalls, Monique M., 2018, *Singing the Congregation*, Oxford: Oxford University Press, p. 7.

3 The other main licence provider is One Licence: https://www.hymnsam.co.uk/the-business/one-license/ (accessed 17.5.21).

4 News item, 2013, *Church Times*, 9 August .

5 Ingalls, *Singing the Congregation*, p. 177.

6 Interview with Matt Redman in *Church Music Quarterly*, June 2005, pp. 6f.

7 Ward, Pete, 2005, *Selling Worship: How What We Sing Has Changed the Church*, Milton Keynes: Paternoster Press, p. 1.

8 Spinks, Bryan D., 2010, *The Worship Mall: Contemporary Responses to Contemporary Culture*, London: SPCK, pp. 96–101.

9 Perona-Wright, Leah, 2004, 'The future is eclectic!', interview with Graham Kendrick, *Church Music Quarterly*, March.

10 Ward, *Selling Worship*, pp. 171f.

11 Keith Getty, 2018, quoted in Madeleine Davies, 'Where next for contemporary worship music?', *Church Times*, 7 December.

12 Pete Ward, 2018, quoted in Madeleine Davies, 'Where next for contemporary worship music?', *Church Times*, 7 December.

13 Perona-Wright, Leah, 2005, 'Talking with Townend', *Church Music Quarterly*, September.

14 Interview with Matt Redman, *Church Music Quarterly*, pp. 6f.

15 See 'Source and Sovereign, Rock and Cloud', a hymn by Thomas Troeger which explores the many titles of God in Scripture.

16 Ingalls, *Singing the Congregation*, pp. 75f.

17 Ingalls, *Singing the Congregation*, pp. 98–102.

18 See Appendix 2 for details of this and other worship song collectives and sites.

19 There is another contemporary version, 'O laughing Light', by the Canadian Sylvia Dunstan.

20 Interview with Matt Redman, *Church Music Quarterly*, pp. 6f.

21 See further Chapter 18.

22 Gay, Doug, 2019, 'Renewing the church's worship', Church Service Society *Record*, 54, p. 15.

23 Jeremy Perigo, 2019, quoted in Madeleine Davies, *Church Times*, 29 November.

24 Davis, Charles, 1976, *Body as Spirit: The Nature of Religious Feeling*, London: Hodder & Stoughton, p. 4.

25 Gay, 'Renewing the church's worship', p. 13.

26 Gay, 'Renewing the church's worship', p. 12.

27 Maggi Dawn, 2019, quoted in Madeleine Davies, *Church Times*, 29 November.

28 https://www.missioalliance.org/8-reasons-the-next-generation-craves-ancient-liturgy (accessed 17.5.21).

29 Hunter, Graham, 2017, *Discipline and Desire: Embracing Charismatic Liturgical Worship*, W233, Cambridge: Grove Books.

30 Appleton, Gordon, 2011, 'When the congregation is the choir', *Church Music Quarterly*, June, pp. 27f.

31 Hugh Morris, 2019, quoted in Madeleine Davies, *Church Times*, 29 November.

32 Matt Redman, 'The heart of worship'.

# The Choice of Music for Worship

# 6

# Traditional or Contemporary?

## *Getting the balance right*

The church today is engaged in making bold and imaginative responses to a society where patterns of belief and belonging have undergone radical change, where heretofore unassailable authority is challenged, and where a community is as likely to be formed round digital signals as round pulpits, tables and altars. Its approach to mission and outreach is being re-formed, giving rise to new models of being the church and of worship: fresh expressions, café churches, pioneer ministries, art installations, the eclectic styles under the heading of alternative worship, and various forms of 'public liturgy' such as the pilgrimage movement. These generally do not displace customary churchgoing. Cathedrals – mounting projects to engage with the wider community – are said to be experiencing a strengthening of attendance at regular services, and church-planting continues, even in one location based round a choir,[1] while the thoughtful re-ordering of interiors is common, enabling variety of use and a flexibility which can accommodate different ways of worshipping and of serving the community.

In this ongoing re-formation, the assumption is often made that we should be prepared to be radical and steel ourselves to retire the traditions of worship which are seen to inhibit us. Tradition is often seen as retrospective, stifling, deadening and limiting, and the laudable desire to be more open to our contemporaries, to be more inclusive, more welcoming, often results in the dismissal of the old in favour of the new. Since alteration of formal liturgies or patterns often takes time, skill and synodical consent, music – the easiest and quickest component to change – is often first in the firing line. There have been many stories of clergy and councils closing down the choir, dismissing the organist, introducing new technologies, investing in new hymn books, often without much consultation. This movement also takes other forms, such as the concept of blended worship in which the new music is used alongside the old. There is nothing wrong with that in theory, not least because already the music of the church is a blend of the newer, the older and the very much older! However, a danger is that blended worship can justify uncritical acceptance of contemporary material simply because it is contemporary. It also can leave tradition undisturbed when perhaps it needs to be called in question.

This is by no means new. Throughout history, at times of seismic shifts in society, worship has undergone change. An example was the Protestant Reformation as society and church regrouped around the opening up of culture and learning, along with its attendant spirit of critical enquiry in all fields, all of which took a quantum leap through the invention of printing. These, along with the self-determination which followed social and political change, led to a re-envisioning of worship, one based on hearing and learning, where all were their own priests in that anyone could approach God without intermediary. It was in music that this had its clearest expression, in the metrical psalms that underlined the fact that worship was less a spectacle than an event with the singing faithful actively participant in body and mind. Although this might seem a break with tradition in favour of new practices, in fact much was continuous: the Christian Year with all its festivals continued to be printed in the new psalters, the song schools very quickly regrouped, the canticles remained (albeit in metrical form). Yet in retrospect much was lost, not least the accustomed forms of the music, along with many customs and artefacts which had nurtured devotion.

In spite of this, the new ways can be seen, from later perspective, as being continuous with the old. Ecumenical convergence has contributed to this in that we see in each other's worship practices the same strong shapes and Spirit-inspired formulations as our own. For example, at the Second Vatican Council, the new weight given to the active participation of the faithful as they worshipped looked as radical as did the Reformation emphasis on the congregation as a priesthood of believers. Commenting, however, on the changes brought about by the Council, Anscar Chupungco OSB took issue with those who accused the Council of throwing out history, claiming that its decisions read further back into history than its critics had done, finding 'active participation' as present in the older, more classical liturgical forms.[2] The truth of this was confirmed during the recent wide-ranging and comprehensive Experience of Worship project led by Professor John Harper, which involved re-enactments of Sarum liturgies both in Salisbury Cathedral and a small Welsh parish church. One outcome was to give the lie to the belief that lay people were largely passive in worship. Indeed, the enactment suggested a 'far richer, more fluid and distinctive individual and collective experience and engagement among the laity in the medieval Mass'[3] than is often assumed.

The important building block of the church known as tradition is often sold short. When people use the word, what is often meant is something like: 'what we do now – which of course is the way we have always done things'. Tradition is seen as something fixed, proven, arrived at, an outcome – whereas it is really flow rather than sediment, the distilled essence of the imaginative discoveries of the past. Paul Vallely, visiting Iona Abbey, was struck by the history of innovation going back to the sixth century that attaches to this ancient place: the marking of a grave with a stone bearing a cross, the symbol reaching new levels of creativity with the massive four-metre-tall crosses with their elaborate double-sided carvings which spread from Iona to the rest of Britain; or the scriptorium, new dyes and inks discovered, able to produce the magnificent Book of Kells; or the first glass ever made in Scotland.[4]

A later community in Iona Abbey was Benedictine, and it is possible that there would have been found there examples of liturgical innovation similar to that in the cathedrals of Europe and Britain during the tenth and eleventh centuries. Found in the Winchester Troper (the trope being a way of embellishing or extending existing song and prayer) is both the text and an eye-witness description by the (Benedictine) bishop of a dialogue and enactment added to the early-morning office on Easter Day.[5] He describes the unobtrusive entry of one, representing the angel, who waits by a sepulchre constructed in view of the people, being followed after a reading by three others 'stepping delicately as those who seek something' (the Marys). Beginning 'Quem quaeritis', they sing:

> Whom do you seek in the sepulchre, disciples? –
> We seek Jesus of Nazareth who was crucified, O heavenly one. –
> He is not here; he is risen as he foretold; go, announce that he is risen from the tomb. –
> Alleluia! The Lord is risen!

At this point the angel throws back the veil; one of the Marys displays the cloth abandoned in the tomb. All then sing the antiphon, 'Surrexit Dominus'. This has been described as the kernel of all Western drama, as it developed into similar scenes for other festivals and ultimately moved into public places as mystery plays.

The Christian Year, already a renewing of tradition as it has fused with or incorporated pre-Christian folk festivals, has developed new festivals, most recently the Reign of Christ the King (1925) and Creationtide, the latter in process of being finally established following the initial proposal from the Ecumenical Patriarch of the Greek Orthodox Church in 1989. Both these were a response to movements or crises in the world, an interaction between the established Calendar and the bringing into worship of Christian concern.

In music there was the sea-change when monophony began to turn into polyphony, later leading to harmony-based structures. At the beginning of the second millennium, a second voice was being added to the plainsong melody, travelling parallel a fourth below, that voice in time being duplicated an octave above, creating a succession of 6/4 chords. It is not difficult to see how contrary motion between the voices might creep in and take hold, preparing the way for the polyphony of voices independent of each other.[6] An entirely different example of musical evolution was the result of a deterioration. The lining-out of the psalms could result in both a destruction of the fluency of the sense and, as contemporary accounts reveal, a cacophonous sound as hit or miss voices reached for the melody. As this vanished from the mainland, it continued and evolved in the Highlands and Islands of Scotland to become the characteristic style of Gaelic psalmody, a musical form of ethereal beauty.

The danger is not tradition itself but traditions which have become hardened and no longer have within them the resilience in which they were birthed. As Jaroslav Pelikan put it: 'Tradition is the living faith of the dead; traditionalism is the dead faith of the living.'[7] In *The Language of Mystery*, Edward Robinson approaches the matter from the context of art. He argues that a tradition is only kept alive by the constant injection of new imaginative insights. To be resisted is a spirit of antiquarianism that is not open to the possibility that the contemporary imagination may carry a revelation for our own century that the artistic language of an earlier period would be unable to provide. He remarks: 'It is only in retrospect that we can see the great innovators like Berlioz or Wagner, Constable or Cézanne as being deeply in debt to their tradition; to their contemporaries they seemed more often to be subverters of it.'[8] Tradition, rightly understood, 'changes in order to remain the same'.[9]

None of these innovations have remained as first conceived, since tradition continually renews itself. Museums do not house a cold heritage but enable us to be stirred by beauty and skill that can offer us new places to begin. Heritage embodies change, otherwise there would be nothing sufficiently creative to mark the moment that is conserved. Elaine Scarry argues that when justice falters and society is fractured, beautiful things from the past keep visible the manifest good of balance and equality, and are a force in nudging us towards restoring justice and peace.[10] We might find an illustration of this in the public martyrdom in 2015 by ISIS of Khaled al-Asaad, head of antiquities at the ancient city of Palmyra, a UNESCO World Heritage Site, who refused to reveal where he had hidden its treasures. The reason was that he saw it as crucial that these should be preserved undamaged as something from their own culture expressive of a fair and peaceful society, still to be there as a backcloth for rebuilding justice when the present troubles were over.

The choice, then, is not between the traditional and the contemporary. Our worship traditions do not hand on 'the remains of the day' so much as capture a constantly unfolding and living encounter with God, to which people have brought the best of their gifts, and of which we today are a still evolving part. But there is another dimension to the concept; it is not simply the link between past and present. As John Zizioulas reminds us, tradition places both past and present in relation to the Parousia: 'The true criterion of Tradition is ... to be found in the revelation of what the world will be like in the kingdom.'[11] If anything encourages continuing imaginative work on worship and music, the idea that we have still to uncover the fullness of our traditions surely does.

How many of the developments in recent years have been recoveries or fresh versions of an old model: gathering round a table for Communion, house churches, pop-up monasteries. There is the midnight service on Christmas Eve (could this be echoing one of the earliest forms, the Easter Vigil?), the nine lessons and carols format, the Christingle – all recent 'innovations'. Or take the Sanctorale, the feasts of the saints, now being creatively revisited. The Calendar of the Uniting Church in Australia is not just a filling out from another tradition of the traditional list of canonised saints, but a reinvigoration of it, where those traditional saints of universal approbation are retained but joined with categories of uncanonised saints relevant to the constituent denominations of that Church or to the nation in which it is set. The categories do not just recall people and their contribution but open the way to seeing ourselves as potentially among them, assisted by the way the categories are named. In addition to apostles and martyrs there are: reformers of the Church, Christian thinkers, renewers of society, faithful servants, persons of prayer, witnesses to Jesus, and Christian pioneers.[12]

Tradition can be a quarry, but it can also be a corrective. It can spark our imagination, and it can critique from long experience what we are reaching for. We have been this way before. 'The new song can be an old song sung by those whom God is making new.'[13]

## Notes

1 Davies, Madeleine, 2018, 'Choir to be core of church-plant', *Church Times*, August 2018. This refers to an initiative shared between St James's, Milton, Portsmouth, and Portsmouth Cathedral.

2 Chupungco, Anscar J., OSB, 2016, 'The vision of the Constitution on the Liturgy', in Alcuin Reid (ed.), *T & T Clark Companion to Liturgy*, London: Bloomsbury T & T Clark, pp. 263, 281.

3 Harper, John, 2016, 'Enactment and the study of late medieval liturgy', in Sally Harper, P. S. Barnwell and Magnus Williamson (eds), *Late Medieval Liturgies Enacted: The Experience of Worship in Cathedral and Parish Church*, Farnham: Ashgate, pp. 306f.

4 Vallely, Paul, 2017, 'New paths to familiar destinations', *Church Times*, 28 April.

5 Reese, Gustave, 1941, *Music in the Middle Ages*, London: Dent, pp. 194f.

6 Reese, *Music in the Middle Ages*, pp. 254f.

7 Pelikan, Jaroslav, 1984, *The Vindication of Tradition: The 1983 Jefferson Lecture in the Humanities*, New Haven and London: Yale University Press, p. 65.

8 Robinson, Edward, 1987, *The Language of Mystery*, London: SCM Press, p. 34.

9 Paton, Ian, 2019, 'Ordination – an Anglican perspective', *The Record* (Church Service Society), 54, p. 27, paper given at the Society's Study Day 2019.

10 Scarry, Elaine, 1999, *On Beauty and Being Just*, Princeton, NJ: Princeton University Press.

11 Zizioulas, John, 1993, 'The Church as Communion', in T. F. Best and G. Gassmann (eds), *On the Way to Fuller Koinonia*, Faith and Order Paper 166, Geneva: WCC Publications, p. 109.

12 *Uniting in Worship 2*, 2005, Sydney: Uniting Church Press, pp. 567f.

13 Stein, Jock, 1988, *Singing a New Song: Fresh Resources for Christian Praise*, Haddington: Handsel Press, p. 3.

# 7

# Choosing the Music

No-one who has had the good fortune to be in the audience at a live performance of Benjamin Britten's church opera *Noye's Fludde* – a musical setting of one of the fifteenth-century Chichester miracle plays – could forget the moment when through a rising storm, brought to deafening life by percussion and screeching violins (aided by the younger children playing tin mugs with spoons), the tentative strains of 'Eternal Father, strong to save' are heard through the melee. As the spectators rise to sing, the hymn gradually strengthens over a heaving passacaglia-like figure in the lower instruments, until finally the fury of the elements is overpowered. The prayer is answered. It is one of three hymns, where the audience become performers – the others, the penitential 'Lord Jesus, think on me' as the Ark sets sail, and 'The spacious firmament on high' as it makes landfall under a shining rainbow. The feel and flavour of the hymns resonate with the story. In a similar way, J. S. Bach made his audiences part of the narrative. In the *St Matthew Passion*, at the point when Jesus identifies a betrayer among the disciples, the composer captures their anxious guilty clamour as they shout over each other in jagged counterpoint, 'Lord, is it I?' The audience can no longer keep silent in their shame, breaking into a chorale, 'My sin it is that binds thee'.

We have examined the different genres of music that have a place in Christian worship (Chapters 3–5). In discussing principles that govern choice, it will be helpful to consider the inner workings of an act of worship and how music may not only fit but also help shape and bring it to life. To find the right music is a sensitive, imaginative, often intuitive task. Erik Routley comments that in *Noye's Fludde* the people are on the edge of their seats waiting for the moment to leap to their feet and sing. 'The hymn is precisely what they want to say. No other hymn would have done.'[1] He is setting the bar high; our task is no less than to select music which changes people from spectators to actors, hymns and songs that they are poised to sing. Music for worship is not like a series of items in a concert but is more akin to the recitatives and arias which are integral to an opera, which carry the story and move it, and us, towards the climax. In this delicate and creative process, in addition to the musical resources available, we have three things to keep in mind:

- The shape of the service.
- The Christian Calendar.
- Associated biblical themes.

## The shape of the service

Over the centuries, the church has developed shapes, patterns and formulae which map out a space where worship can take place. Even for those who eschew formulae and have free and spontaneous worship there is an underlying pattern which can be quite constant. Some traditions, like the Roman Catholics and the Anglican Communion, have set forms, even though customised in various ways to suit context and occasion. Others publish worship books containing orders clothed in model texts, orders that are deemed more likely to enable worship that is true to the Word of God, pastorally sensitive, inclusive, passionate and contextualised. This ordered liberty may be 'authorised' or 'commended' (rather than decreed) by higher Councils, leaving room for further creativity and spontaneity. Yet across traditions the fundamental order of Christian worship – word and sacrament together – can be recognised. It is interesting that even in the 'prayer book churches', wider choices of form and content are now offered.

What is the nature of the shape, of the order? What it is not is a sequence of events, a list of items. Some describe it as a drama, wishing to capture the dynamic nature of worship, where there is not only progress but potential transformation. Here are people gathering; they listen for and hear the Word of God in Scripture reading and preaching; they make response to the Word in creed and in prayer for the world; with offering and thanksgiving they celebrate the new life of baptism or gather round the table of the Lord; they are then sent out with blessing to live out the faith. Alternatively we may see worship as replaying the great drama of the salvation of humankind: we come, representative of a fallen world to seek pardon and peace, we encounter God crucified and risen in Word and Sacrament, and are constituted afresh as the body of Christ, now a sign, instrument and foretaste of the Kingdom of God.

## The Christian Calendar

Through the Calendar, beginning on the first of the four Sundays of Advent, we are reminded each year of the whole sweep of the Christian story, the story of salvation: told in Scripture, personified in later thinkers, reformers, pioneers and those who gave costly service, played out in feasts and festivals. The main festivals are marked with colour, drama and story, to feed our spirit and strengthen our faith. Well known are the principal seasons lasting several weeks: Advent, Christmas, Epiphany, Lent, the Easter season. Others are single festivals which commemorate a key incident, like Pentecost or Candlemas. This Calendar still changes and develops; new contours are added as the Holy Spirit leads the church into new challenges. As already noted in the previous chapter, one example is the last Sunday of the Year, the Feast of Christ the King, observed since 1925. Until then the Year ended without any ceremony; we had rehearsed the hope of the gospel, but still we looked out on a broken world, unreconciled people, a devastated environment, rampant disease, where humankind gave homage to other rulers. 'The harvest is past, the summer is ended, and we are not saved' (Jer. 8:20). This new festival offers a more positive ending, a symbol of the realisation of the Christian hope. It reassures us that our discipleship has not been in vain, our love and service not wasted. Something *has* changed; outcrops of the Kingdom of God are indeed seen in our time. Another, even more recent addition is Creationtide (1989) when, between September 1 and October 4 (appropriately, St Francis of Assisi's feast day), we pray for creation and explore lifestyles that will go towards meeting today's climate emergency and rescue those who particularly suffer from our despoliation of the earth.

Some will confine their observance of the Calendar to one or two festivals only while sitting lightly to or ignoring the rest. It is understandable, for example, that the timing of Christmas, so near the turn of the year and the associated holidays, should push the beginning of the celebrations back into early parts of December to accommodate different groups and age ranges. This can be at the expense of overlooking the very powerful themes that traditionally fill Advent, the recognition of evil and danger in the world, reflection on which helps create an expectancy that builds towards the celebration of the Nativity. Again, it is good that today there is a growing co-operation between denominations to observe not just Good Friday but the drama of Holy Week, along with groups meeting throughout Lent, often ecumenical, where there is both self-examination and the examination of the church's own life and witness.

## Biblical narratives and themes

There is more than one way of deciding which Bible passages are read as part of worship: working through a whole book, approaching choice through world events or local community observances, pastoral situations, the private study of the preacher. Most main churches now adopt another practice, not necessarily excluding any of the above, and that is the use of a lectionary. Much used in the English-speaking Protestant churches is the Revised Common Lectionary (RCL), compiled by an international and ecumenical body called the Consultation on Common Texts. This had taken as its starting point the Roman Catholic Mass Lectionary, one of the fruits of the Second Vatican Council, and, after trialling versions of this through many years, published the final version in 1992. In both of these world lectionaries, for every Sunday there are specified: an Old Testament reading with a thematically related psalm (for singing or communal reading), and a passage from an Epistle, and a Gospel. In the RCL, from Advent to Trinity Sunday the Old Testament and Gospel readings are closely related. Thereafter, till the end of the cycle, two streams of Old Testament and Psalm are offered, the first in which the relationship continues, the second where the Old Testament readings are semi-continuous, regardless of Gospel themes. Also, for the Easter period the Old Testament reading is replaced by one from Acts. The cycle runs for three years, each of these working through one of the synoptic Gospels but with the fourth Gospel, that of St John, being drawn upon through the whole period. This is not to overlook other lectionaries with different focuses, such as the Narrative Lectionary.[2] Some lectionaries, like Spill the Beans, accompany the readings and themes with ideas and material for worship, including worship across the age groups.[3]

An advantage of lectionaries is that they allow Scripture to speak for itself and save it from being read selectively in accord with our own favourite themes or preferred theological approach. Lectionaries also illuminate the Christian Calendar and enable particular Christian seasons and festivals to unfold in a way that their meaning is clear. There are other advantages. The RCL, for example, is *ecumenical*, enabling single denominations and several denominations together to share in their study, prayer and praise. It is *pastoral* in that it enables worshippers to base their private prayer and study on the Sunday readings and thus prepare in advance, perhaps with the help of a lectionary-based scheme devised to accompany personal devotion. It is also *practical* in that it gives organists and others who undertake the planning of worship advance notice of the themes and emphases of a particular Sunday or season, so that they can choose appropriate choir music and settings, suggest hymns to the leader of worship, or select suitable organ music. Its practical uses also include offering the opportunity for *linking the programmes* of Sunday Schools and other groups with the worship of the congregation, or providing a focus for *local clergy* who may wish to meet to plan their preaching in common. Many fear that a lectionary might cramp their style, but many more attest to the surprising experience that, even though set in advance, the readings so often engage with issues of the day, sometimes bringing unexpected insight.

It needs to be emphasised that what will be suggested below is not a slate of hymns and songs which faithfully refer to the themes for the day. A service of worship is not primarily the delivery of teaching, the exposition of ideas, although this takes place. Worship is far wider than this, and those who worship engage with it in many different ways. What is being said is that an act of worship is bound together with coherences, between song and speech, between song and song, and music and ritual, maybe only lightly stated. A recognition of a reference in verse 3 of a hymn to one of the passages heard or expounded, for example, may make a connection in the mind. So while we do not set out to find, say, four hymns that are a perfect match, it is helpful to study the scriptural index that is now commonly found in hymnals and see what it offers.

Because of the spread of denominational practice and the rich variety of contribution music can make to worship, it is not possible in what follows to be exhaustive but only to offer pointers.

## Making choices

The following four or five 'movements' embrace the shape, conscious or unconscious, that worship takes in most parts of the church:

- The Gathering/Preparation.
- The Word of God or the Service of/Ministry of/Liturgy of the Word.
- Response to the Word *or*
- Holy Communion (or Baptism).
- The Dismissal/Sending Out.

## The Gathering/Preparation

Following any processions (Bible, choir, clergy), the leader greets
the people (who may respond) in God's name and calls them
to worship. Alternatively, there may be a responsive sequence
which enables the transition to worship. The prayers may be
the well-known collect for purity or longer prayers of *invoca-
tion* (asking for God's presence) or praising God in *adoration*.
Prayers of *confession* or *penitence* lead to a *declaration of forgiveness* or *absolution*, followed by a collect specific to the day
or other prayer. The Gloria may conclude the section. In some
settings there may be included a children's or all-age talk.

*Hymns, songs and psalms.* The first hymn is sung as on a
threshold and helps to bring the worshippers into the presence
of God. Most commonly it focuses on God in adoration and
praise, 'big' in its statements and its tune. Or it may express
delight in being in God's house and more quietly prepare the
mind to recognise the presence of the One who promised to
be where two or three have gathered together. On special
Sundays, it can strike the appropriate note for the day or
season. At a time of sorrow or threat, it may express contrition,
searching or longing – a time when an opening metrical psalm
may be particularly appropriate. Alternatively, a processional hymn (dignified in rhythm, similar in theme) is announced,
during which choir and clergy enter. After a children's/all
age address a children's hymn might follow. This may be one
written specifically with children in mind or it may be one
of the vivid hymns of the church, with clear images and a
telling tune, which children can appreciate and respond to as
well as adults. There are also styles of music (participatory,
using percussion, rhythmic – often from other cultures) which
particularly engage children (see 'Shorter songs and chants'
below). A criterion might be that such hymns should be
capable of being sung by adults and children together. Some
hymn collections offer an index of such hymns.

*Service music.* In this section are settings of the Kyrie and Gloria. As well as fuller versions sung by the choir, simpler congregational settings in various idioms are available, as well as stand-alone settings of individual texts. The service might begin with an introit. For this, a choir might offer a composition which expresses the nature of the day or the time of year or festival, whether in a composed anthem or a suitable hymn. Alternatively it could reflect one of the biblical themes of the day. For this and other parts of the service, see further in Chapter 4.

*Shorter songs and chants.* There may be chants, canons and choruses as people gather. There are simple participative settings of the Kyrie – such as that from Ukraine which may be sung in four parts, or versions in English beginning 'Lord, have mercy' – and the Gloria in excelsis, such as the one from Peru ('Glory to God'), which easily and ingeniously builds into a tower of sound. For this and other parts of the service see Chapter 3 (section on Songs) for more suggestions, and the parts of hymn books headed Short Chants, Short Songs or Liturgical Settings. Be alert to the fact that some items can also be found in the bodies of these books in appropriate sections such as Penitence, Eucharist, Sending Out.

### The Word of God/The Liturgy of the Word

This section can sometimes begin with an introduction which briefly alerts people to the season and to themes that are to unfold in the service. The readings may include all, or some, of a passage from the Old Testament (on which the psalm for the day is a reflection or echo), one from an Epistle, and one from a Gospel. Where there is Communion, it is expected in some traditions that all three readings will be used, or, if fewer, the Gospel must be included. The readings are followed by a sermon, reflection, homily or address. Other ways might be used to convey the content of the passages or to enable reflection on them (drama, art, multimedia resources, silence, as well as song).

*Hymns, songs and psalms.* The psalm usually comes after the first reading. There is now considerable variety in psalm settings, as outlined in Chapter 4, where there is also a description of the responsorial psalm and Anglican chant. Alternatively, a hymn which quotes from the psalm for the day, identified through the scriptural index of your hymn book, may be chosen. It is also possible at this point to select a hymn which is a prayer for the Holy Spirit to illuminate our listening to readings or sermon, or a hymn which celebrates or reflects on the nature of Scripture. Suitable might also be one of the now increasing body of hymns about the life of Christ, as opposed to his Passion and death.

*Service music.* In the Proper of the Mass this section contained the Gradual prefacing the readings, and the Alleluia. Today it is common to surround, or to follow, the Gospel with the Gospel Acclamation, typically consisting of psalm verses and alleluias. *Music for Common Worship* (MCW) has a variety of settings from chant to contemporary style, pp. 52f.[4] See also 'Laudate', nos. 534f. Here too an anthem is commonly placed as continuing the listening to the Word.

*Short songs and chants.* There are many settings of Alleluia. There are also songs about hearing Scripture, like the responsive, 'Listen now for the Gospel'. Other chants which express expectancy or readiness like 'Jesu tawa pano' or 'Jesus, name above all names' are suitable. Readings or sermon might be followed by songs like 'Your will be done/Mayenziwe' or affirmations such as 'Goodness is stronger than evil'.

### Response to the Word when Holy Communion is not celebrated

This may be followed by one of the Creeds (or a contemporary affirmation of faith).[5] The offerings may be presented followed either by a short prayer or by Prayers of Thanksgiving and Intercession (or 'prayers of the people', in some traditions lay-led), including a prayer of offering, and ending with the Commemoration of the Faithful Departed. When there is no service of Holy Communion, this would lead, after a hymn, to the Benediction and Dismissal. It is not uncommon for any general announcements to precede the final hymn, a point in the service where they are less likely to feel like an interruption.

*Hymns, songs and psalms.* A hymn following the sermon, especially when the Creed is not said, could be credal in theme. Or it may take its theme or mood from the sermon, whether praise or lament, or contain reference to the Scripture passage being expounded. It also could be seasonal. Alternatively a hymn could point forward to the prayers of intercession, or it may be one of thanksgiving. A hymn could be sung in association with the presentation of the offerings, perhaps remaining seated.

*Service music.* MCW has traditional and contemporary settings of the Creeds, including Timothy Dudley-Smith's 'We believe in God the Father', found also in hymn books.

*Short songs and chants.* An Acclamation could be used as part of the response to the sermon. A prayer chant, such as 'Stay with me' (Taizé), could be used in association with spoken prayer. An offering song such as 'Take, O take me as I am' (Iona) might be sung several times as the offerings are brought to the table.

### Holy Communion (or Baptism)

When Communion is celebrated, the acts of offering, intercession and thanksgiving are grouped in this part of the worship.

*Hymns, songs and psalms.* A hymn or preparation for the Sacrament may come at the beginning of this section. In some Reformed traditions it may accompany the 'Great Entry' (of elders bearing the elements), often to Psalm 24:7–10,

'Ye gates, lift up your heads on high' sung to St George's, Edinburgh.[6] There are, however, many other options available. Eucharistic hymns may be sung during the Communion, while people are going forward or returning. This doesn't work quite so well when the elements are shared along rows, when often silence is kept.

*Service music.* Where a Communion setting is not being used (see Chapter 4 for sources), the Sanctus and Benedictus are often spoken by all together. The Agnus Dei is spoken responsively. Where it is sung, this may be during the reception of the bread and wine, or following the Great Prayer just after the breaking of the bread.

*Short songs and chants.* Given that people may already join in the Sanctus and Benedictus (spoken), they may be prepared to sing one of the short versions, such as the popular Argentinian Santo, albeit not setting the complete text. For the Agnus Dei, there are settings of 'Lamb of God'. Songs suitable for after or during the reception of the elements are 'Eat this bread' (Taizé) sung repetitively, the Argentinian 'God bless to us our bread', begun by a cantor, or 'This is the body of Christ' (Iona).

## Dismissal/Sending Out

Although brief, this section is of real importance, as, having heard the Word (and shared a meal together), we cross the threshold to live out our faith in the life of the world. The Dismissal may be extended and might be drawn from the themes of the service.

*Hymns, songs and psalms.* A closing hymn may express praise, dedication and commitment, encouragement, discipleship and service. It may in some way echo the themes of the day and the Calendar season. It is likely to be one known well to the people so that they are confirmed by the familiarity of the song as well as the promises and hope of the act of worship. It may also be a post-Communion hymn, like Fred Kaan's 'Now let us from this table rise'.

*Short songs and chants.* There is a dismissal song from South Africa ('Send me, Lord'/Thuma mina) with a cantor or the Central American 'Sent by the Lord'. Blessings include, from China, 'May the Lord, mighty God', and, from Scotland, 'May the peace of God go with us' to a tune used by Robert Burns, and there are many doxologies and amens.

## Resources

Those choosing hymns now have more assistance than ever before. Biblical indexes are now becoming standard in hymn books. Reference to the Scripture passages used in the service often throws up many possibilities. Thematic indexes also help. There are publications like the excellent and comprehensive *Sunday by Sunday*, which not only lists suitable hymns – with special sections for 'Iona world songs and short songs' and 'All-age worship' – but choral music and organ voluntaries as well. The hymn books *Ancient and Modern* (2013) and *Laudate* have suggestions for each Sunday of the three-year lectionaries, as do Church of Scotland and Methodist websites (see further Appendix 2).

## Fine tuning

There being so many options risks overloading worship with too much music. In addition, there are several different styles of worship included in the above and they don't necessarily belong together. Further, bearing in mind the principle that what we ask people to sing is what they need at that point to sing, we must choose well, but sparingly. Sometimes, one brilliant choice lifts the whole act of worship.

This certainly applies to hymns. Too many can be wearisome, especially to people for whom singing and getting up and down are difficult. Four might be plenty, especially if there is other music that invites people to participate. Five is common in some traditions but even then we are approaching what is dismissively called the 'hymn sandwich', when it can look as if the hymn has the function of giving the ear and brain a rest from the spoken sections. Here and elsewhere it has been suggested that song is embedded within the liturgy rather than consisting of items which come in between other parts. If there is a culinary metaphor for the right use of hymns in worship, it would be not so much a hymn sandwich, more a hymn soufflé!

## Notes

1 Routley, Erik, 1968, *Words, Music and the Church*, London: Herbert Jenkins, pp. 157f.

2 This was created at Luther Seminary (USA) and is based on a four-year cycle.

3 See www.spillthebeans.org.uk.

4 *Music for Common Worship 1: Music for Sunday Services*, 2000, Dorking: Royal School of Church Music, pp. 52f, 123, 127.

5 The Nicene Creed is usually specified for Communion services, but the Apostles' Creed (the creed for baptisms) is commoner in general use because shorter and easier for people to remember and follow.

6 This psalm has problems in performance in that, while it depends for sense on a musical dialogue ('But who of glory is the King?'), the melody is in the tenor, which can be quite weak. The organist needs to highlight the melody by duplicating the tenors' and basses' question in the right hand so that some may be encouraged to sing and restore the sense.

# Ministries of Music, Their Tasks and Responsibilities

# 8

# Apprentice Angels

## *The Music Ministry of the Congregation*

That an organist, a choir, a precentor or cantor, or a praise band and its worship leader should exercise a music 'ministry' will occasion no surprise. They are, after all, characterised by having musical skills and a discipline to develop their offering, their gift. A congregation, however, tends to be seen more as a consumer, in that music is provided which helps them worship. Even when hymns are claimed as the people's part (a misleading term in any case), there is the sense of following a lead, doing the best we can with our limited musical abilities. The suggestion that there are initiatives we should take, responsibilities we should recognise, understanding that we should develop – *together* – is not immediately obvious. How, we say, can we exercise a music ministry when really we are the ones ministered to? There are three possible circumstances which could give rise to this view.

One is that we have a tendency to see ourselves as a gathering of individuals with needs to be met. We seek for ourselves forgiveness, peace, the renewal of our spiritual lives, instruction in the faith, a sense of being valued. In prayers of intercession and in preaching, individual consciences are stirred, resolutions made. In this we are echoing the common view in our culture that religion is an individual matter, private, our own business – an approach driven not just by centuries of emphasis on personal morality but in the modern prioritising of self-improvement, health and well-being, in which even spiritual growth comes in a choice of colours. Of course we are not entirely wrong about this, in that Christian tradition values both the festive gathering and the solitude of the seeker. In the Sermon on the Mount, we are urged to pray in our room with the door shut (Matt. 6:6) – but there is also the promise that, when two or three gather, Jesus is in the midst (Matt. 18:20).

Scripture teaches, however, that what the numbers add up to is not a multiple but a unit, the body of Christ. St Paul makes it clear that it is the body that is paramount, not the components (us) who make it up. When he writes, 'all the members of the body, though many, are one body, so it is with Christ' (1 Cor. 12:12), it is not our numbers or diversity, 'the many', that is the focus but the obvious truth that if there is a body (ours or Christ's) there must be limbs and organs with differing functions. It is not that we add up to something, but that by baptism we are made indissolubly into a body of members, both mind and muscle.[1] This is underlined in teaching about the gifts of the Spirit. All members of the body are spiritually gifted but these are gifts given to the whole body. Persons with their giftedness interlock to serve the whole body and to build it up. This is not a talent competition, or a grouping where there are separate roles which must not be trespassed upon; rather, there is a dynamic which flows between gifted persons, preventing the body ossifying into a fixed shape. It is first and foremost *one*, but it is enriched by difference.

A second factor that may inhibit a congregation from grasping their role as an agent with a ministry relates to the many other gatherings we participate in – clubs, rallies, associations, crowds in shopping malls, or audiences for concerts and dramatic productions – which unwittingly become models for us. The American liturgical theologian Gordon Lathrop characterises our participation in these as *consumers*, and suggests that the Christian congregation is distinctive in being 'transformative', both for its participants and for the world from which, and on behalf of which, we gather:

> This is a meeting, an association, that is transformed in its mode and its content by being gathered by the Word of God which calls the assembly together, gives a centre to the meet-

ing, and criticises and transforms the mode of mutual relationship.[2]

It is a congregation 'constituted through Baptism and continually renewed through the use of Scriptures and the Eucharist'.[3]
The worship in which we participate is necessarily communal.
It requires others' voices, convictions, minds, bodies, love,
strength, speech, imagination, hospitality (the latter so that
it always remains open and inclusive). As Thomas Troeger's
hymn begins, 'We need each other's voice to sing / the song our
hearts would raise.'

It was in singing that congregations at the time of the Reformation period found their voice and status as a priesthood
of believers who, by the grace of God, could approach God
on their own authority, and pray and praise with their own
unmediated voices. At the Second Vatican Council, music was
also seen as one of the vehicles for 'the full, conscious and
active participation of the faithful'. However, to define the
nature of the local congregation is not to make it so. We are
very aware of how far we can fall short of this high calling.
The Revd J. W. Stevenson, writing of his induction into a new
parish in the Scottish Borders in the 1950s, tells of how he
first saw his new congregation, as they approached the church,
through the differently tinted sections of the glass of the vestry
window, now clear, now distorted: 'I did not understand then
the mystery of the Church ... that (God) sets us in the community of His love while we are yet, by all the signs, unfit for it;
that He binds us one to another before we seem ready to be
bound. In the years that followed ... I was to learn also why
these things are so; why, under one aspect, the Church seems
to be made up of men and women no better than the rest, and,
under another, has the look of heaven.'[4]

A third reason for passivity in congregations may be said to
be a result of a gap in the provision of the church. A frequently
recurring theme at conferences and in articles at this time is the
need for what is usually called liturgical formation, the latter
word suggesting that this is not intended to teach people about
the nuts and bolts of a service but to allow worship to play

its part in 'forming' the Christian life. For this to occur, there needs to be understanding of the nature of worship but also of how we prepare body and mind to participate fully in it and how we are to carry the flavours and modes of that worship with us as we leave – that is, how liturgy resonates with the life of the world.

In conducting workshops on worship, I always begin by acknowledging that I am talking to experts. Those who have worshipped faithfully for decades know more than they realise about its meaning and its content. This never fails to surprise them, who look on themselves as 'only' in the pews. Gordon Lathrop tells of one of the native peoples of northern Canada called the Yellowknife, who have named themselves Tetsot'ine – 'those who know something a little':

> Their name reflects the respectful and careful common life of a people surrounded by a vast and mysterious land marked by powerful natural forces: no one knows everything about such a land. But their name also reflects a community that treasures the life-giving, survival-enabling skills of the things they do know together.[5]

If it is true that seasoned worshippers know a great deal about worship, could it be that our usual assumption is correct – that to worship is natural and does not need to be taught? St Paul did not think so, as shown by his excoriating critique of the way the church at Corinth handled its meetings. The practices they had developed were making nonsense of the core message, emphasising the class divide in their fellowship. 'When you come together, it is not really to eat the Lord's supper', he cries (1 Cor. 11:17–21, 33–4). In earlier centuries, it was accepted that people needed to be primed to worship, to understand what it all meant (in medieval times this tended to be highly allegorical), and to know the words and learn the music. The song schools attached to the collegiate churches or to a town's grammar school prepared young people for active participation in worship, and universities also had courses. Stephen Mark Holmes has brought to attention that liturgical interpretation was a significant element in the religious culture both before and after the Scottish Protestant Reformation of 1559–60, and figured largely in preaching.[6] Today sermons about worship – how to take part in it, how to let it form you – would be the exception rather than the rule, with the weight on biblical exposition and its connection with contemporary culture and with individual conduct.

## Affirming the congregation

One way of encouraging a congregation to take seriously its role as a musical body might be to introduce a more direct form of enabling their song. At the moment the role falls to organists, who direct them through the medium of sound, they themselves usually out of sight. A choir is often spoken of as leading the congregation; this too, however effective the singers, is through the sound they make, which can often be lost by the weight of congregational numbers. In times past song would be 'taken up' by the precentor, with whom the people would interact directly. Anyone who has taken part in a *Songs of Praise* programme knows the different feel when there is a conductor in the pulpit combining those present into a unity and enthusing them to engage fully in their contribution to the whole. We see this too where there is a praise band and worship leader who interacts personally with the people. In Iona Abbey, with a changing congregation every week, it is unusual for a service to commence without someone facilitating people's participation by demonstrating and rehearsing a song it is not likely that, as visitors, they would know.

The example of two internationally known musicians is worth paying attention to. The late John Currie, lecturer in music in the University of Glasgow and dubbed 'Scotland's choirmaster general' for his work with a wide range of choirs here and in the USA, was happy to work with both the greatest and the least. As organist and choirmaster at Govan Old parish church, Glasgow, in the 1960s and 70s, he used to write music – an original composition or the arrangement of a hymn – which he would rehearse with choir, congregation and instrumentalists simultaneously before the Sunday morning service began.

Another example is that of the composer Sir James MacMillan, who similarly has dedicated himself to the week-to-week worship of a Roman Catholic parish church in Glasgow. The membership of his choir is open to all singers regardless of age, gender, religion or musical experience (in that sense patterning the composition of the congregation). In recent years, he has been accustomed to composing a new responsorial psalm every week, rehearsing it with the people in the three minutes before Mass starts. 'They're designed to be picked up quickly ... This is one thing I sometimes just don't get right. And that's why, although this is one of the most difficult things I do as a composer, it's also one of the most enjoyable.' More recently he has been exploring with the congregation 'the church's traditional reservoir of beautiful chant that can be adapted for the reality of the contemporary church'.[7]

When a musician in any of these ways works with a congregation to help them produce their music, there is a sense of expectation upon them to deliver a sound it is uniquely theirs to utter.

## The congregation's ministerial duties

What responsibilities then fall to the congregation? In the Introduction to his lively Companion to the first *Australian Hymn Book*,[8] Wesley Milgate lists what he calls the 'obligations' of clergy, of organists and choir leaders – and of the congregation. This is not to talk only of a few enthusiasts scattered among the pews but rather some responsibilities without which the congregation's participation in worship, and all that means in the strength of its witness and service, will be weak and their 'lays feeble'.[9] What follows builds on Milgate's initiative.

## 1 *Browse through the hymn book*

When a new hymn book is adopted by a local church, it is too often the case that the known is located with a sigh of relief while unfamiliar material is passed over. A first responsibility is to browse through the contents of the main hymn book used in your local church. Previous generations saw the hymn book not only as a tool for worship but as a devotional resource, providing material for personal prayer and meditation. Some people decide to read through the whole Bible; in the case of a hymn book, to start at hymn no. 1 may mean never reaching hymn 800. Begin with the Contents page and choose one of the sections – a theme like 'the stewardship of the earth' or 'enlivening and renewing the church', or a season of the Christian Year. Renew acquaintance with those you already know (and in some cases maybe reflect on editorial alterations made to what you used to sing and work out why), but give more time to those that are unfamiliar. Here, denominations may need to provide material to assist, either in the weekly order of service or separately, or online.[10] (By the way, don't omit the Preface of your book, which is usually of more than passing interest, and sometimes even contains surprises.)

As well as the words of a hymn, it can be helpful to note the other information on the page and what it can tell us about the hymn. This is particularly true with regard to the author of the words and, from the dates given, you might consider what was happening in the period the hymn was written. The composer or the source of the tune too should be noted; sometimes there is a story behind this. Increasingly today, hymn books appear in a melody edition (as did the earliest Psalters) as well as words only or full music. Some, over and above listening to the tune on a website or on YouTube, or having a friend play it over, might consider learning to read music. This is not so outrageous as it might seem! In nineteenth-century Scotland when the tonic sol-fa method of reading music,[11] devised by Sarah Glover and promoted by Congregational minister John Curwen, swept the country, it engendered enthusiasm for choral singing to the extent that a General Assembly precentor formed a 'Choir of

a Thousand Voices' back in his home city.[12] A good proportion of a congregation, even into the twentieth century, would
have sung from a sol-fa edition. In my earlier years, sol-fa was
taught in primary school to all pupils. To read music from staff
notation may be found to be equally within reach and is preferred today for teaching music. The reason for members of
the congregation undertaking this is partly so that when the
minister or organist wishes to introduce a new hymn, you are
halfway there, not least because the melody edition of your
book is beginning to make sense. But another equally important reason is that it would make it possible for you to suggest
new things to try in your church. It is also more than likely that
you will find hymns that are helpful to you personally, phrases
that bring you up short, and echoes of Scripture to nourish the
spirit – offering ways to pray, to meditate, to be at peace, to
find equilibrium, to be better able to meet the demands of life.
For the thing about browsing in a hymn book is that it very
soon stops being a duty and, like John Wesley, himself a hymn
maker, we may feel our 'hearts strangely warmed'.

## 2  Sing well

Members of congregations quite often find singing difficult,
especially the top notes by the men. This has been partly
explained by suggesting that the vocal range of the average
male does not correspond with the treble range exactly and
that their top and bottom notes are – generally speaking –
lower. Some organists transpose hymn tunes downwards when
they are playing for a congregation singing in unison, especially when they are not also having to take a four-part choir
into consideration.

Then there is the matter of a congregation believing they
are 'not a singing church', perhaps because a former minister
chided them for not singing out, for not putting their heart into
it, or an organist has complained that they always lag behind.
These strictures may have been quite undeserved, but they have
stuck. Or perhaps it is 'Bell's rule of proximity' quoted in an

earlier chapter, which states that if there is a gap between you and others you won't sing in case they hear you, but if you are standing next to them you'll sing because you can hear them.[13]

Another problem can be running out of breath. This results in taking a breath in the middle of a phrase, or even a word, which means we are not singing sense. Recent sightings (or the auditory equivalent) have been: in 'Abide with me' – *when other helpers (breath) fail, and comforts flee*; 'Lord of all being' – *before thy ever-(breath) blazing throne*. It also spoils our enjoyment in singing. There's a cure, however.

Remember the psalmist's last word: let everything that breathes praise the Lord! This final verse of the 150th psalm is meant to be inclusive of all living (and breathing) things, and the invitation is that they should use their breath to praise. If teachers or choir directors wish to improve someone's singing, it is breathing they go for first. The sad truth is that generally we tend to ration our breath, sufficient for normal conversation perhaps. Singing, however, requires a more sustained drive. What we do is use the top front part of our lungs and thus only call on a fraction of available breath. A colleague,[14] asked to lead a two-day workshop for men who claimed they couldn't sing, had them lie on their backs and take a deep breath through the floor (i.e. 'through' their backs). She reports that within 24 hours they were all singing top Fs (think Pavarotti) and enjoying it, and one expressed anxiety about returning to his own church and everyone tutting their disapproval. (Yes, good question! Why do they?)

Having got the mechanism right, we have to use it wisely, using what we need when we need it. We look to the next comma, notice if a phrase continues into a second line, or save something for the longer climaxing note at the end of a verse. Standing up straight makes for better delivery. Singing into the book doesn't. Screens can help, but so can using the book as a cue but singing with the head up and the mouth open. Breath control is helped when the throat too is open (as when we yawn) and, as teachers of singing emphasise, when the core muscles of the body are consciously supporting the voice. An operatic singer acts as she sings, but there is a sense in which we are all acting – bringing the body into play – when we sing properly. Studies have variously equated the effect of singing to a seven-mile jog, or to a whole-body massage, since every muscular system is involved.

You might also say that this breath consciousness is part of our offering in an act of worship; if normally we don't give breath a second thought, here we feel it is a gift and a blessing, and we offer it in praise, as the psalmist enjoins.

Therefore, we are to sing with regard to the meaning of the words, which for some may open up a hymn that they thought they knew, whereas so often what they were enjoying or responding to was the music.

> Lord, keep us safe this night
> beneath the stars and moon.
> Pay thou no heed to what we say;
> we only like the tune.

Quite apart from the meaning, the sound of the words is satisfying and is part of our feeling of satisfaction in the act of singing, but, above all, the sentiments of the lyrics stimulate insight, renew faith, strengthen discipleship, embrace us within the community of saints. We sing too because our faith is not just rote-learning but involves our feelings and our wills. As St Augustine said: singing is for lovers.[15]

## 3 Listen to each other

Perhaps the first skill drawn upon by people who sing well together is not so much a voice and ability to hold a tune but the grace of attentive listening to each other. A feature of the Church of Scotland's General Assembly always remarked upon is the strength and fervour of its singing, which is often unaccompanied and precentor-led. People are packed close to each other and that helps. However, there may be another factor. Here is an annual gathering, together for a week, where matters of moment are tackled, decisions made and strategies undertaken which can only take place when people listen to each other. It is a listening which is even beyond the chamber, symbolised by the sound from the quadrangle below where distant trumpeters are heard announcing the arrival of Her Majesty's representative, the Lord High Commissioner (knocking the pitch of the first note of the impending psalm out of the precentor's head, as I can testify). During the Assembly the beyond also comes through committee reports where global and social issues are tackled, from moving messages live on the screens from critical situations, or from the fifty or so guests who represent other world churches. Other denominations will recognise this too – an excitement at breaking the routine and coming together which prompts an enhanced listening, a 'body listening', which means that there is a propensity to hear also from those with us in that space. What is being suggested is that it makes a difference in the local church similarly to think of this gathering of God's people as something out of the ordinary, something momentous, enabling us, rather than stumbling along on our own, to be aware of others' voices and, at the same time, of their different giftedness and identity. We also listen to the organ or ensemble of instruments, picking up signals as we sing. This double task might seem to make unreasonable demands. Yet think of Isaiah, who knew that an ability as performer was enriched the more we were open to receive.

> The Lord GOD has given me
> the tongue of a teacher,
> that I may know how to sustain
> the weary with a word.
> Morning by morning he wakens –
> wakens my ear
> to listen as those who are taught. (Isa. 50:4)

## 4 Sing new songs

The command to 'sing a new song' rings from the psalms, through the prophets, and right on to the last words of the Bible, for the book of Revelation also speaks twice of the new song, the angels' song. Revelation is a not so much a book as a colourful mosaic of how the world will be when it is reconciled to God and humanity at one with creation, but it is a book with a soundtrack, the new song. John Bell offers this as a candidate for the 11th commandment which allegedly Moses was not able to include because there was no more room on the stone tablet! 'Sing a new song' is a phrase which occurs 19 times in the Bible.[16]

The importance of refreshing the repertoire is argued in other chapters. It is usually assumed that congregations don't want to learn new tunes. We are generally willing to meet new people; why not befriend new hymns? Every hymn has been new once. The experience, in fact, of those who work with congregations is that people are quite ready to learn fresh material. The question is, how do we go about this most effectively? Several methods are commonly used in local congregations, with various degrees of success.

Some will hear the musician play over the tune twice before the congregation joins in. Or, the tune is played over, the choir demonstrate verse 1 and the congregation then begin the hymn from the beginning (or continue with verse 2). A soloist may sing in place of the choir. There are many variations on this: the melody *only* is heard, without the distraction of chords and perhaps played in octaves; a soloist with accompanist sings the first verse, which is then sung by the choir, then finally the congregation joins in with verse 1 and continues from there. Another way is for a new hymn to be sung as an introit or anthem on one or more Sundays before it is sung by the congregation.

By far the most effective way is to teach the tune directly using one's own voice, even though it is a very ordinary voice (which in itself can be reassuring for the congregation), and persuading the organist not to play until you have established the tune. (This is not to say you cannot call on an organist or pianist to support you at appropriate times.) There is advantage in not inviting the people to look the number up at that stage in their own books (or to put the words up on to a screen), since this interrupts the direct relationship between your voice and theirs; have people sing to 'la' or similar. It is particularly helpful when hand gestures, primary-school style, are used, the eye supporting the ear.[17] Who can do this? The teacher/demonstrator may be the organist (having temporarily left the console) or choir leader, if there is one, or a cantor, or indeed someone who knows how to relate to groups of people, like a school teacher who is also a confident singer, or the *fear-an-tigh* at the local ceilidh.[18]

The leader will offer the tune in short sections, a line or half line, then, when ready, it is sung in its couplet, and so on until the whole verse can be tried. *Then* they can look up the words. It can help to show the structure of the tune – that the first, second and final lines are virtually the same, for example, or how an idea appears in another guise or at another register. It helps people to know that having grasped one part, they are more than halfway there. It is often relevant to give some background to a new song, not in a laboured introduction at the beginning (best to start straight in and get people singing before they know it), but to relieve the musical concentration as you go through. Sometimes a new song is in harmony, as are many of the world church songs. The parts are rehearsed separately, but never leaving another part unattended for long. It is sometimes appropriate for all to learn the top part together – to get a sense of the overall shape – before, say, dividing the voices, and beginning to build up the parts in layers. Those who have learned their parts can hum them quietly while a new part is prepared. If you have assistants, each can lead one of the parts. It is important to prepare quite carefully before teaching new material, dwelling with the tune yourself, thinking through what might work best in introducing *this particular* tune. Be encouraging (you will usually find that you are encouraged in return) and in so doing, as well as introducing fresh sounds, you may well be rehabilitating a congregation which is not confident in its ability.

When is it best to do this? Worshippers often find it disturbing to be asked to rehearse during a service. Before the service begins is a good time. Even better is on an occasional Sunday to designate part of the time together (up to half an hour perhaps) as a time of learning, followed by a shortened act of worship. Or it may be that special evenings from time to time may be planned as a Big Sing, a time of enjoyment and encountering new sounds.

## 5 Don't speak to the organist!

Four responsibilities that lie with congregations as they lay hold of their ministry of music: browse through the hymn book, listen to each other, sing well, and sing a new song. Milgate in his own list of 'obligations' adds this: never try to engage organists in conversation while they are playing a voluntary. And many will bless you!

### Notes

1 Robinson, John A. T., 1972, *The Body: A Study in Pauline Theology*, London: SCM Press, p. 96.

2 Lathrop, Gordon W., 1999, *Holy People: A Liturgical Ecclesiology*, Minneapolis, MN: Fortress Press, p. 39.

3 Lathrop, *Holy People*, pp. 39–48.

4 Stevenson, J. W., 1960, *God in My Unbelief*, London: Collins, pp. 7, 9.

5 Lathrop, *Holy People*, p. 101.

6 Holmes, Stephen Mark, 2015, *Sacred Signs in Reformation Scotland: Interpreting Worship, 1488–1590*, Oxford: Oxford University Press.

7 Ferguson, Michael, 2015, *Understanding the tensions in liturgical musicmaking in the Roman Catholic Church in contemporary Scotland*, PhD thesis, University of Edinburgh, pp. 173, 176.

8 Milgate, Wesley, 1982, *Songs of the People of God*, London: Collins Liturgical, pp. 11–15. A revised and expanded edition to accompany the second Australian Hymn Book, *Together in Song*, is edited by D'Arcy Wood and published (2000) by the Australian Hymn Book Pty.

9 Hymn 'O worship the King' v. 6. Some books, to avoid the now less familiar term 'lays', have modified the couplet in which it appears.

10 See Appendix 2.

11 Each note was designated by its place in the scale. It was immortalised in the song 'Do-re-mi' ('Let's start from the beginning') from the musical, *The Sound of Music*, by Rodgers and Hammerstein.

12 In the north east of Scotland, William Carnie drew some 2,000 to a lecture on psalmody, resulting in the formation in 1870 of the Choir of the Thousand Voices which held a weekly practice of psalms, hymns and anthems.

13 Bell, John L., 2007, *The Singing Thing Too*, Glasgow: Wild Goose Publications, p. 22.

14 In the preparation of this section, I am indebted to the Revd Marion Dodd, director of the Roxburgh Singers, for sharing with me her long experience in persuading choirs and congregations to sing well.

15 St Augustine, sermon 336.

16 Bell, John L., 2000, *The Singing Thing*, Glasgow: Wild Goose Publications, pp. 83f.

17 Bell, *The Singing Thing Too*, is largely given over to techniques of teaching new material and empowering congregations as singing bodies, and is well worth study.

18 The Gaelic *fear-an-tigh* translates roughly as 'the host' and is the name given to a compère at a ceilidh, an evening of dance and song in Highland communities in Scotland.

# 9

# Your Church has got Talent!

## *The Ministry of the Choir*

One of the most beautiful insights of Scripture relates to gifted-ness (1 Cor. 12). From the examples given we know that Paul is not only referring to people we tend to see as especially talented, a category in which we often put musicians, but more broadly the skills of heart and hand, the experiences which form us, particular enthusiasms. Paul urges his readers to look on these 'gifts of the Spirit' not for individual enhancement but for the benefit of the whole body of Christ, enabling a unity which is textured and contoured by diversity. The idea may be extended. A choir itself can be a gift to the church. The church choir is not simply an outlet for singers to exercise their talent but a body which gives itself to the church to shape, beautify and bring to fullness the gift of praise bestowed upon the whole body.

One of the features of the nineteenth-century surge in church music was singing in choirs. In Presbyterianism the market was fed by precentors with pretensions who published their own psalters (modestly adding some of their own compositions), causing denominations to bring out definitive collections of tunes to try and curb the variety of harmonisation and stem the flow of the second rate. Yet there was always an ambivalence which harked back to the Reformation principle of the congregation's voice being paramount. An Ayrshire church allowed a choir only if it conformed to the following restrictions: it should be confined to church members or their children; it must be limited to twelve persons on any one Sunday; membership must be by invitation only; and it must never, ever, coincide with the precentor's congregational psalmody practice.[1] A frequent mantra in the reports and writings of the time was: 'Ideally, the congregation should constitute the choir.'

Today, there are signs of a new ambivalence about the choir, which is often seen as part of a world we want to leave behind. The communications revolution has helped to popularise other styles, traditions and sources of music, bringing a corresponding desire to be in touch with the generations who live nearest to these expressions. This has sometimes been deemed to be contrary to what choirs stand for. The result can be stand-offs between different styles of worship and music, and some reforming clergy have put their choirs on notice. Sadly, full exploration of the attitudes on both sides is often bypassed, so that the profile of the choir as a gathering of musical gifts in the service of worship is not acknowledged, the possible role of trained singers to help the congregation pilot the often difficult rhythms and melodic gaps in worship songs is unexplored, and the possibility of a range of sound textures being provided in an act of worship is not considered. There is desperate need to widen the conversation in the church.

Yet the evidence is that in other spheres choirs are flourishing, as the television series *Last Choir Standing* has dramatically proved. Proof there too that singing in choirs clearly appeals to the young as well as the mature. Not only that, but what an amazing range of styles and repertoire you can form a choir round. In recent years on the BBC Gareth Malone has grown choirs from seemingly unlikely soil. His series *The Choir* won a BAFTA. Its sequel *Boys Don't Sing* only served to prove the opposite. The contribution of the Kingdom Choir at the wedding of the Duke and Duchess of Sussex took the nation by storm and renewed interest in the Gospel Choir movement. The justly celebrated National Youth Choirs of the four nations stand at the pinnacle of a comprehensive nationwide structure of local choirs and training opportunities with which children can begin to connect at an early age, even 'catching them young' in mother and toddler groups. The Royal School of Church Music's Voice for Life scheme offers church choirs and individual singers opportunity and a structure to develop their skills, while building in a sound education programme.

What is more, that initiative both crosses denominational barriers and reaches into the wider community.

## The heritage of music

The repertoire available to the present-day church is quite remarkable in its size and quality. It is humbling to realise that in our week-to-week worship we may hear music which is equal to anything available in the concert hall or over the air waves. What's more, there is music to suit a range of skills and experience. The choir exercises custodianship of this gift by selecting examples from across the centuries, bringing them again to life, and showing their worth in a performance as fine as they are capable of.

## Choir and congregation

The choir does not think of itself as a musical elite, with the choir stalls as worship's business class while the rest of us have to jam our knees up against the pew in front, worthy only of the plainer fare on the musical menu. Choirs themselves can sometimes slip into this view, for example when too many of the hymns on a Sunday are in unison and can lead them to feel, as one choir leader overheard, that they should 'not bother coming'. Yet choirs have the privilege of symbolising and high-lighting the fact that the whole congregation is made up of people who are musical in their different ways. Its aim is to enhance the experience of worship for all, to make music to touch the heart with the words of Scripture, to be adventurous on the congregation's behalf and to seek new sounds to express a twenty-first-century faith – a body, what's more, for whom the sort of music into which the whole congregation can join easily is not beneath notice. This does not reduce the choir's task. Its sound is not drowned in the assembly's voice; it also soars as it sings for the congregation, challenging it to value its own musical gift.

The choir thus ministers to the congregation as its musical mentor. To grow and mature in Christ (Eph. 4:13–16) is not just with one's understanding but one's sensibilities. The choir can by judicious choices challenge people to appreciate more imaginative music, breaking down the clichés of what 'nice' music should sound like. This is not only in the music it provides itself but in the hymns we are asked to sing. The choir is the first body to scour a new hymn book and share its delights and its mysteries with the whole body. (This is a task that will continue throughout the life of a hymn collection, as the church seeks more from its hymns, or as the expanding repertoire of a congregation opens the way to new idioms and more imaginative writing.) In offering the best of music, the choir engages the whole assembly musically and spiritually, always acknowledging that people are at different points of their personal musical journey. There is also the music that asks for the particular contributions of choir and congregation, sometimes a cantor too, to sound together – another way of drawing the congregation into worship. The core of all our worship is *doxology*, the utterance of praise, and it has always been understood that it is in the unique mix of word and music that the authentic sound of praise resides. There are so many ways of sounding doxology in worship but also not enough ways fully to declare it. The choir reminds us of this inadequacy but at the same time enriches our praise-making and offers to take us to new heights.

## The choir teaches through its music

The Word of God is read, preached, but also sung – in hymns, of course, but also in anthems and motets sung by the choir. The anthem is usually a setting of a biblical verse or passage, and, as *Sunday by Sunday* makes clear,[2] it is not difficult to find examples which, if they do not specifically quote from the readings of the day, in some way reflect them. Thus it is part of the hearing of the Word and an opportunity offered to the people of digging deeper into the words of Scripture, as they are skilfully set by the composer and clearly and passionately sung by the choir. They are in effect expounding Scripture as the composer and then the choir offer their interpretation of the words. It is common for the anthem to be sung in conjunction with the readings or sermon, but the sense of the words may mean on occasion that it belongs in another part of the service. The anthem is not to be listened to passively as if in a concert (a mistake that some clergy perpetuate by thanking the choir at the end) but should be entered into prayerfully. How the anthem is introduced can help, but in particular to provide the words on an order of service (or screen if used) will be helpful.

Listening prayerfully to a choir is not a passive activity. Music becomes part of us just as strongly as we listen as when we participate directly. In some Roman Catholic churches today there can be suspicion of choral groups, seen as usurping the proper role of the congregation. Paul Inwood, of the St Thomas More group of composers, suggests that there was a misunderstanding, following the Second Vatican Council, of what was meant by 'full, conscious and active participation' by the congregation, 'which resulted in large numbers of parish choirs being disbanded by well-meaning priests who thought they were an obstacle to singing by the people'.[3]

## Enlivening the tradition

Style and content of worship has a certain constancy whatever branch of the church you are in, but it requires to be renewed by all together each time it is celebrated. Music changes with the culture and is a way of contextualising an act of worship. The choir's ministry is to renew and refresh the ancient texts of worship, the Kyrie/Lord, have mercy, Glory to God in the highest and other texts of the Services of the Word or of Communion, or the Aaronic Blessing at a baptism, a doxology at the offering, or a glorious final amen. Here the choir is bringing to life rites and rituals that so easily can be ossified, offering fresh perspectives through live music. For example, it may be heard in the introit, linking that day's worship with the season of the Christian Year. In former times, this would have been a bridge between the worship of the day and the lives of the people, since the festivals of the Calendar had a strong presence in the life of society. It brings out the special music that characterises different seasons, and we should remember too that carols are not just for Christmas!

## Alternative structures

Some choirs give public concerts where the sacred and the secular commingle. But perhaps their most important ministry of outreach is in their recruitment and welcoming of new persons to the choir. These may be adults who simply want people to sing with, or, even more importantly, they can be younger people or children, who through this can become committed to the church and to music. Participating in choral music changes lives.

For many local choirs, recruitment has been a problem. Often a choir seems a shadow of its former self. Dwindling numbers have meant that it is weak in one or more sections (beginning with the tenors). Its members are ageing and do not have the resilience that once tackled more imaginative and demanding music. Attempts to recruit additional and, especially, younger members have failed, a circumstance with many causes: smaller congregations reduce the catchment area; it may be that the repertoire is not attractive to a generation used to different styles of music; millennials and Generation Z are listeners to music rather than makers. Some choirs may be surprised to hear that they themselves are the problem even though they do want people to join them. A choir can become set in its ways and does not yield enough to embrace new members. Lower numbers in the procession into worship does not encourage people to think of joining.

There are, however, some steps that can be taken. The truth is that people are more likely to agree to participate, even on a trial basis, if they are approached individually – talent-spotted if you like. It means research on the part of the music department, and some turning of the soil. This could go hand in hand with a celebratory occasion when potential members are invited together, at the end of which singing takes place. It may be necessary to reduce one's usual requirements of choir members and settle for a widening of membership where more work needs to be done on the voices and musical grasp of the members. It is at least better than going out of existence, and it means, more positively, that some who would say they were 'not really a singer' will find their voice.

In an age when people have to meet many demands, requiring intermittent absence at weekends, commitment to regular attendance at church and choir practice is difficult to guarantee. There may come a time in a particular church when the norm of all choir members being together Sunday by Sunday has to be varied and new patterns sought. There are probably some in a congregation who would sign up for two or three weeks of concentrated rehearsal before festivals, so that the high days of the Christian Year are given their profile. Again, it may be that a monthly pattern rather than a weekly one can be tried. In one congregation, the women are on duty one Sunday, the men on the next, both together on the third, with the congregation fending for themselves on the fourth.

It is often not the best solution to retire people when their voices lose quality, and when what keeps them coming is loyalty to the choir and a feeling of responsibility for keeping things going. One way to proceed is to arrange that other forms of choral grouping are created, complementing the faithful few, sharing out the Sundays or festivals, together serving the whole body. These may become choirs as usually understood, a committed group meeting with regularity, or they may be groups of singers who prefer to come together in a more ad hoc way, encouraging people to drop in and drop out as their circumstances dictate. Their purpose may be to explore new congregational music and become able to introduce such material to others. It is also possible that they may not want to sing exclusively religious music.

There is another growing pattern today that may be suggestive. Both as a way of better meeting the needs of communities and of mustering a greater strength within the church to resource this, patterns other than the single-congregation parish are being explored, such as clusters of congregations in a natural wider community. In such arrangements, members of staff may not be confined entirely in one congregation but their time spread between several churches and groupings. Might such a cluster also share one well-resourced choir which is equally at home in several locations, offering themselves in different weeks to different groups of worshippers and ministering at greater festivals when all can come together as one?

This is also a time when there is a movement to look outside the demanding life of a busy congregation to the many who are not within the church, many of whom are sympathetic to it and have a level of belief and commitment to others which is akin to that of regular churchgoers. Several congregations today are expressing this in extending their interest to forming community choirs.

A recent initiative in one parish was the founding of a church/community choir, Celtic Sounds, in response to a felt demand by people in the community for an opportunity for choral singing. This included people who said they had 'never sung before but wanted to sing'. Repertoire ranged from Iona material (including songs from the world church) to secular items such as an anti-war canticle by Simon and Garfunkel. These, with the church choirs, took part in an annual concert. The directors commented that it was a large task to 'keep all the groups happy' with material they liked to sing or play and required a broad knowledge of resources. Another congregation advertises an ad hoc opportunity to meet before a service to prepare an introit with whoever turns up, the group then remaining to boost the congregation's singing, while a dedicated small group of four, all with music in their background, meet by mutual agreement to prepare more complex music.

We should not forget the Anglican model of the choir which is made up of children (boys or girls) and adults, rightly celebrated for its distinctively beautiful sound, and which affirms the generational breadth of the church. Churches not in that tradition may benefit from exploring this and many have:

Dunblane Cathedral (Church of Scotland) has long nurtured an excellent choir of girls, boys, women and men. If, however, we specifically establish a junior choir, we must use them, and not just for special child-orientated occasions such as Christmas and a prizegiving service when Sunday School closes for the summer. Sometimes adult choirs can be slow to move aside to allow this.

## The choir practice

The first thing that needs to be said is that for a choir to exercise its ministry effectively there should *be* a practice! Since we have been entertaining the idea of different structures of singing groups, the description 'practice' may not always suit, but the purpose is the same. Even when the local variant is come-all-ye nights for trying out new songs, there is more satisfaction if people feel they are singing well and intelligently. From signs on the page to songs of praise is not a simultaneous translation. Rhythm needs to be internalised, there is the grammar of the phrasing, the blending of the voices, the shape of the whole work – even when 'just' a hymn tune. To find a practice time that everyone can commit to is challenging in today's world. For many choirs, a week-night practice is difficult to achieve and they meet on a Sunday morning only. If this can be achieved without disruption or being caught up in the preparations for the service, it can be a valuable time, but it can feel pressurised. Consider bolstering this with an evening once a month when solid work may be done, starts made on future tasks and room given for social interaction. Of high importance is how time is used when choirs come together to practice.

In preparing this chapter I recalled the time when, for the purposes of writing an article, I shadowed the well-known Greenock conductor, the late Ian McCrorie, at one time director of the Scottish Philharmonic Singers, founded to sing with the Scottish Chamber Orchestra. McCrorie was celebrated for the rapport he enjoyed with his choirs but never attempted, or was unable, to put into words how this was done. Many of the insights in what follows were gleaned from observing him as he led a choir workshop. For him, the atmosphere was of paramount importance. 'When I am calling a choir to order to begin a practice, I keep in mind the remark of the late Arthur Oldham[4] that the amateur choir comes together after a hard day's work and they will not thank you for seeming to make this time of contrast more of the same.' Humour has its place. Lightening the learning of a tricky passage relaxes the concentration and can lead to redoubled effort. Singers may make suggestions, ask for clarification, offer interpretations. Monologues from the maestro shut the choir up in more ways than one. The choir director is interacting all the time with what is coming back from the singers. What we are talking about here is dialogue. The music is made somewhere between you.

That said, as directors know, choirs will not be satisfied if they don't feel that they have worked hard. Basic 'note-bashing' is necessary. Do it quickly. Even better when there is someone in the choir who can take a section away to another room and work on their part. Shirking accuracy does not only make the music suffer but it affects the confidence of the choir. Knowing that the line you are singing is correct, as opposed to suspecting that it might not be quite right but you are not sure why, provides the security from which you can go on to sing not just accurately but musically. To be able to pick up faults as they happen (preferably at the end of a section rather than in full flow) and deal with them quickly without blame or shame will keep the fluency going; of course, this ability arises from hard work by the conductor in advance in getting to know the score intimately. It is not a bad idea for people to mark reminders in pencil on the score, but the conductor should avoid spending ten minutes doing that with them before they have even had a chance to sing. The aim is not to lecture about what the music should sound like; that is to be shown through the music as they sing. It can help to begin with a warm-up, which can be a time of hilarity before settling down to work. Collect exercises from other choir leaders or from workshops you take part in. Singers would remain seated but can be asked to stand when the choir leader feels extra concentration will get past a difficult spot, or when the time seems ripe for a final go. Rehearse unaccompanied as much as possible for extra confidence. If you can have an accompanist standing by to demonstrate passages, support one of the parts as they work at a tricky sequence, or just give the note, that is a bonus.

One of the most important abilities a choir can develop is that of listening to each other. Achieving a good blend is most satisfying for a choir, and for this they are doing the tricky thing of concentrating on their own part and hearing each other's at the self-same time. As the conductor, you have that blend in your head, but it is they who achieve it.

People should be made to feel they have an identity within the choir, and a good conductor will try to learn people's names and something about them. If you are working in a situation where the choir has high demands made upon it, auditions may be the norm. These should be seen not as simply tests but a way for the conductor to get to know the singer as well as the voice. In some choirs, auditions may take place more frequently and not only when someone first joins, their purpose not just to see if the singer still can make their contribution but to receive feedback more generally. Perhaps as a result the director might realise that someone who has so far simply sung in ensemble might now be able to take a solo role. It also reminds or identifies who each one is, his or her name and personality. There should be no favouritism; others should be given a chance to flower.

The choir pays continual attention to the conductor. Conducting does more than keep people in time; it communicates the director's intention for the music; it also communicates 'back' to them, reminds them, what they know about the music and how it should be sung. The conductor should not just be the arms but the eyes, and the body too. One's physical attitude can help engage the choir in the meaning of what they are singing. The sound follows suit. Directors don't just conduct in a technical sense, but offer their own personality, their love for the music, their enthusiasm, as a resource for the choir. A choir can then develop its own personality, and, it is hoped, share and pass on that love and echo that enjoyment. The director's own appreciation of the music is evident. If the choir do not yet know the piece or are still learning it, seeing that someone has already got somewhere on a road they are still travelling on will increase their expectation of the end product.

It is no fun for a choir to be confronted continually with undemanding music. On the other hand, there will be music which is too difficult at that point for a particular choir. The conductor's skill is to be able to choose what they will be able to tackle, even if the choir at first acquaintance is sure they can't! There are now many publications that cater for different strengths and compositions of choir and preferences of style. There will also be options in the hymn book used in the congregation, items perhaps which are not yet able to be sung by the people.

Many choirs have just hymns to practise, although that should not stop them working up a particular item in the hymn book not usually sung locally and offering it as a possible anthem, prayer response, introit or reflection on a Scripture reading. However, it is a missed opportunity just to sing through hymns so that the tune is known and the parts are accurate. The conductor should introduce it, give some background (period, writer, composer, theme), comment on the tune and how it works. In other words, raise the expectation of the choir for this hymn they are to sing. Have all voices sing the tune to appreciate it before learning the parts. Select a particular verse or two and focus on the words. The choir's extra understanding will communicate itself to the people. There is nothing wrong, if this is more suitable to your resources, with singing the tune well, in unison, with meaning.

Lastly, as you have begun with warm-ups and exercises, consider leaving time to end with a piece that is quite different from what you have been rehearsing. Eighteenth- and nineteenth-century psalters sometimes included a handful of 'glees and catches' at the end of the book, which may well have rounded off a practice, perhaps to be brought out again at a ceilidh or other social occasion. If this is not in your usual repertoire, consider a worship song, an African-American spiritual, a shape note melody, one of the songs from the world church, a Taizé chant, or something from the Iona Community's Wild Goose Resource Group.

## Conclusion

In another place the suggestion has been made that what can enable a congregation or an individual in it to 'connect' within an act of worship, to receive an insight, a blessing, a hope, is when some kind of 'break' occurs in the even tenor of the delivery. This can be a child's artless comment, a juxtaposition of unexpected words in prayer or sermon, the way the reader that morning voiced an otherwise unknown and unnoticed passage of Scripture, something is done differently, something in one's own life that week, all the way to that shock during the enthronement of Archbishop Justin Welby when a group of Malawians erupted into the chancel and triumphantly and clamorously bore the Gospel to the place of reading – something that breaks through, something unexpected that ruffles the surface, something surprising.

For many, and often, it is the music that serves this function. The odd thing is that this element of surprise that reaches into the soul results from something that can seem to singers and players quite routine, even boring – when they work at the weary business of getting things precisely right: the shape of a phrase, the exact duration of a note or a rest, the enabling of words to be heard, the timing of a pause, the contrast in dynamics, making a melody sing through or a harmony to blend – the whole choir listening to each other so that, even though many individuals sing, only one voice is heard.

It is then, in the mellowness of a line, in the pause which opens a new space, in the expressiveness which causes the gasp of astonishment in the soul, in the concentrated beauty of a cadence in which all is gathered up, through all these things that the divine voice speaks through and between the notes. It is then that happen the things that can't be captured on the printed page. A choir does not always know what it has contributed to a service. Its members may sometimes feel they are just going through the motions. They may feel there is no pleasing some people. They are a bit like the children in the market place calling to each other:

We piped for you and you would not dance.
We lamented, and you would not mourn.[5]

We should never overlook, however, the cumulative effect of a costly music ministry, nor assume that no-one's heart was touched, their soul soothed, or a possibility stirred in them through the music we make and enable, even though they might not always know it. Jesus was speaking about John the Baptist and about himself, early in his ministry and before the outcome was known. But we know now. 'We piped and you would not dance!' Yes, they surely did, and they do now.

### Notes

1 I am indebted to John Bell for drawing my attention to this.
2 See Appendix 2, section Sunday by Sunday.
3 *Tablet*, 2 October 2004.
4 Founding director of the Edinburgh Festival Chorus.
5 Matthew 11:17, REB.

# 10

# To the Chief Musician

## *The Ministry of Those Who Plan and Lead the Music*

This heading to so many of the psalms in the Old Testament captures well the multitasking nature of the person appointed to lead a congregation's music. The many modern titles highlight different roles and emphases: director of music, organist, choir director, master of the choristers, rector chori, pastoral musician, cantor, worship leader, precentor, pianist or maybe even known simply by their name. The chief musician is a pivotal figure – on the one hand facing towards the clergy and church councils and beyond to the world of music, on the other towards the choir, the congregation and even beyond to the wider community.

This is surely one of the most demanding and potentially fulfilling roles that a musician can be asked to undertake. The church musician may be expected to play music for the organ, to accompany – and often to direct – a choir, to enable the congregation to sing with meaning and conviction, to provide, possibly through improvisation, music to accompany liturgical events or rituals, and even to find ways of navigating unexpected faults or long-standing inadequacies of the instrument that is provided, as well as overseeing its care, repair and tuning. In addition to these musical tasks, the organist is placed in relationships that have to be negotiated, with clergy, with governance bodies within and beyond the congregation, with worshippers who have views about tunes or tempos. As well as the expansion of the musical repertoire the musician may be a teacher, seeking opportunities to increase the musical knowledge and abilities of worshippers. There may also be responsibility for developing the church as a location for public musical events, not only to make fuller use of an attractive building but as part of the church's outreach to the community. Erik Routley has remarked that 'A good church organist ought to be one of the most cultivated, humane, well-rounded musicians alive, for it is given to few to practise in equal proportions the virtues of obedience and of invention.'[1]

It is tempting to look back to a golden age when roles and tasks were clear, unquestioned and well supported, but the truth is that each period brings its challenges. Currently, the church is adjusting itself in relation to a landscape of change, which in musical terms affects resources (in people or finance) and also repertoire. Beginning in the middle of last century, new musical idioms emanating from popular culture have broken into the church and have been found expressive and appealing (not that this hasn't happened before). Mainstream hymn books now incorporate music of different genres and the internet supplies a steady stream of fresh examples. Different styles of accompaniment bring new tasks and opportunities: writing parts for instruments, facing technical issues regarding amplification, and the management of groups of musicians. It is for this reason that local congregations increasingly advertise not simply for an organist and choir leader but a 'director of music'. Sometimes of course, different musical roles may be given to more than one person, as when there is a separate choir director, or someone to work with instrumentalists or a praise band. Often, however, it is one single musician who has to be a general practitioner.

A more recent title adds another dimension. The designation 'pastoral musician' grew in popularity in the Roman Catholic church in the USA after the Second Vatican Council, where there was a new emphasis on the full participation of the people. Those who favour that title, as some in the UK do,[2] see their role as wider than simply working within a 'music department' but more broadly in the congregation, encouraging them in their own music ministry, with the intention of helping them bring the best of themselves, body, mind, and spirit, to worship. This can involve widening the repertoire to include material that the people will be able to learn, remember and sing, and which allows them to contribute not only to the hymns but also in the service music.

## The place for organ music

The person who said that music in worship should never be regarded as absolutely necessary unless it is clearly and demonstrably better than silence might seem to be undermining the importance of the organist's calling, but it contains some truth.[3] It implies that thought needs to be given to what we are playing and at what point we are playing it. Sometimes organ music can be used as no more than a diversion to cover untidiness or undue noise. Some Roman Catholics complain that they have to improvise to cover an action within worship but as soon as the priest is ready to move on they are unceremoniously stopped whether or not the music has come to an end. Organists have become adept at wrenching emergency cadences out of nowhere! In Presbyterian worship, music is often played to cover the bringing forward of the offering or the distribution of Communion or the exit of the Sunday School. That is not to say that it is mistaken to play at these places, only that we need to be clear what we are doing and allow this to dictate what we should play. Our music should be intentional, related to what is happening, and be the means of drawing people more fully into worship.

The word 'voluntary' appears in titles of organ music of earlier composers such as Purcell and Stanley to indicate a piece that was improvisatory in style. Today we use the term to cover any music played on the organ in worship. We are generally aware that voluntaries have different functions or characters. United Reformed Church minister and theological teacher Nathaniel Micklem once said that introductory music on the organ achieves for Protestants what incense does for Catholics – that is, it 'lifts them over the threshold'.[4] It is not invariably the case that a soft and more devotional style of piece is best for the beginning of a service, while a loud and rousing style is right for the end. Having in mind the Christian Calendar, we might sense that sometimes a big announcement is called for at the beginning (Easter, perhaps, or the Feast of Christ the King) and that during Lent a buoyant final voluntary is less appropriate than one that is thoughtful and searching. It is not only the Calendar that pilots us through the year, of course; themes within worship or circumstances in society at large may set the tone.

In traditions where the offerings are presented, we should bear in mind that this is not a moment for entertainment, nor a break in proceedings, but the point where people solemnly give themselves once again to the service of Christ. If children go out of the service to follow their own programme, music which would be recognisable to them can be appropriate: a hymn they know, a song they sing in children's church or Sunday School. Alternatively, you might find a good organ piece which you feel children might respond to, which could become a ritual as they hear it each week. That way, you have already begun building their knowledge of organ music.

Organists should make their core repertoire music that is actually written for the organ rather than transcriptions from music in other genres (accepting that there are compositions which particularly lend themselves to adaptation for the organ). You may have a personal enthusiasm for and knowledge of opera or Broadway musicals, or be steeped in the cinema organ repertoire. You yourself may be able to see past the immediate provenance to value the skill and the art behind these musical genres, but for others preparing to worship it sends confusing messages. Some play choruses or hymns prior to a service. Perhaps the intention is to help people prepare for worship by bringing to mind the words we sing to these melodies. It might be argued that this is not so different from playing a chorale prelude (a reflective setting of a well-known hymn melody). Yet even if hardly longer than the melody itself, in the hands of a J. S. Bach it is still long enough to give the composer's originality room to move and represents a challenge to attentive listeners to aspire to that creativity as they worship. Greater length means there are internal structures which enable the play of themes, gives room for ideas to develop, for feelings to be established, for a momentum to be created towards engaging in worship. Music written for the organ is written to capitalise on the unique properties of the instrument. However, let this not rule out the many splendid transcriptions of music you may judge as suitable (and, in any case, many pieces of music are provided, even by their composers, for several instrumental contexts). Consider ways of making known what you are playing – and not necessarily just the title and composer and dates. Part of our role could be to find ways to teach people how to listen to this kind of music.

In playing opening voluntaries, we may have to choose registration not purely in respect of the music but the noise level in the church. On some occasions – a festival where there is excitement or more people than usual, perhaps – we might need a firmer or more penetrating sound. The trouble is, however, that the louder we play the more the voices will be raised to compete, and a compromise needs to be found. One of the most difficult things to handle for the less experienced player is finishing when all are in place and the service is ready to start. Ideally, you wish to end in the home key and not take too long to get there. In preparing the piece beforehand you will be noticing how it is divided: points where you could go back to, just to get that little bit more music rather than going back to the beginning and then finding you have to screech to a halt; noting where the cadences are at which, even though there is a page to go, you might discreetly slip in a full stop; or where it is a full stop you make it an interrupted cadence and go back a little to try again, like a horse refusing a leap. But make sure what you do does justice to the music; there are times when you just can't stop without discomfort to those who are following it. If you go deliberately on, without rushing, until the end, it will look as if you intended a little music for people to settle to before the first words are spoken. Better, however, to time your piece beforehand and begin in time to end on time. It is better to end early, and play something else in the minute or so that is left, perhaps improvising, but do finish it properly. It can be appropriate to increase the volume as a procession is approaching so that people's attention is captured and a signal sent that worship is about to start. What we want to avoid is any idea that we are greeting the choir or the minister like a television game host. Some organs have a warning light to tell when an entry is to take place; if none, it is probably easy these days to instal one that can respond to a remote signal without having to take up the floorboards.

Some suffer from nerves when having to play without the cover of the people singing (or even when they are). It is better to play something simple competently than risk 'something before you are ready. It is not the end of the world to play manuals only until the pedals become second nature. Remember too that you could be the only one to notice if you play a wrong note or two, unless you are playing a tune that is very well known.[5]

## Improvisation

It is usually assumed that the roles of composer and performer are quite distinct. It is true that the motivation and time required to do either well often precludes the other, but in reality the two callings shade into each other. A composition will take shape either in the imagination and/or as composers play freely on their instrument, trying new sounds, making shapes, developing ideas. Sometimes the two converge, as in the cadenza in a concerto where soloists let the themes of the piece lead them into new treatments, culminating in a final coda. Improvisation is a feature in jazz forms of music where the virtuoso player is given the floor, even for several minutes, to the acclaim of the audience, where the improvised passages are as important as the written part. What we aspire to is not simply filling gaps with shapeless music that seems to go nowhere, which the French organist and composer Widor characterised as so much *macaroni au fromage*. But don't be put off trying; cooks have to learn to boil an egg.

How therefore do we approach these points in a service when even brief improvisation is required, where music can enhance a moment, focus a movement, create time for reflection? For those who have not been introduced to this skill, it is rather like skiing off piste. To strike the first sound and continue without the safety of a score can be terrifying; what if I run out of ideas, what if I cannot find a way to stop and everyone starts to look at me, what if I fumble the notes? Yet we are musicians. We come with a facility for enjoying and making music. We have listened to an enormous amount of music in our time. We also come with a life experience and, usually, a commitment to being at worship. These things give us confidence. It is a whole person who improvises. As the great jazz musician Charlie Parker put it: 'Music is your own experience, your thoughts, your wisdom. If you don't live it, it won't come out of your horn.'

Yet there are good places to start which are within the grasp of all of us. It is not a bad idea when you arrive to practise, to spend time 'just playing' and developing confidence in playing without music. In a service, rather than try and make it up from nothing, you can use a tune, a hymn tune perhaps, but one that is second nature to you. You may write the melody down – just the melody so as not to be distracted by the rest. Don't write it out from beginning to end; divide the ideas up, so that you have another idea to fall back on when you have done all you can with the first. However, this is not a skill that can be described in words. There are short courses available which show with examples how one might find one's feet, so that to improvise becomes second nature. A link to a short course of proven popularity by Brigitte Harris is included among the resources in Appendix 2.

## Practising

An organist remarks: 'In my years of playing the organ, I've been in more trouble for wanting time to practise than anything else!' Where this can be felt most keenly is when lists of hymns are late in arrival, leaving little time to negotiate an unusually demanding tune. Sometimes the most awkward are worship songs which, beguilingly tuneful, may harbour vicious syncopation and require some editing before playing on an organ.[6] Added to accuracy there is the matter of interpretation; you will wish to spend time studying the hymns so that you can accompany them imaginatively and in a way that helps worshippers interpret the meaning and join in more fully. Few of those who listen Sunday by Sunday will realise how much time has to be spent in practice. Some are lucky enough to have an electronic organ at home to practise on. If choosing one, make sure it has a full pedal board (usually 32 notes).

The most valuable practice is not measured by how many times you play through a piece. All you may be doing is confirming the mistakes. Practice times need a structure.[7] If you are about to learn a new piece, step one, strangely, is to leave the organ firmly shut and just browse through the music. You may be able to hear it in your head but, if not, what you can do is notice what shape it has, whether sections are repeated, whether there are characteristic patterns of notes which are repeated, albeit in different registers. Does the title tell you anything? Is there indication of mood? Do the dynamics suggest that this will be a gentle piece, or a bold, or impassioned one? Note the key, any points where it seems to go into a new key, tempo, changes of time signature, transitions, potentially tricky fingering. Even if you take in only some of this, you have surveyed the landscape. This is very different from just starting at the first chord and battling through.

The first time you try it, play through to the end, without stopping if possible, just to get a sense of how it sounds. You might want to do this again, maybe rather slowly, noticing different things. Then start work! Your read-through and play-throughs may have identified some sticking points. Work on these, spending all the time you need on each one – but knowing it is always possible to come back for another spell. To work on just a few bars at a time removes the impatience that wants to get to the end and have something to show for it. At this point, some prefer to work with hands separately, then together, pedals on their own, manuals only, then with pedals. It is quite a good plan to play really slowly and deliberately, fixing the moves in your mind, but keeping nevertheless a steady pulse; we need to learn the rhythm as much as the notes. When everything is right, or you know they are going to be, increase the speed. Note anything that is still tentative, and go back to that point and spend a bit of time on it.

## The organist's homework

In Chapter 8 members of the congregation are encouraged to become more familiar with the hymn book in use in their church (assuming there is one), but the organist can bring more to the same task. The purpose, apart from one's own interest and nourishment, is to be able to make suggestions to clergy and worship planning groups for psalm settings, hymns and other songs which would be suitable for your church. Going through the book from beginning to end is less productive than taking a section (study the index and choose). Browse through, play everything, study the details on the page that give information about authors and composers and dates, fill in your own knowledge by referring to websites that provide background notes.[8] Then do the same with another section or with the hymns that relate to a particular festival – well in advance so that there is time to get your suggestions into the system.

When an item looks a little strange – words under the music, passages for a cantor, verse and chorus, an antiphon, anything unexpected – take a closer look. You may be the only person in that church to work out how it is meant to sound and be sung, and you may be uncovering a hidden treasure.

## The organist as worshipper

Organists sometimes refer to their difficulties in participating fully in the worship for which they play. The presiding minister frequently has the same problem. Both in different ways are enabling people to worship, and this requires a certain detachment which allows the monitoring of the flow of the worship, which sees what is coming before it happens, which prepares the support for what is to follow. The organist's tasks can thus prevent participation on the level of the people in the pews. How can you stand for the benediction when you would have to struggle back along the organ stool in time to accompany the choral amen? How can you be moved to new insight by a hymn when you are poised to change registration to bring out the meaning of the next verse? How make confession when you have to shuffle the music, which often defies the meagre ability of the music stand to hold it in place, so that the anthem is on top and open at the right page? You are in your place before the people gather and do not experience the welcome they are giving each other to worship, renewing their expectation by mutual greetings and conversation. If your family comes to church, you can't ever sit with them, or maybe only at the sermon (when you may arrive late and leave early). In some churches you may not even be in a position where you can hear or see properly, and indeed may be attached to the gathered congregation by video link.

Yet in a way your unique role offers you an advantage others will not have – namely, that you are coming prepared. Organists will be much better acquainted with the hymns because they have had to examine them, their argument, their high points, beforehand so that they can help them come alive in the mouths and minds of the people. Again, if the congregation uses a regular lectionary, and you know in advance what the week's passages are, this provides another way in which one can prepare. Both may contribute to a heightened alertness which can allow you more quickly to latch on in the time you have.

It is also helpful to bear in mind that the organist at least shares the same pre-worship baseline as (potentially) do other worshippers. Prayer in worship is in verbal form, whether traditional collects and litanies or modern compositions or indeed extempore prayer which, like improvisation, is brought together in a particular moment of time from a vocabulary of prayer which is established and available. However, long before the prayers were formalised, they existed, hardly heard, in the many duties, encounters and accidents of the week. Before a prayer finds a formula, it is *felt*, often only in passing, but real enough: small spasms of need, of joy, fear, emptiness, love, completeness, that may not at first occurrence be translatable into coherent prayer. Spoken liturgical prayer is a continuation and a generalisation of such whispered prayers-in-life. Formal thanksgivings find precedent in the mute thank you when one feels a satisfaction in one's skills (manual or mental), or at the end of the working day or when a new day begins; the joy in relationships with colleagues; the loving word or gesture which brings the relief of being accepted; the stirring of the spirit at a performance or an exhibition. Then there are our confessions, supplications and petitions which find their origins in the demands to which we do not feel equal, frustration at a setback, emptiness after a difficult encounter, unease at the compromises in which we are implicated, the times when we cry, 'I can't do this', or even, 'Why hast thou forsaken me!?' Or a shaft of compassion for a family member, an agony of frustration at injustices before which we feel helpless – these and many other thoughts and experiences prime our formal intercessions.

For other worshippers, these may reach worship if participants have fanned the flame by being able to call them back to mind, and if the public prayer is skilfully enough made and led so that they connect with these self-same remembered feelings. The organist, however, is handicapped in having other things to keep in mind before and during the prayers. Might it be possible to find a few minutes at another time to reflect on the week, its events and encounters? This may help to tune in more quickly when there is opportunity as the spoken prayer unfolds, even if one only can achieve the attitude (of thanksgiving, confession, etc.) rather than follow the specific content.

Alternatively, or in addition, is it too far-fetched to suggest that while others listen and are stirred to prayer by leader or liturgy, your musical offering may be a physical expression of prayer? Might your playing be a bodily act of adoration and thanksgiving, your intercession made through the effort (in a voluntary or carefully prepared hymn) to awaken the congregation to greater attentiveness as they worship, your confession in your regret at a fumble or in feeling a lack of preparation, your heartfelt petition when you start the voluntary which has been challenging to prepare, the feeling of blessing as you play the final cadence? You cannot so easily give yourself the space in worship to connect with what is being said, but in what you do, your acts confirm the embryo prayers of the week and translate them not into words but into sound.

## Being part of a rota

The time commitment demanded of an organist, compared with other members and leaders in a congregation, means that at the moment there are as many gifted organists willing only to deputise occasionally as there are in actual posts. Other weekend demands, of family or leisure or work, lead to many congregations establishing a rota of organists, sometimes as many as four, who share the task. Such a community of musicians can be very effective, not just in practical terms but in signalling that music ministry is by teamwork, and indeed the team is as wide as the congregation. Yet it is important that this arrangement is given the careful planning similar to that which goes into the drawing up of the tasks and duties (and remuneration where appropriate) of a single organist. One aspect that must be taken into account is that a congregation's musician does not simply play an instrument but has the opportunity of developing the quality and reach of the musical life of the church. The team of organists needs a structure where this is taken into account.

## The organist as community musician

Many amateur singers and other musicians find their only opportunity for developing their musical skills and their enjoyment of music in the local church. In previous centuries, it was the local choral unions, often church-inspired, or the church choirs expanded to put on oratorios, that provided the occasion for people to come together for the making of music. In some circumstances now as then, the church musician might be the only person who can offer musical leadership and expertise for wider community ventures which are not faith-based – although secular choirs often embrace religious works, such as oratorios, as well. Another example is assisting in community festivals. Here is one way of being in touch with people who at the moment are out of reach of the church, for one reason or another – which doesn't at all mean they are inimical to it. The musician therefore, as well as contributing to the personal, even spiritual, development of those who have been beyond reach, could become a conduit for musical talent in the community to enrich the church by arranging for their contribution to a special season, perhaps. It may be that the church choir too can occasionally offer a concert or event, with a varied programme.

## Other roles

As well as, in some cases, teamwork with other organists, there are various roles where one finds partnerships in the work of leading the music. If there is a *choir*, or the remnants of, or the makings of, a choir, it is in most cases the organist who is expected to oblige. You may feel, though, that directing a choir may not be your skill or suit your personality, although you do at least know about music. Some would say that the best kind of person to direct a choir is someone who has sung in choirs, and there is much truth in that. Could it be that, even in the wider community, there is someone who might take on this task as your partner, whether it is to prepare the choir for weekly or occasional use? If the choir is only an embryo, this may be a time to consult with others about whether to recruit or whether to devise a different structure. Some churches develop children's choirs, with or without a separate leader. This can be a refreshing addition to services, and show how the church community values children, while at the same time developing active musicians for the future. This is of course already the case in cathedrals and large churches where children and young people are an integral part of the choir. Also, in cathedral and similar settings, the choir is already the responsibility of the director of music, and there would usually be an assistant organist or an organ scholar to accompany.

Similar issues are raised if there is a *praise band*. It has recently been common for organists to keep their distance, feeling the two approaches to music in worship to be incompatible, and perhaps threatening. A similar stance may be taken by a band and those promoting contemporary worship song. This is changing and many organists put their training and their musical knowledge at the disposal of the band, able to write parts, accompany on keyboard, offer advice about presentation and about what is singable by a congregation. There are times when the organ has to come to the party and accompany the worship song, or join in with the band to enhance the experience.[9] A praise band is one of many forms of instrumental group, and reminds us that there are other ensembles that can, perhaps on special occasions, enrich worship – and thus involve more, possibly young, musicians. We may want to use even single instruments, like a flute or a fiddle to, say, provide a descant within a hymn for the occasional verse.

You may or may not feel like the kind of person who stands in front of a congregation and gets them miraculously singing something they have never heard in their lives before. At least you can play the melody (perhaps section by section) and invite people to imitate it, but you can also be alert to, or seek suggestions of names for, someone else who is accustomed to using their personality to communicate to a crowd. Therefore another partnership could be with a *cantor or precentor*, who might be already in the choir and who might be the one to teach new material, and also to be the person to lead the several new choir/congregational settings in today's hymn books which are in the form of a dialogue. You may yourself deal with *copyright matters*, or arrange for someone else to do this. Again, it would be helpful in some circumstances to have a *choir manager* or secretary, who as well as administrative tasks could also be the librarian for the music. There are also the people who prepare the words on the *screens*, where that is appropriate, and those who produce the *orders of service* or 'pew bulletins', in which you might wish to insert information about organ music or hymns. There is some strength in involving others with you in delivering the music from week to week. An important additional role could be someone knowledgeable about music who could represent the musicians on the *council* that is responsible for the governance of the local church – kirk session, vestry, circuit. It would be a bonus also for the musician to be given an invitation to attend once in a while when the council would make room for a discussion about the music.

## Relationships with clergy

An important partner is the priest or minister with whom in different ways we share responsibility for the music. Even if we have the same tastes in music, the roles are different: the organist focuses on the music, while clergy have responsibility for the worship as a whole. Inevitably there will be need for discussion and clarification, as well as joint planning.

The pattern of relationship will inevitably be different in every case. It could simply be agreed that email exchanges will be considered sufficient, and the two parties could undertake to give prompt replies, and be willing to consult in person should such a need arise. Even better would be to meet regularly (even twice a year or quarterly), preferably in a congenial place and possibly away from the church. Difficulties, if any arise, are easier to deal with when you are not having an emergency meeting solely for this purpose. It would be helpful to have an agreed agenda, or some regularity about the ground to be covered, such as: reflecting on recent services, especially when something new was tried; discussing the introduction of hymns and songs that are not yet known, perhaps thinking quite far ahead to the next big season (the organist could bring a list and talk about it, and of course vice versa); a slot for sharing difficulties either has perceived or encountered; an 'ask me anything' session which allows each to ask the other why they do something the way they do – no holds barred, which could give rise to one or other sharing something of their own understanding, insights or tasks, or to imparting useful information; ending with a time, perhaps, to put forward new ideas (like forming a youth choir, having a congregational musical event or mutually identifying people who might support the music in some way, such as an instrumentalist who has come to light).

If you feel you are being asked to do something you don't approve of, one way is to agree to do it as long as you and the priest meet afterwards to review it, allowing you perhaps to suggest another way in which what is being asked for might be approached.

### Is it necessary, or desirable, for the organist to be a church member?

This is often a rhetorical question in that a musician can be difficult to find. Nevertheless, it is a reasonable question, and requires three approaches to answer. The first is the fact that a church needs a competent musician, but it does need someone who, if a stranger to the ways of the church, is willing to learn the ropes. If faced with an organist who has no church connection but who would be willing to learn, and a volunteer-member who is not yet equal to playing what is required, one option would be to appoint the former but find a way of involving and encouraging the latter. They might be your, or someone's, future musician.

The second approach to an answer is along the lines of 'Who are we to judge'? A congregation is likely to have many levels of belief and commitment within it. There are times in one's life when doubts arise about the faith or one feels dissatisfaction with the local church. Some might hang in, hoping that this will pass or new insight be found; others will cease to be involved altogether. There is often little real difference between those who are no longer churchgoers and many who remain in the church. Those 'outside' may still identify themselves with the church on a wider basis, or at least bear it no ill will. It sometimes happens that when something emerges that they can contribute, they may happily offer it.[10]

A third approach to this question is simply to note how many people are now part of the church who first came to be in touch with it through music, whether as a child or adult.

## Should an organist be paid?

It is a common belief, stronger in some denominations than in others, that an organist (or other musician), especially if from within the congregation, should offer their services free. Behind this may be a feeling that music should be a hobby rather than an occupation, and this is aggravated by its link with worship, which all take part in. Not far from this is a belief that 'amateur' is somehow more suitable in the context of the church. We are all playing our part and sharing the tasks. Why should the organist be different? This feeling surfaces also in relation to paid choirs. Are they really taking part in worship or just enjoying singing? In this view, the professional player or singer is focused on music to the detriment of prayer.

To pay the person to whom you give responsibility for the congregation's music is to acknowledge a number of factors. Consider, first, that you are asking a time commitment which is often more than asked of a member of the congregation, not only being there every week but not free to decide not to come on any one Sunday. A second factor is that you may expect your musician not only to be able to play music to last over many months without too much repetition but that you hope that the music will develop in its reach both in terms of the organist's own musical growth but also the congregation's. Then, further, you are requiring an ability to draw on a bank of some 800 hymn tunes of greater or lesser difficulty, and not only that but when they are played they are bound up with words that await release – requiring time spent in studying the content as well as the music. Together with the hope that initiatives may be taken, new things tried, and often planning for and preparing a choir, this adds up to a deal of time and energy. If there are times when one's post as an organist becomes a chore or conflicts with other responsibilities, to have the steadying influence of a salary is worth more than its size. A congregation has invested in you, you are accountable to them, and they to you. Above all, it is important to remember that a great many young musicians are reliant on multiple tasks or appointments to make up a living wage.

Here also the matter of contracts is raised. Denominations vary, some leaving things to the local situation, others recommending that all churches should consider formalising the arrangement. Some denominations have a model contract that can be modified to local circumstances. What this does is that, first, it affirms a partnership, then it clarifies the relationship within this – what the local church council's responsibilities are in this, what is the minister's or priest's obligation – not just to the organist but in terms of worship as a whole, and of course what is expected of the organist, including holidays. This last is of as much importance as the rest in that where this is not stated, there can be resentment on both parts: organists feeling they cannot take time off because they will be letting the congregation down, especially if cover is difficult, and the congregation getting it wrong and thinking that someone is 'always' taking time off. When a model contract is used, it is an opportunity for the church council to consider carefully what they are asking the organist to do – ideally in consultation with the organist, a rare opportunity for them to become more aware of the music of the church and how it is delivered. It is also important that local circumstances are fully taken into consideration when finalising the contract so that an unworkable template is not forced on a situation to which it doesn't apply. Two other aspects are also important: a door left open, however it is couched, for development and for initiatives to be taken seriously; and also that there is mention of other people with whom the organist is brought into partnership so that difficulties are less likely to arise as they together tackle the important and complex task of leading a worshipping congregation in praise.

Particularly it should be clear how the roles of organist and clergy dovetail. The last word is used advisedly since in some denominations at least the organist seems to be line managed by the clergy or a body like a cathedral chapter. This is not so much a matter of personal authority as that the clergy are given a different and wider role. They represent the disciplines and practices of their branch of the church. They have responsibility for the whole flow of worship, and an act of worship is far more than the sum of its parts. It is immediately clear, however, that another expertise is essential in the delivery of this, one that can vouch for the music. Clergy will defer to the judgement and ability of the musician to propose, prepare and bring to performance the musical parts of the service. What the organist might find it helpful to bear in mind also is that in a sense the minister represents the 'unmusical' to the 'musical', and could well be able to assess how well particular music is playing its part. Clearly a balance needs to be found within these different roles and responsibilities. Finally, it has to be remembered that although a contract is cast in legal terms, it has to be interpreted in the light of the gospel of grace.

### Notes

1 Routley, Erik, 1968, *Words, Music and the Church*, London: Herbert Jenkins, pp. 81f.

2 Stuart Muir of St Paul's (Scottish Episcopal) Cathedral, Dundee, is one. See Stuart Muir, 'Why I prefer to be a pastoral musician', *Different Voices*, no. 7, Lammas 2010.

3 Routley, *Words, Music*, pp. 196f.

4 Routley, *Words, Music*, p. 197.

5 See Appendix 2 for a link to a bank of simple versions of hymn tunes.

6 See Chapter 15.

7 I am indebted to a tutorials given at Scottish Churches Organist Training Scheme local workshops, particularly those by Walter Blair of Holy Trinity Church, St Andrews.

8 See Appendix 2.

9 See Chapter 15.

10 Aisthorpe, Steve, 2016, *The Invisible Church: Learning From the Experience of Churchless Christians*, Edinburgh: St Andrew Press.

# 11

# Embodying the People's Praise

## *The Music Ministry of the Clergy*

That they have a ministry is a concept fully understood by
clergy. That they might have a *music* ministry may be a step
too far. Some will claim they are 'not musical', a stance much
challenged today when studies and natural observation show
that musicality is a basic component of being human. Not to be
knowledgeable about the technical side of music is a different
matter. While some may not be able to hold a tune, or believe
so,[1] most count music, in a wide variety of idioms, as one of
their pleasures. In the world of music, amateur has no negative
connotations, but fully lives up to its Latin root meaning –
'lover' or 'friend'. Yet many clerical friends of music abdicate
responsibility when it comes to the music of the church, save
the inevitable duty of picking the hymns.

It is not, however, easy to avoid a commitment to music in
worship. One may think of several places where the spoken
resonates with the sung. Hymns, for example, can add to
*proclamation*, both with their density of scriptural reference
and their contextualisation of Christian witness. Fr James
Quinn SJ belonged to a preaching order and saw his hymns as
fulfilling that commitment: 'Hymns form a catechism in song.'[2]
This could also be said of anthems. James Montgomery's
several hymns on *prayer* call us towards a high standard in
our preparation for leading prayer: that our words should seek
to draw out 'truth in the inward part'; that we – reminded
that 'prayer is the burden of a sigh, the falling of a tear, the
upward glancing of an eye' – may touch into the intimate life
of the worshippers; that we might combine 'the simplest form

of speech that infant lips can try' with the 'sublimest strains', so that in the end all of us together 'through the Spirit and thy Son, shall pray and pray aright'.[3] Hymns enshrine every mode of prayer: confession and forgiveness, intercession and offering, thanksgiving and supplication, a sense of the saints praying with us, as well as furnishing inspired utterances of that most difficult of modes of prayer to convey in words alone, adoration. Above all, in the very *singing of the people*, we are continually reminded that we do not provide the worship but ourselves worship within a wider priesthood, the faithful people of that place.

More particularly, the presiding minister (often nowadays, just 'presider' – a term first used by Justin Martyr in the second century[4]) prepares the ground in which the music is planted. Just as an architect's design for a dwelling inspires the lives that inhabit it, so the order of worship, its returning memories and comforting words, its surprising angles and opening out of perspectives, enable a hymn, song or setting to come to life. The interlocking skills of the presider enable a liturgy, whether captured in a prayer book or held in the shared memory, to be reincarnated, fresh and relevant, among a particular people at a particular time. The varied elements are fused into coherence, a progression not only of logical sense but of emotional drama as the story of salvation sweeps up the personal and communal stories of those who have gathered, pointing forward to their culmination in the Kingdom of God. Thus in our presiding the song is clearing its throat to become the 'new song'.

In her sharply observed *Memoirs of a Highland Lady*, Elizabeth Grant describes going to church in the early part of the nineteenth century in her home parish in Rothiemurchus:

> The stir consequent on our entrance [the laird and his family] was soon hushed, and the minister gave out the psalm; he put a very small dirty volume up to one eye, for he was near sighted and feeble sighted, and read as many lines of the old version of the rhythmical paraphrase (we may call it) of the Psalms of David as he thought fit, drawing them out in a

sort of sing song that was very strange. He stooped over the pulpit to hand his little book to the precentor, who then rose and called out aloud the tune – the 'St George's tune', 'Auld Aberdeen', 'hondred an' fifteen' etc., began himself a recitative of the first line on the key note, then taken up and repeated by the congregation; line by line he continued in the same fashion, serious severe screaming quite beyond the natural pitch of the voice, a wandering search after the air by many who never caught it, a flourish really, of difficult execution and plenty of the *tremolo* lately come into fashion with the tenor singers in particular. The dogs seized the occasion to bark, for they always came to the kirk with the rest of the family, and the babies to cry. When the minister could bear the din no longer he popped up again, again leaned over, touched the precentor's head, and instantly all sound ceased.

Two matters emerge from this vignette. One is how hymns should be announced, of which more later. The other highlights the difficulties ministers face in conducting worship, as much in our time as in Georgian Speyside. It is a daunting role, and calls for skills that we continue to hone throughout our ministry.

While discussing the music ministry of the congregation (Chapter 8), note was taken of the way other contemporary models of gathering could affect a congregation's understanding of itself. Gordon Lathrop has suggested that rather than being a body of spectators or consumers, the Christian community gathered for worship is distinctive in being 'transformative'. Lathrop goes on to suggest how these cultural models could, willy-nilly, influence those who preside over these gatherings. This arises from our own recognition of the deficiencies of these models of community, and our understanding that it is the very meeting together that is itself the content. Lathrop suggests that the response of many presiders is to affirm that distinctiveness by seeking to create 'genuine communities', which can mistakenly assume that this must mean 'intimate community, a collection of friends and lovers'. This, he finds, can shape current liturgical practice: 'Intimate, familial speech and narratives of the self, for example, often replace formal and stylized expression in the work of preachers.'[5]

If this is true, it is not helped by the greater informality which characterises both contemporary social media and day-to-day relationships and transactions. Added to that is the changing nature of Sunday morning which, as we have seen, may be attempting to incorporate several different former aspects of church life into one occasion – groups and guilds, education, social gatherings. Clergy when they visited these groups, to lead, participate or encourage, would bring different parts of their personality to bear: teacher, public speaker, counsellor, chairperson, friend, compère, the life and soul of the party. But which are we on this new Sunday morning? Or in what combination? The growing practice of streaming church services also brings a dilemma, as we feel a clash between conducting a service in a church building while simultaneously speaking to people at home. Proclaimer from the pulpit, presenter on the small screen, how do we, with all our undoubted skills as communicators, combine these seemingly contrasting roles?

Our own sensitive pastoral concern can play a part. Aware that our usual worship practices are no longer part of the communal memory, we fear people may be put off by the ritual and rubric of the traditional service of worship and believe that part of that is the priestly voice and stance, which seems to be remote from the styles of modern life. There is a temptation, therefore, to play down some of the registers of presiding and instead introduce a simpler vocabulary, a lighter touch, a disarming humour, a greater informality. Is it possible, though, that we are in danger of creating our own modern Rothiemurchus, as American Presbyterian theologian Edward Farley suggests in this devastating picture?

To attend the typical Protestant Sunday morning worship service is to experience something odd, something like a charade ... Lacking is a sense of the terrible mystery of God, which sets language atremble and silences facile chattiness

... If the seraphim assumed this Sunday morning mood, they would be addressing God not as 'holy, holy, holy' but as 'nice, nice, nice'.[6]

The well-intentioned and laudable desire not to stand in the way of people's engagement in worship has been given an alternative description, namely 'the refusal to preside'. In his classic study on conducting worship, Robert Hovda recognises how recent developments in thinking about church, ministry and worship have led many to play down their leadership role. The causes may be legitimate, but to abdicate in this way will not contribute, in his view, to the necessary ecclesial reform. In fact, we have to lay hold of our ancient role more firmly in our time, albeit differently. Worship is the action of a community of persons and requires a person to hold it together.[7]

A symposium to assess the contribution of the Church of England's *Common Worship* on its tenth anniversary, *God's Transforming Work*, contained an important introductory essay by the then Archbishop of Canterbury, Rowan Williams.[8] In it he reminds readers that leading worship is more than finding the right words and following the correct practices: 'Learning liturgical behaviour is learning to *use your body significantly*. A great many people emerge from our training institutions with very little sense of what that might mean, or of how the use of the celebrant's body enables or disables the whole community's worship.'

Hovda suggests that the bodily *style* of the presider is a dimension to which we should pay urgent attention in these times when worship's tectonic plates are shifting. To the puritan in us the idea of adopting a style has a ring of falsity, the suggestion of posturing, pretending to be something we are not. Surely the time for the pulpit tones, the sacred alias, the authoritarian demeanour is well and truly over. We have, however, to ask how much we can tell about people by the way they enter a room, walk along a street, stand waiting at our door, and how we may often be able to tell from, say, the demeanour of a doctor or a member of the police force whether the news is good or bad. People's bearings speak volumes and affect how we react to them, to keep out or to welcome, to dismiss or to give all our attention.

We may assume that worshippers notice without noticing what messages minister or priest is sending. Kimberley Bracken Long reports that to ask people from a variety of denominational backgrounds what they hope for in a leader of worship is to get surprisingly similar answers:

> Ask, 'What qualities do you appreciate in a worship leader?' and you will hear things like presence, authenticity, warmth, grace humor, reverence. Ask what characteristics you hope you never see again, and the list is usually even longer: lack of energy, easily distracted, no eye contact, distant, dull, verbose. As with good art or great music, we may not be able to explain what makes a good worship leader, but we often know it when we see it – and when we don't.[9]

She elaborates: 'Certainly there are things to say about the proper use of the voice and evocative gestures and appropriate words, but much of what lies at the heart of the matter is less about correctness and more about passion.' Without this, she suggests – that is, without being present as the whole (passionate) person that you are – something is missing, 'some inclination of mystery, perhaps, or of deep joy'.[10] Two questions are raised: what is the source of this passion and what messages have our bodily postures, our style, to convey?

Regarding the first, Bishop Kevin Pearson recalls the moment when Nelson Mandela, after 25 years of incarceration on Robben Island, emerged to face for the first time ranks of photographers and television cameras. There could have been no greater contrast than between the previous solitude and this sudden exposure to the world's clamour: 'Yet there was no uncertainty in his bearing. He was utterly himself. He came before them directly from out of an interior life.'[11] Only later was it learned that this had consisted of physical exercise, extensive reading and daily prayer. Pearson experienced this quiet presence as a gift offered to himself and others, in enabling them to see how the integrity of body and spirit can carry one through even the most adverse of experiences – and, we might say, contribute to the formation of the person who embodies and leads the worship of the people.

What do we hope this bodily 'presence' will convey? Hovda explains how we carry in our posture, our voice, our attentiveness, signals and invitations which open up pathways into the presence of God. We are striving to be at the height of our God-consciousness and therefore at the height of our human-consciousness, the latter both in our awareness of our own humanity and our knowledge of those to whom we minister: 'It is an awesome thing to face the mystery of the Other and the mystery of ourselves.'[12] Above and beyond the rubrics that usher us on is an awareness of the limits of our words and teaching, the music and the polished ritual, but also our awe at the generosity of the divine response. Ministerial educator Stephen Burns, reflecting on Hovda's legacy, recalls Evelyn Underhill's eulogy of an indefatigable docklands priest. She writes that he was not such a good preacher, but people did not come to church to hear his sermons but 'to look at his face'. It was, perhaps, his face, his 'atmosphere', that held people, that taught them of God's esteem for them, of their status as beloved. Burns continues:

> Presiders should, maybe, think much more deeply about what they teach by their look – what they are seen to look at, what they are seen to reverence, behold, take delight in, yield and surrender to, be wary of, shy away from. Presiders might teach the faith as much by when they smile and what they smile at; what they turn away from, when they grimace or flinch; what they incline towards, when they keep their distance, what they hold and carry, whom they face. And so on and so on. I would give away a lot of what often passes as formation for ministry in order to be able to concentrate communal attention on these things.[13]

One quality that Hovda particularly identifies in the presider is an attitude of reverence: 'The numinous must be tangible.' This will immediately sound warning bells for some to whom it may signal distance, stiffness, even pomposity. Yet you only need to experience worship in other cultures to know that reverence has many guises. Exuberance and informality, and much vocal participation, may be both strengthened and balanced by being offered in reverence. A writer on worship suggests that whatever reverence is, it is not disturbed by people taking more part. Instead, he would say that reverence is our means of becoming *right-sized, creaturely*. It begins when we no longer confuse ourselves with God. So you might say that what chases out reverence and drains a sense of transcendence from worship is when human beings, worshippers – and their minister – take centre stage.[14]

This right-sizedness comes not only from the presider's own spiritual life, but from the understanding that this particular act of worship is not a closed sequence of particular acts and offerings but, as Williams reminds us, a point of transition for the people gathered, moving them 'from one context or condition of heart and imagination to another' and saying 'something about the new humanity within the new creation'.[15] Further, we are aware that we are presiding not only at this one act of worship but participating in the greater worship of the church catholic. Especially at these times not just of ecumenical interest but of denominations' growing need of each other, we are pointing beyond this congregation and this particular worship tradition to the worship of the great church. It should be possible for people of other denominations and of none to recognise themselves in our company. This is not expressed solely in a welcoming posture but in words carefully chosen to include and by drawing on resources which come from many traditions.

In what is written so far, it may seem that too great a weight is put upon the presider's own spiritual life. The reality is that, like anyone else, those charged with the leading of worship may be going through a transitional period in their own faith and may experience the absence of God more strongly than God's presence. At such points they may not feel capable or worthy to focus a people's worship yet continue because they are called and trusted to do so. An Irish musicologist, Thérèse

Smith, spent a year or two in the company of the Clear Creek Missionary Baptist Church, near Oxford, Mississippi, studying their worship and their music. Particularly she was interested in the way that prayer or preaching could turn into music as the speaker moved beyond words to intone what he was saying. But in one sermon she recorded, the preacher as he approaches the end of the sermon has a moment of self-doubt: 'Dear Lord, seem like to me you're not sure, this thing that got on to me. Won't let me act right sometime, every once in a while.' But as he intones this, a voice is raised among the Hallelujahs, 'Oh that man is alright, oh the man is alright.' Smith writes: 'They were owning what he was doing, owning his ability to interpret their thoughts, anxieties, desires, their precarious hold on faith. They trusted him. Maybe they even loved him.'[16]

American Methodist Constance Cherry has written that 'it is less a matter of our *doing* worship – of the capabilities we think we bring to the event; rather, it is more a matter of our *yielding* to the actions of Christ who facilitates our worship to God' (Cherry's italics).[17] Our role is one that not only makes demands on our spiritual resources and our creativity, but also on our humility. The second report from the church music study group Universa Laus emphasises that 'listening is … an essential component of liturgy', and suggests that 'ministers … are the "listening ones", and they create … the conditions necessary for the ear of the assembly to be opened.'[18]

## Announcing hymns

Before, therefore, we even announce a hymn, we have led the way to it. If cues are needed, they should be just enough and no more. The Rothiemurchus way (see above) of reading several verses, and even a common contemporary practice of reading out the whole of the first verse, not only distances the hymn from the point we have reached in the service but it misunderstands the nature of a hymn: that it is made up of music and words and neither component stands on its own. Some believe that the best way is not to use words at all, but let the opening phrases on the organ be sufficient announcement, although this will depend on people consulting the hymn board or the service sheet, and this takes time, and is also difficult for some. To use a repeated formula (another common practice), can reduce anticipation and sound dull. I grew up with the then common but stereotypical 'Let us sing to God's praise and glory the hymn two hundred and thirty-nine, ... the two hundred and thirty-ninth hymn.' This, five times in a service, did not help us spring to our feet. What might be considered is to combine an announcement with a brief sentence to say why the hymn was chosen, or to draw attention to a subsequent verse, clarify a difficult phrase or identify an allusion or reference, or alert people to a point when words are difficult to fit to the music. But not too often. Where the psalms have been incorporated in the current hymn book and bear hymn numbers as well, consider identifying it as a psalm, coming as it does from a distinctive corpus of material. Please don't sing over your microphone; it can play havoc with the organist's (and congregation's) tempo. A last comment: in these more inclusive days when it is realised that some find it a struggle to get to their feet, make it known that it is not the end of the world to stay seated to sing, which means that the other very common formula, 'Let us stand to sing hymn ...', is not appropriate.

## The musical duties of the clergy

As we have explored the ministries of other groups and individuals, we have built upon the preface to an Australian hymn book Companion which outlines what the author calls the obligations of each. What of the presider?[19]

### 1 Browse through the hymn book

In times past, when people brought their own hymn books to church, and took them home with them, the book was seen, along with the Bible, as a companion to private devotion. To approach the book this way, which means time is taken with a hymn rather than a quick glance to see if it fits next Sunday's service, can suggest a number of contexts the hymn might satisfy, and a note could be made to return in the future. In the weeks before a season or a festival we might focus specifically on the hymns offered. Consider making a date with your musician to do this together. Or in any given week, with modern hymn books now tending to include a comprehensive index of biblical and thematic references,[20] time could be set aside to see what hymns quote verses or echo themes from the coming few Sundays' readings or psalms. In the course of this investigation, one could seek information about the author and composer and check in a hymnary companion or other source[21] for information about their background and the situation in which the hymn was written. It is advisable to keep a record of the hymns chosen to prevent too much repetition.


## 2 Move beyond your own preferences

The second duty is, in choosing hymns, consciously to go beyond those that are well known to you yourself, and not just your familiarity with the words and tunes but also the idiom. It is quite difficult when you have grown up with a particular range or style not to feel most at home among these when choices have to be made. Notice the variety, or lack of it, in the hymns you choose. Some seem drawn to hymns of six or eight lines, some only to worship songs, some go for those that can be sung heartily, while some seem in thrall to tunes in E flat! (It is good not to have all or most of the hymns in the same key. You would think that wouldn't matter, given that they are separated from each other, and most in the congregation probably don't read music, but the sameness of pitch can be 'felt', and may have a deadening effect.) The growth of mature Christians requires being challenged by new ideas and new experiences; don't deny them this with safe choices. Someone has remarked, considering the tendency to keep within the radius of the known, that a business which makes no use of a third of its assets would not last long!

### 3 Make sure your director of music gets the hymns on time

This seems trivial, yet it is the burden of frequent complaint from organists. This is of course not necessarily due to clerical procrastination; often a service only 'comes together' late in the week. Perhaps at least some preliminary choices might be made and forwarded. Especially for an inexperienced player, there can be pitfalls in seemingly straightforward tunes which need particular attention. This is especially true for worship songs. Many an organist has felt undermined by not having played as well as one would have wished, made all the worse by having too little time to practise. Be prepared for your organist to ask if a chosen hymn could be kept for a suitable future occasion, allowing time to prepare. An attentive organist will also wish to accompany in a way to bring out the meaning, and this needs time to study the words. With regard to other music in the service (such as the need to choose and prepare anthems or introits), your musician needs to know themes well in advance. If there is an agreed lectionary in use, both minister and music director can work to this.

### 4 Meet regularly with your musician

If not in place, encourage your church council to draw up a contract with the musician, and you should be involved in this.[22] Make time to meet with your organist or music director on a regular basis. It could be once a quarter, or twice a year, or in good time before key festivals or main seasons. This is an expression of the fact that both parties have musical responsibilities which at some points dovetail. It might be helpful to have an agreed agenda, with not every item required each time. It might include forward planning, review of past events or new ideas that had been tried, the development of the musical life of the congregation, the consideration of any problems that have arisen. In addition, the minister or priest might encourage their musician to take opportunities to develop their craft, whether encouraging the making of time to prepare for an advanced diploma or to participate in organist workshops (with the church even footing the bill), depending on the experience of the musician so far. The minister may wish occasionally to drop in on the choir or any other choral group, perhaps allowing an opportunity for questions. When first arriving in a parish, it is good to make the music director or band leader one of your first ports of call.

### 5 Learn to read music

Consider the suggestion that you might learn to read music sufficiently to sing the tunes in your melody edition. In a course on church music I taught for ministers and lay leaders in training, each session began with a short segment when music notation was explained and students tried out what they had learned. This was one of the parts of the course most valued, not just for the new skill acquired but for the confidence it gave them in relating to the musicians in the parishes to which they went. Learning to read music is discussed further in Chapter 8 (the ministry of the congregation).

### 6 Preach about worship

Just as in preaching and teaching we offer biblical and theological support to the people in their faith and witness, we should consider from time to time preaching about the nature and content of worship. There is a rising awareness today of the need for 'liturgical formation' by which worshippers are enabled, with the help of greater understanding, to draw more deeply on their experience of worship for their own spiritual growth and for sustenance in the life of faith and discipleship. This is a task (which also is discussed further in Chapter 8) which had a higher profile prior to the Reformations of the fifteenth and sixteenth centuries.[23]

## Conclusion

If we have a choir, perhaps that moment of quiet prayer with these musical colleagues before a service is one of the most important pieces of presiding we do. Methodist minister Frederick Pratt Green (d. 2000), looking back on a lifetime of leading worship in partnership with many a choir and musician, wrote this:

How often, making music, we have found
a new dimension in the world of sound,
as worship moved us to a more profound
*Alleluia!*[24]

*Notes*

1 Bell, John L., 2000, *The Singing Thing*, Glasgow: Wild Goose Publications, pp. 95f.

2 Interview with James Quinn, *Different Voices*, No. 3, Candlemas 2009, pp. 32f.

3 'Lord, teach us how to pray aright', 'Prayer is the soul's sincere desire'.

4 Long, Kimberley Bracken, 2009, *The Worshiping Body: The Art of Leading Worship*, Louisville, KY: Westminster John Knox Press, p. 2.

5 Lathrop, Gordon W., 1999, *Holy People: A Liturgical Ecclesiology*, Minneapolis, MN: Fortress Press, pp. 26–8.

6 Farley, Edward, 'A missing Presence', *Christian Century* (March 18–25, 1998), p. 276. Also http://findarticles.com/p/articles/mi_m1058/is_n9_v115/ai_20460250/ (accessed 17.5.21).

7 Hovda, Robert W., 1976, *Strong, Loving, and Wise: Presiding in Liturgy*, Collegeville, MN: The Liturgical Press, pp. 53–4.

8 Papadopulos, Nicholas (ed.), 2011, *God's Transforming Work*, London: SPCK, p. 12.

9 Long, *The Worshiping Body*, p. 6.

10 Long, *The Worshiping Body*, p. 2.

11 Sermon broadcast from St Mary's Cathedral, Glasgow, Epiphany 2020.

12 Hovda, *Strong, Loving, and Wise*, p. 63.

13 Burns, Stephen, 2012, 'Yearning without saying a word', *Worship*, 86, No. 1, pp. 2–15.

14 Mitchell, Nathan D., 2004, 'The amen corner', *Worship*, 78, No. 1, pp. 67–72.

15 Papadopulos, *God's Transforming Work*, pp. 2, 11.

16 Smith, Thérèse, 2004, *Let the Church Sing: Music and Worship in a Black Mississippi Community*, Woodbridge: Boydell & Brewer.

17 Cherry, Constance, 2010, *The Worship Architect: A Blueprint for Designing Culturally Relevant and Biblically Faithful Services*, Grand Rapids, MI: Baker Academic, p. 28.

18 *Music in Liturgies*, Universa Laus Report II, https://universaolaus. org/documents/ (accessed 17.5.21).

19 Milgate, Wesley, 1982, *Songs of the People of God*, London: Collins Liturgical, pp. 11–15. A revised and expanded edition to accompany the second Australian Hymn Book, *A Companion to Together in Song*, is edited by D'Arcy Wood, Sydney: The Australian Hymn Book Pty Ltd, 2000.

20 *Ancient and Modern* (2013) and *Laudate* also suggest hymns for each particular Sunday.

21 Appendix 2.

22 See also similar observations in Chapter 10 made from the perspective of the organist.

23 Holmes, Stephen Mark, 2015, *Sacred Signs in Reformation Scotland: Interpreting Worship 1488–1590*, Oxford: Oxford University Press.

24 From the hymn 'When, in our music, God is glorified' by Frederick Pratt Green, v. 2.

# Skills

# 12

# What Kind of Organ?

The organ is one of the oldest musical instruments still in use, the earliest remains dating from the third century CE. Organs have been known in the British Isles since the tenth century, although the oldest surviving instruments date from the seventeenth. Three of these connect England and Scotland. The carvings on the case of a Flemish organ built in 1602, now in Carisbrooke Castle on the Isle of Wight, are intertwined with the initials of John Graham, the 3rd Earl of Montrose, the probable original owner, a conjecture supported by finding the same initials and thistle markings on the front of the keys, with the thistle repeated on the pipe stoppers. Another connection is through the organ builder John Loosemore of Exeter, who is long thought (although hard evidence has yet to be found) to have been the maker of the organ now on display at Blair Castle in Perthshire, dated 1630, and from whose instrument in Exeter Cathedral (1665) the present-day cathedral organ is descended. Again, the earliest organ still in use in Scotland is in St Adamnan's Episcopal Church, Duror, originally built around 1700 by 'Father Smith' of London.[1]

Prior to the religious upheavals of the mid-sixteenth century, organs were not used in the way to which we have become accustomed. Vocal polyphony is likely to have alternated with plainsong, and sometimes the organ would provide further variety, especially at festivals, playing in lieu of some of the singers' verses. Thus there was no natural transition to accompanying the congregational singing which developed at the Protestant Reformation, and organs were removed, or destroyed, or allowed simply to decay. Invective against the organ in Scotland came a century later along with a strain of Calvinism that might have alarmed Calvin himself, and any remaining organs were finally removed, like that in Holyroodhouse, 'an unprofitable instrument, scandalous to our profession'.[2] In England and Wales at the time of the Reformation it is estimated that there would have been around 7,000 instruments. Over 800 would have been in monastic institutions, some of which might have suffered along with the buildings at the dissolution of the monasteries.[3]

Another difference in use was in how organs were played. John Fethy was organist at the Town Kirk of Aberdeen towards the middle of the sixteenth century and is referred to as 'the first trim organist that ever was in Scotland' (in the sense of 'neat', or 'accurate'). Fethy had studied on the continent and had brought back a 'curious new fingering and playing on organs', the novelty being the use of all five fingers.[4] (An organ had been in place there at least by 1437, there being a burgh record in that year of a payment of twenty-six shillings and eight pence for the blowing of the organ.)[5] Fethy was also a composer and wrote both 'note and letter' of the penitential 'O God abufe', based on which the late Peter Maxwell Davies wrote a short organ voluntary, an austere and almost frightening piece.

The church organ had a sibling in the cinema or theatre organ, which was employed to fill out the drama of the silent films. The late Tom Fleming, the actor and broadcaster, when in the Royal Navy, tells of playing for the 'other denominations' service while billeted at Butlin's in Skegness. This had to be in the local cinema, where there was a magnificent white and gold Compton Theatrone organ, 'complete with bells and whistles'. He remembers: 'It was a somewhat alarming experience in that it had "double touch": press down so far and you had a resonant diapason, press a little further and you could get something like a train leaving the station!' Church music commentator Erik Routley had a similar experience playing for a Scout service, also in a cinema, when he encountered a stop marked Aeroplane. But whether pulpits or picture houses, the instruments were similarly constructed, and equally versatile.

For many new players, especially pianists who have agreed to help out at a church with no organist, the instrument facing them seems like a large and puzzling piano. In time they find stops that suit them and are loud enough for the congregation to sing to, while others are left well alone. This chapter is about making the best use of the instrument you have. To understand, also, the nature of the instrument and how it works helps both organist and church council to identify faults for the tuner to address and to make informed choices when larger repairs are indicated. Since that may involve considering replacement, the various options, including the purchase of a digital instrument, are explored.[6]

The organ has experienced something of a renaissance in recent years. In broadcasts, in frequent public recitals, and through an ever-increasing number of recordings, the organ has consolidated its place in cultural life. There are many aspects to an organ. Its case, display pipes and woodwork can have a pleasing aesthetic appearance and contribute to the ambience of the church. Those who are knowledgeable about the instruments know the high level of craft work that has gone into the unseen workings of the instrument. Above all, there is its remarkable range of tone colours. Many church buildings are listed as of historical importance, but there are also some organs which are listed in their own right.

The organ has its place in churches because of its suitability for leading congregational singing. A pipe organ is generally of a size and tonal design to envelope, surround and support the congregation. The additional lower extension of range that the organ pedals allow, with their deep reverberations, gives almost a physical foundation for the singers, while the high notes lead from the top. The fact that each note, unlike those on a piano, controls several pipes from lower to higher pitches gives the organ a penetrative power which has an enlivening effect on singing. Bellows store the wind so that many pipes may sound at once without fading and be powerful enough to fill the building.

## What is a pipe organ?

It is helpful both to a player and to those in a church with responsibility for the care of the instrument to understand how a pipe organ is constructed and how it functions. For the player, this can add to the enjoyment of handling the instrument and help make better use of the sound palette available. For the decision-makers and purse-holders, it will assist when estimates for repair are received or if the organist has to report faults. For the member of the congregation, it will lead to an appreciation of the skill and artistry of the makers as well as the players.

A pipe organ consists of a number of pipes planted in a wind chest and controlled by a player from a console: a keyboard (called a manual), or set of keyboards, and a pedal board. Usually there are two manuals, the Great and the Swell, the latter most commonly the one above, its pipes being enclosed in a box whose shutters can be opened from the console, thus swelling the sound. While a piano has one sound per key, each of the 61 keys on the manuals and the 32 on the pedals can activate several pipes at once, depending on what 'stops' and which 'couplers' are drawn. (Stops are essentially switches that determine which pipes are brought into play when a key is played; couplers connect together the manuals and pedals or the key an octave above or below the one played.) Thus a 4-note chord of C major in root position, with the bass note reinforced on the pedal (5 keys in all), on a small organ of five stops on the manual and one on the pedal, will activate 21 pipes. If the manual to pedal coupler is drawn, this will add a keynote from the manual, out of reach of your hands, making a total of 26. You can imagine how many pipes might be playing at once in a larger instrument – and sometimes they can be very large, with anything up to five manuals, each able to be coupled to each other and, by means of other couplers, to the keys an octave above and below the ones you are playing.

The sound is produced by air vibrating in a pipe in the same way as in a recorder. The pipe may be constructed from wood or metal. The air is not passing through the pipe. What happens is that the air, at a controlled pressure, enters the foot of the pipe and strikes a lip at the open mouth of the pipe, causing the air in the rest of the pipe to vibrate. The frequency of the vibration gives the pitch, and this is set by the length of the pipe. The lowest note on the keyboard is a C, and this pipe is 8 feet tall. This measurement explains the number added to the stop name. For example, a stop may be marked Open Diapason 8ft. As you go up the keyboard, each pipe is slightly shorter until at one octave it is 4 feet in length, at two octaves 2 feet etc. (but it remains an 8ft stop all the way up). Some pipes are 'stopped' (this can be acknowledged in its name), which has the effect of doubling the length of the pipe and thus sounding an octave lower than its actual length suggested. In most instruments, the lowest pedal pipes would be 16 feet in height.

The collective name for the set of 61 (sometimes 56) pipes which answer to one stop is a 'rank', a name explained when you imagine each set of pipes standing one behind the other on the soundboard. (Most of the pipes are out of sight, behind the front pipes, which themselves may be decorative and not meant to sound.) A rank differs from the next one because of either its sound quality or its pitch, or both. If you were to add to your 8ft stop a Flute 4ft, and play the lowest note, you would hear an additional note one octave above, the two playing simultaneously. It is this mixture of sound quality and pitch that gives the organ its range and colour. In fact, with stops of varied sound quality similar to wind, string and reed instruments, a large organ can resemble a whole orchestra. The instrument is housed in a 'case', open at the front (or sometimes two matching cases facing each other), which serves to focus and throw the sound.

Connecting console and pipes is the *action*, of which there are different types. In *mechanical* action, the key is physically attached to the soundboard by a system of levers. Within the case, pulling out (or putting down, if your organ has stop keys) a stop will move a slider to make openings under the chosen rank, while pressing the key will open the feet of the individual pipes you need. Then there is *pneumatic* action where instead of levers there is a wind system, distinct from the main system which feeds the pipes themselves. In pneumatic action the keys and stops are linked to the main organ by tubes. Depressing a key increases the pressure in the tube, which opens the valve at the foot of the pipe, while *exhaust-pneumatic* action empties the tube, with the same result. It should be noted in passing that this method tends to be susceptible to heating damage. The action on many of these instruments is now electrified. Earlier electric actions have been superseded, in organs built during and after the 1970s, by a solid-state system.

A medium-sized organ is likely to contain a range of tone colours. What are often called the foundation stops, which you would find on all organs, will have titles like diapason or principal or fifteenth (respectively 8ft, 4ft and 2ft), and are basic to hymn playing. Also arranged over these different pitches there are several kinds of *flutes* (a gentler sound) and *string* stops (dulciana, salicional, viola). These three families are classed as flue stops. Then there is the extensive *reed* family, whose sound is generated by the air causing a reed to vibrate, which also results in the air in the pipe vibrating. They can be chorus reeds (suitable for playing in chordal textures) or solo. They have such designations as oboe, trumpet, clarinet, trombone. In all stop families, organs constructed by overseas firms or based on certain traditions may have different names.

Another distinctive sound is given by *mutation* stops. These are based on the fact that a sound wave consists not just of its basic pitch or the pitches one or two etc. octaves above, but also contain other resonances within that, such as the third or the fifth of the chord. Mutation stops are pitched at different points in between the octave, where the lowest pipe may be two-and-two-thirds feet (sometimes called a twelfth or nazard), or one-and-three-fifths feet (tierce) or one-and-a-third feet (larigot). Since these are in between the 'clean' sounds of 8 and 4 etc., they bring extra colour to the sound when played along with the more basic pitches. Finally, there are *mixtures*, where more than one rank play simultaneously. The number of ranks may be stated instead of a pipe length – so you get names like Mixture IV (activating 4 pipes at once) or Sesquialtera II. The composition of the ranks is sometimes printed on the stop-knob instead, so you might see Mixture 19.22.26.29 (which refer to the place on the acoustic range of each of the four pipes relative to the basic pitch). Again, these have to be judiciously mixed with more basic sounds or they are just shrill and unpleasant.

Reference was made above to the susceptibility of pneumatic action to heating damage. The Scottish Federation of Organists advises that 'Pipe organs do not mind cold conditions, but they suffer from dryness caused either by excessive central heating, sub-zero temperatures in winter, or occasionally dry warm weather in Spring. The most important aim should be to keep the relative humidity level within the building above 55%, which can best be achieved by confining central heating to periods when the church is used, by changing the temperature as gradually as possible (within reason), and by actively refuting the myth that heating an empty building is bound to be good for the fabric. Small hygrometers can often be bought from gardening suppliers.'[7]

## Repair and replacement

Reference to a volume like *Organs in Scotland*, which lists every instrument there is and has been in every church, chapel, house or public building in that country, with their original builders and full history,[8] provides both evidence of the long life of a pipe organ and of the periodical repairs and refurbishments that typically take place. It also records the movement of instruments from one building to another as the need arises, testimony to the quality and longevity that attaches to a well-made instrument. Some congregations keep a running organ fund so that when the time comes the appropriate repairs can be made. This precaution means that the unwelcome day when a more substantial repair is required is longer in coming round.

Sometimes this can lead a local church council to take the plunge and propose replacing the organ with a digital instrument more suited to modern times. This often can be for the wrong reasons, based on the assumption that the digital is more versatile and suitable for contemporary worship. The versatility of the pipe organ was mentioned earlier, but it is advisable to check first if the current instrument needs repair. This applies also to instruments with tracker action, which may require attention before they can be at their best.

It also needs to be borne in mind that organs are played by organists, who may be unfamiliar with the idioms in question. There is certainly no shame in that. Accompanying worship songs is a new skill many have to learn (see Chapter 15). Again, the organist may have strong views on the merits of modern hymns and be reluctant to play them. Thoughtful and sympathetic dialogue is called for before expensive decisions are taken. Such organists may be making an important point out of their knowledge, experience and commitment to music and its role in worship, and should be enabled to contribute to the discussion. Equally, they may need to listen to other genuinely held views and perhaps benefit from a widened perspective.

If serious repairs are called for, it is best to ask more than one firm of builders what the instrument needs, and what it would cost. If a church would have financial difficulties in pursuing this, there may be a less ambitious scheme which could be undertaken. Alternatively, the necessary work might be phased over a few years. This is where your denominational organ advisory service can assist.

Adding stops to the existing organ – for example, to give a brighter sound at the top end of the pitch spectrum – has quite often been done, not successfully in all cases. With such proposals, care must be taken not to spoil what is at the moment an artistic unity. Many instruments have been unbalanced by adding to the existing specification, destroying the tonal design and detracting from the historic value of the instrument. The organ in question might be a good example of a particular school or builder – a small part, if you like, of our national heritage. The effect can be similar to adding a wing to a historic building without properly designing it to merge with the style of the original. Here expert advice should be sought. The practice of adding stops can also prejudice the award of grants from the Heritage Lottery Fund and other sources and thus make eventual restoration unachievable. Unaltered organs have the best chance of being awarded grants for restoration.

## Electronic or digital organs

### Financial considerations

Where, however, all agree that substantial work is required which the church cannot afford, what comes quickest to mind is to select a digital instrument. Indeed, organ advisers have made this recommendation themselves in some cases, particularly when the existing organ is not of great merit. A well-made organ will have pipes which will last indefinitely. The action required to activate the pipes, particularly if it is mechanical, will last, when in good repair, for 70–150 years. Electronic organs (analogue or digital) have often had a far shorter life. Twenty years has been common, sometimes less, sometimes longer. This is not surprising in that the technology is similar to that of a computer, which both ages and becomes redundant. There is also the danger of companies going out of business and the difficulty of finding spare parts. While some digital organ companies affirm that they keep parts for instruments dating back as far as the 1950s, in practice it has been shown that complete replacement after 30 years often makes better economic sense.

### Musical considerations

Present-day digital organs are now able to produce a much truer sound than before, and they can also be much more reliable, especially now that sealed (rather than open) electrical contacts are the norm. But although it is claimed that a particular make of digital organ stores and reproduces the actual sounds of real pipe organs, too many of these instruments can still sound characterless. This is partly due to the fact that the sound is delivered through a speaker or speakers, which means that the sound is more confined than the more pervasive sound of a pipe organ with hundreds of individual pipes acting as their own resonators. Partly it is also due to the fact that digital sampling of sounds is not done for every note in the scale; two or three per octave at the most is usually thought to suffice. The pipe organ depends on the voicing of pipes and wind pressure to give enough volume, while the digital organ is measured in watts. Although clever use of speakers can assist, the lower the wattage the more distorted the sound can be through speakers.

Congregations understandably will be likely to choose an organ with what looks like a large range of stops – value for money. Often this is far more than would be found in a pipe organ appropriate in size for that building. In providing this more marketable package, compromises have often had to be made and the actual delivery of volume and variety does not always match its pipe equivalent. For example, a single diapason stop on a digital organ with a large specification will not in any way match the volume of the diapason of a small pipe organ suitable for the same building.

Some digital models are fine pieces of engineering and make good instruments. They may not be affected by low humidity levels in a building in the way that pipe organs undoubtedly are. Some firms do not follow the practice of simply marketing a variety of standard models but build the digital organ after study of the building and local requirements – referred to as customising. It is quite possible – though it all too rarely happens – for a digital firm to build its consoles from traditional materials, including natural woods and reclaimed ivory, bone or wood (rather than plastic, which is non-porous and which some find a little uncomfortable to play) for the keys. Good digital organs, customised or not, are still quite expensive for what they are, and a congregation may find that what it might pay for such an organ could in fact finance a rebuild or restoration of their existing organ (or a good redundant pipe organ). It should be kept in mind that, the larger the building, the greater the number of speakers that will be required, especially of those which are able to reproduce the deeper pedal sounds. To make a digital organ truly effective in a very large space can be demanding, and the finished instrument could turn out to be far more expensive than it looks in the brochure.

## Artistic considerations

Placing the speakers for a digital organ is an aesthetic matter and may require advice and approval from the relevant denominational body. Since they could be highly visible and require to be mounted at different points in the building, it is likely that this will require formal approval – as will the placing of the console. To keep the pipe façade of the former organ and to hide the speakers behind it seems a neat solution but it may give the wrong impression that it is the pipe organ that is being played. If this is done, however, care must be taken to avoid damage to the workings, which could prejudice any future restoration of the instrument, either in its existing location or elsewhere. However, in some denominations and some parts of the country, organs and their cases were often installed in places (like behind a central pulpit) which now are felt to be less appropriate since they take the focus away from pulpit and table. An opportunity might then be taken to remove the redundant instrument and restore the original design of the building – which might even reveal an interesting window which had been blocked for many decades.

## The player of the instrument

It is important that the views of the regular organist of a church are taken into account when decisions of this kind are taken. Although there is a good number of organists with enthusiasm for these instruments, many churches have found that the purchase of a mass-produced digital instrument deters applications from some musicians when a post falls vacant, who may be seeking an instrument with individuality and what they consider a unique sound.

## Other solutions

Another solution, when faced with crippling costs, is to explore the possibility of installing a good redundant pipe organ. With church closures, there are now numerous excellent instruments awaiting new homes, and sometimes with no other cost than that of removal and rebuilding into the new location. The Institute of British Organ Building maintains the most comprehensive list of redundant organs in the UK.[9] Local denominational organ advisers will also know what is available, and will be able to match one of the existing redundant organs to the building. An organ builder will then be asked to give an estimate for moving and, if necessary, making any repairs to the instrument as it is installed. This option is not pursued as often as it perhaps should be. Instruments built in the High Victorian era (c.1870–1900) were often made with extremely durable materials and have an inherent quality likely to outlast organs built in the leaner inter-war or post-war years. An older organ with mechanical action may also be more reliable than a later mid-twentieth-century organ with pneumatic or electro-pneumatic action.

Despite the huge cost of purchasing a brand-new pipe organ, a surprising number of churches have pursued this option over the last thirty years or so. Just to take one example, in central Edinburgh no fewer than five churches have taken this route, all with substantial instruments from a variety of builders. These organs are a great asset to worship and to the musical culture of the city. However, it can at the time of construction be a considerable drain on a church's financial resources. It is the kind of project which can be brought to fruition if a specific legacy has been left for the purpose, if not dedicated fund-raising.

## When there is no organist

Modern digital organs have one particular advantage in that they may have attached to them a *MIDI* system by which hymns or indeed whole services can be prepared in advance. Most new digital instruments have this facility built in. This can be a useful solution where it is difficult to find a regular organist, and allows someone to provide accompaniments to cover for absence, although it is desirable that he or she knows the congregation. Some pipe organs with modern electric actions can also play music without an organist. In conjunction with this, commercially produced disks can be bought which store a large selection of hymns.

A related solution is the digital hymnal, an instrument in itself which stores a huge number and variety of hymns. A search on the internet will yield the most up-to-date versions. This might seem an ideal solution for country situations where an organist, say, is only available for special services, and indeed in many circumstances it will be. Some comment needs to be made, however. The style of playing may not be what a congregation is familiar with, and the sound produced often is equivalent to a much larger instrument which can sound incongruous in a small church. Further, with the necessity for setting up the system so that the right tune appears in the right order for the service, with the right number of verses, at the right pitch and at the right speed, some skill is required of the operator. A congregation has to get used, also, to the rather disconcerting style resulting from the sounds being produced by mechanical means. The robot-like accompaniments can make no allowance for a congregation in starting verses, cannot observe sense or grammar, or produce change of tempo to shape the final verse towards the end.

Another comment relates to the desirability of seeking other solutions involving people before what should really be a last resort. Music in worship is a co-operative effort between people and leader(s); in this partnership there is give and take as each adapts to the other. With a machine this is less easy. Nor is it essential that an organ sound be used in worship. If there is no-one among the regular attenders, is there a local singer or instrumentalist (fiddle or flute, say), or a member of a local band, who might help – and perhaps be glad to have a role in the local church? Also, young people learn instruments at school; is there one who could play the melody line and provide the momentum required? Or a group of instrumentalists? The most common solution is to acquire a piano, since more people are able to play this than can play an organ.

Sometimes a keyboard or digital piano is proposed. This would be suitable for a small building but can have a low output that does not sound so well when amplified to the level required to support a congregation in an average-sized building. They work well in the context of other (usually electrified) instruments.

## Conclusion

It is not just the playing of the organ, or the singing of a congregation led and supported by an organ, that constitutes the offering of praise in worship. The instrument itself is the result of the offering of intricate crafts using materials from the created world – animal, vegetable and mineral. The hymn 'Angel voices ever singing', written by Francis Pott for the dedication of an organ in a colleague's Lancashire parish, celebrates both aspects of the instrument:

craftsman's art and music's measure
for your pleasure
all combine.

But there is more than that. For a recent project to enact the medieval Sarum liturgy, seeking to learn how the people of the time experienced worship, a new organ was built in an earlier style, not just in appearance but with regard to how it worked and sounded, based on detailed technical research. The case was similarly recreated, drawing on both Christian and natural imagery. In addition to the doors celebrating the Virgin Mary there are deer, insects, leaves, shepherds and sheep – beautiful carvings, all representing creation come to worship. Recording the project, Dominic Gwynn speculates on a wealthy donor making a gift 'in the knowledge that the veil between earth and heaven had been pierced'.[10] Thus even the physical instrument contributes to and brings to expression the meaning of any act of worship, which is not simply human skill and voice but the whole of creation uniting in praise of its Creator.

## Notes

1 Buchan, Alan and David A. Stewart, 2020, *Organs in Scotland*, Edinburgh: Edinburgh Society of Organists.

2 Inglis, Jim, 1991, *The Organ in Scotland Before 1700*, Schagen (Netherlands): Uitgeverij 'De Mixtuur', pp. 20f and 40f.

3 Gwynn, Dominic, 2016, 'A new pre-Reformation organ for the church of St Teilo', in Sally Harper, P. S. Barnwell and Magnus Williams (eds), *Late Medieval Liturgies Enacted: The Experience of Worship in Cathedral and Parish Church*, Farnham: Ashgate, p. 79.

4 Sachs, Barbara and Barry Ife (eds and trans), 1981, *Anthology of Early Keyboard Methods*, Cambridge: Gamut Publications, pp. 7–19.

5 I am grateful to the Revd James Stewart, former minister of the Town Kirk, for this information.

6 Much of what follows draws on a pamphlet for congregations written by the present author and colleagues. It has since been updated by other hands, particularly as regards digital organs. The author is grateful to the Organ Advice Committee of the Scottish Federation of Organists (SFO) for their encouragement to draw from this. The pamphlet itself, which contains additional material, can be seen on the website of the SFO, www.scotsorgan.org.uk, but other denominations will have access to similar guidance.

7 Alan Buchan, SFO Organ Advisory Committee.

8 Buchan and Stewart, *Organs in Scotland*.

9 www.ibo.co.uk.

10 Gwynn, 'A new pre-Reformation organ', pp. 87f.

# 13

# The Accompaniment of Hymns

There are many organists in Scotland who would describe themselves as 'reluctant' – not, I hasten to add, because they grudge having to do it. Indeed, they may well be enthusiastic and grateful for this opening which gives them the opportunity of contributing to worship in a way appropriate to their gifts and their call to discipleship. The frequently used description 'reluctant organist' usually refers to those, pressed into service, who do not feel quite equal to what might be demanded of them, either because their proficiency might be on another instrument or because they do not feel they have the right skills or the right kind of experience. Others might identify with the aims of an organisation like SCOTS[1] – which are 'to encourage emerging organists as well as to assist those already in post who wish to develop their skills'. This chapter has such emerging organists in mind, even though they might have been emerging for some time! Its intention is to try to harvest some of the skills of veteran players and pass these on. On the other hand, experienced musicians do not always know why they do what they do, and they also may wish to read further to consider whether what is recorded here matches their experience. Finally, since this section takes the view that *understanding* the music we play will make a difference in how we play it, some people in choirs and congregations might find it of interest to read about something they know so well from a different perspective.

A composer may burn the midnight oil to finish a score but there is no music until it is performed. The performer does not simply translate signals into sound – i.e. 'play the right notes' – but shapes it into a coherent musical utterance. For the organist or pianist accompanying a hymn, there is also the wild card of those who are making that music with you, namely the congregation, and you aim to play the music in such a way that it enables a musical response from the people. Then again, the music does not stand alone; the words to which it is set, whether hymns or service music, have to be interpreted. The tune may have been written for that hymn, the sounds magicked out from these particular words. Alternatively, match-making editors will have carefully and creatively put the words together with a particular tune so that they are 'right for each other'. For all these reasons, the score has become more than simply dots on a page.

The thrust of this chapter – the deepening of the people's experience of worship through the quality of the accompanist's musical offering – has an undertone of urgency. Many churches have seen a move away from the traditional repertoire, along with its usual support structure of choir and organ, in favour of more popular styles. Development and change itself is welcome and necessary, and church music history makes clear that the music which accompanies the life of the world has always enhanced the worship of the church. But is it possible that one of the circumstances that allows 'brighter' music 'more suitable to the times we are in' to displace (rather than add to) older, stronger music is the result of missed opportunities in our custodianship of the music that has come down to us? We have inherited, for the most part, a repertoire of fine music that is vivid and compelling, very much fit for purpose. We don't always make it sound so. This chapter makes a plea that we do justice to what we have inherited so that any experiment and development in church music will have richer ground in which to grow.

How do we approach the hymn list for Sunday? Is it by simply looking up the numbers and playing through the music, correcting slips, practising the more difficult sequences, sorting that fumble on the pedals, and then on the day checking the number of verses and repeating the tune as many times as required? If so, we risk monochrome results. How should we proceed?

As musicians, it is understandable that we look first at the music. Yet there is other information on that same page that is just as useful, including of course the words of the hymns themselves (next chapter). There will be found the name and dates of a composer or of the book of hymns or music in which the tune first appeared. A surprising proportion of the music is anonymous, most often because it originated within an oral tradition by which song was passed from person to person, changing and developing in the process, or from a period when there was less emphasis on the ownership of a melody. However, what is true of all of them is that, like participants in the television series *Who Do You Think You Are?*, there are surprises lurking in their family tree.

John Bell, in *The Singing Thing Too*, identifies some fifteen or so different types of hymn tune, and offers notes on how they may be performed.[2] Here the focus will be narrowed down to some of the main categories and their implications for the accompanist. Some, of course, might feel that the original category doesn't matter; all are now hymn or psalm tunes and find a common ground in their purpose in worship. However, melody has its own integrity, drawing from its original purpose and provenance, and, just like appreciating the rich variety among the people gathered to worship who come as they are rather than having adopted a pious veneer, to recognise and respond to the true character of a tune is to bring vitality and refreshment to worship. In other words, our understanding and appreciation of a tune affects how we approach it and play it.

This means being willing to accept the hymn tune as a real piece of music. We have plenty of that already: organ works to rival anything in the concert hall, choral settings and individual anthems which would be worth the time and attention of the most skilled of secular choirs, the psalm chants which demand intricate and nuanced accompaniment. For the serious and committed organist, the hymn tune can seem like 'the least of these' (Matt. 25:40). Its brevity, and the belief that nothing much can be said in such a short compass, or that hymn tunes are purely functional rather than artistic, or that this is music for amateurs, might seem to suggest that it cannot compare with more elaborate compositions. Yet to write a good hymn tune, one which engages with singer and words and does so from the very moment the first note is struck, is potentially a demanding intellectual and musical task. Hymn tunes have musical form and content, even if this is compressed into a small compass. In this they are rather like the collects,[3] those tiny concentrated polished prayers which embrace no fewer than five parts and carry a clout that belies their brevity. For us to appreciate ingenuity of melody, rhythmic drive, variety of metre, progression of harmony, and the internal shape of a tune is to deliver it with more conviction and more insight than if we simply set out to play the notes.

## Melody

The parentage of the classic hymn tune, whose guise has little changed from the sixteenth century to this day, is the metrical psalm tune which emerged during the Reformation period.[4] These tunes were dignified and restrained, with clear lines that a congregation could follow, a melody that fell easily within the compass of the voice, and which could be sung unaccompanied. They were but a short step away from the ecclesiastical modes, shared also by folk song – an example of which is still present in its pure form in the rugged tune *Martyrs*, which is in the Dorian mode (characterised by its 'minor' third and flattened seventh). (Appendix 1 lists all tunes and hymns referred to in this and other chapters, with their numbers in four standard hymn collections.) Already, however, the sea change in European music culture generally had taken place by which more voices could be added, and the way ultimately opened for harmony. In time the harmonies had moved from being incidental, as the parts wove round each other, to being linked with melody and bass, so that the progression was in melody and harmony together. The early tunes of such composers as Calvin's musician, Louis Bourgeois, who wrote for people attuned to the more chordal sound of madrigal and chanson, were precursors for the Scottish and English psalm tunes.

An example of the dignified and simple earlier melodies is *French* (also known in some books as *Dundee*), one of the most widely known of the original psalm tunes from its being wedded to a psalm ($121^5$ – 'I to the hills will lift mine eyes. / From whence doth come mine aid?') often sung at a time of national disaster or rejoicing, or at times of personal bereavement and loss. How apt are the two rising phrases at the tune's beginning, the first moving to its highest note on 'hills' and the second mimicking the lifting of the 'eyes'. From its highest note on 'Be-*hold*', at the beginning of the second half, the melody then descends, ultimately to come to rest on the pitch on which the tune began.

This melodic shaping, sooner or later climbing to its highest point and returning to rest, is found in many different guises through to the present day: *Stroudwater*, *Salzburg*, *St Botolph*, and longer tunes like *Kelvingrove*, *Cwm Rhondda* and *Abbot's Leigh*. Incidentally, organists will be well aware of the problem in the penultimate bar of the fine tune last on this list, where congregations automatically go for F sharp on the third-last syllable. (Note: sometimes it is transposed into the key of C.) Yet this was surely deliberate on the part of the composer; to anticipate the final tonic in the second-last bar somehow gives this long tune a more solid and satisfying return home. The accompanist might try, in playing over, and perhaps in the first verse, substituting the penultimate D in octaves on the first half of the minim, then adding the accompanying harmony on the second half. A very slight lift-off before the problem note can help also.

Dignified and restrained, however, does not mean flat melodies that move step by step. The extraordinary *London New*, which first appeared in the 1635 Scottish Psalter, and which Benjamin Britten used so dramatically in his church opera *St Nicolas* at the death of the saint set to William Cowper's words, 'God moves in a mysterious way', is cast in great striding arpeggio-derived phrases, which are not merely the grabbing of the attention at the outset but a pattern that is skilfully played out through the whole tune. Another of the same is the tune *York* (it was in one of the early English psalters, Ravenscroft's, that tunes began to be given names, often from the town in which they were thought to have originated). It also consists partly of a sequence of gaps rather than steps, and it was no doubt its awkward but unique characteristic first and third phrases that gave it the alternative name, or nickname, *Stilt*, as it seems to stagger this way and that!

While it is invidious to pick out examples of striking melodies, since different ears will be beguiled by different gambits, it does no harm to mention one or two other different ways of constructing melodies, even if just to illustrate that in such small compass enormous invention is possible. From the eighteenth century, *Sheffield* is announced with a stilt-like pattern of crochets which are answered in a running, quaver-dominated phrase which leads to a half close; then when you might in an earlier tune expect a pattern like that of the first half, the continuous quaver pattern continues in short upward-swooping phrases until a strand of familiar melody brings the tune home (notice the imitation in the pedals). Here is a touch of the florid and decorative that is to become a feature of later melodies, but here still dignified and contained. From the nineteenth century comes *Hereford* by the composer who stands out in the crowd of Victorian hymn tune writers, Samuel Sebastian Wesley. It has all the elegance of the drawing-room ballad with its slurred pairs of crochets in triple time; hardly a bar lacks the pattern yet it does not feel in the least overplayed. The melody maintains the restraint of its sixteenth-century forebears in remaining within a relatively narrow compass until, like others we have noted, it reaches to its top note in the second half of the tune and in a leisurely but nevertheless inevitable way proceeds towards its close. In accompanying, it is a tune that can't be hurried.

## Rhythm

Another feature of a tune is its rhythm. The rhythm of a hymn tune may have several origins. There is the metre of the verses, the mixture of stressed and unstressed syllables that make a line and offer the satisfaction of repetition in other lines or pairs of lines. Another is the inspiration of the composer who feels the tune's pulses, and then pushes against them. Finally there is the original purpose of the tune: was it a tune which kept people in time with each other in a shared task or one which made them dance? It is rhythm that keeps people engaged and enables them to sing together. The organist seeks to appreciate the feel of that rhythm, and to play exactly and accurately to ensure that the rhythm is not just heard but felt by the singers.

A tune's *metre* is one of the pieces of information which is given on the page: the number of syllables in each line, e.g. 8787 if the stanza is of four lines – 8787D if it is of eight lines, where the second half (D=double) is identical in metre to the first. The metre may be given in shorthand such as SM (i.e. 6686), CM (8686), LM (8888) (short, common and long metres, the latter two the commonest). A longer line or a greater number of lines can accommodate more complex ideas or even longer words (unless you are a Charles Wesley who, in 'O thou who camest from above', effortlessly fits a word of six syllables into an eight-syllable line – 'There let it for thy glory burn / with inextinguishable blaze'!).

This measuring tool provided in association with the tune can have another advantage. Should we need to seek an alternative tune, this sends us to the part of the appendix where the tunes are listed under their metres. It is not enough to select any 'one they'll know' from the list; there needs to be some correspondence between the sentiments of the words and the nature of the tune. One has to study the hymn and note its themes and moods, and similarly with potential tunes. Sometimes there can be variations in pulse within metres, such as the anapestic line where the words are shaped as two light and a third more marked. It can be appropriate to consider the place of a hymn in the service as well as the time in the Calendar. 'O for a thousand tongues', for example, is a hymn text both of great dignity but also high excitement; it is sometimes offered with both *Richmond* and *Desert*, which respectively enhance these two moods.

Uncommon metres can offer different opportunities to the writer and singer. For example, 66 66 44 44 (*St John/Havergal*) brings a new energy in the latter part of the verse in that the shorter phrases take on the nature of shouts of praise. Similar is 'Ye holy angels bright' to *Croft's 136th* in the same metre. In 'Angel voices ever singing', the sudden truncation of the flow of the metre 85 85 84 3 has the effect of slowing for a momentous climax where phrases seem to be invested with a significance of their own and not simply part of a longer sentence. In another unusual metre, Robert Bridges in 'All my hope' exploits the 87 87 33 7 shape, where statement changes to a gasp in the sudden shortening of the lines to make an awed affirmation. In handling these metres, intelligent playing will have its effect.

One way that a rhythm maximises its effect is when it is disturbed by cross-rhythms or changes of emphasis. For example, *Lauds* to 'There's a Spirit in the air' captures the jubilant note of the words (the instruction at the top is 'jauntily') by choosing waltz time but suggesting that it is really in 2/4 by the way it dwells on dotted crochets in the third-last bar. A true cross-rhythm can be seen at different points in the two versions of *Somos Pueblo*. Sometimes a change of time signature lifts the tune, as in Croft's clever *136th*, where the metre at 'assist our song' changes from common time to a more emphatic three minims per bar.[6] The earliest Scottish psalm tunes were more adventurous in their rhythms than the versions we now use, as we can see in the older version of *French* (CH4 has a number of these original forms with the melody in the tenor) where the second half of each musical line is syncopated, bringing energy in their momentary departure from the evenness of the earlier parts. (Note: for this reason you cannot use both versions in the course of the psalm.) The gathering notes in the older psalm tunes at the beginning of lines, which people often write off as redundant (and in many books they are reduced to an upbeat), are in fact the relics of these more complex rhythms. In tunes which begin on an upbeat of several notes, like *Woodlands*, *Sine Nomine* or *Song 24*, a pedal note at the beginning of the bar before the melody begins can help appreciation of the rhythm. At suitable points, a more detached playing style can enable the rhythms to be heard and appreciated, not least in large buildings with a long echo.

## Harmonic structure

What enables people to follow music is its structure, where tensions are introduced and then resolved. The tune travels on a harmonic journey, generally beginning and ending in the home key. Most frequently, the first half of the tune will end on the dominant. For example, *Crimond*, in the key of F, at halfway stage rests on a root position chord with C at the bass. Those who remember the opening of Beethoven's ninth symphony know the powerful effect of a persistent sounding of a dominant in driving the music to declare its key. Some tunes move to the relative minor or relative major (related in that they share the same key signatures), and work their way back.

So there is *Dunfermline* or *Old Hundredth* moving to the dominant at the halfway mark and then moving to re-establish the home key at the end. *French*, however, saves its dominant until the end of the third line of the verse. Often, the journey to the end in the second half can be quite adventurous. In *Bishopthorpe* an accidental signals a departure which takes us through G minor before settling back in the home key of F major. Tension is increased still further in *Church Triumphant* (in Bb), where the second half moves from the chord of dominant F through G minor, touches on the home key then strays via Eb to the close. The stately *Westminster Abbey* moves to the dominant at the end of the first couplet, to the relative minor at the end of the second, then starts a journey through F# major to B major, then E to a reminder of the home key (A) before trespassing on D before coming to a strong close.

Many criticise the Victorian hymn writers for straying too far from their psalm models and writing elaborate harmonies which were a bit over the top. However, in skilled hands this could make for exciting and satisfying musical passages. John Stainer was a master of the form and *All for Jesus* (from the *Crucifixion*), arriving on a dominant G, continues from the halfway mark with a whistle-stop tour of D minor, G, A minor, C, F, D minor again, then to home C. An organist might find it fun to look at other tunes and spot the keys you pass through.

The ability to appreciate these creative touches, as well as to play them with confidence and flair, cannot fail to be communicated to the congregation and add to their engagement in the hymn.

Still concerned with structure, increasingly common is the *verse and refrain*, whether an old favourite like 'To God be the glory' or a contemporary folk-style hymn like Bernadette Farrell's 'Longing for light' where every verse swings into the refrain 'Christ, be our light!' In this case, the refrain is the prayer which is the response to the needs of the world identified in each verse. The accompanist may want to add a little weight or colour at those points to bring out the shape but also to support more fervency on the part of the singer. There should normally be no break between verse and refrain. 'To God be the glory' can seem long and a bit monotonous if the verses and choruses are played with the same registration, whereas the refrain of *Vulpius*, where the Hallelujahs begin an octave above the last note of the verses, needs no enhancement. In 'One bread, one body', the refrain is a standard hymn shape (although an irregular metre) while the verses are more recitative-like, which suggest a lighter, contrasting registration. The extended final bars of the verses call out for a crescendo as you break back into the refrain, perhaps lifting off the hands just before the first chord, which could be played staccato, to get people started again. 'All glory, laud, and honour' begins with the refrain, and there is no break between refrain and verse. Because of its length and unvarying rhythm, it is difficult to prevent this hymn sounding monotonous. It needs quite a lot of variety in registration in the verses, with perhaps the use of the swell pedal as they again approach the refrain. Much the same treatment might be used in 'All things bright and beautiful'.

Sometimes verses have an *internal structure* that can be pointed up by a contrast in registration. In Horatius Bonar's 'I heard the voice', for the first half of each verse Christ addresses the seeker while the second half is the Christian's response of joy and relief. When set to *The rowan tree* the contrast is the way the setting moves from unison to harmony. Without a very strong choir, this change in texture will not be heard and the accompanist can help the singers be aware of the dialogue nature of this hymn. When set to *Vox dilecti* or *Kingsfold*, the contrast is clearer. A quite different internal structure is where the last line is always the same, like 'come, Holy Spirit, come' from 'Like the murmur of the dove's song'. The writer has skilfully, gradually verse by verse, deepened this prayer by reflecting progressively on the nature of the Spirit, then on its reception in the church, then its effect in bringing healing, love and peace, so that the prayer grows in intensity. One might, at least in the first two verses, highlight this line, perhaps playing it solo on a different manual, or the melody an octave up, or even dropping the pedal; the final time might be firm and confident, pedal and all.

## 'Big' tunes

It is here worth pausing on what can be an anxiety for organists: how to handle the longer compositions that come from the pens of well-known composers for the concert hall, like John Ireland's *Love Unknown*, Jean Sibelius's *Finlandia* or Ralph Vaughan Williams's *Down Ampney* (by the way – if you visit R. V. W.'s birthplace, the 'p' is silent). Such tunes are characterised by being denser in musical invention than the classic hymn tune, as well as for their freedom from the tight rhythmic structure that comes down from the metrical psalm tunes. Because of the spaces in the music, these tunes can feel heavy and can falter without strong leadership. The organist has the difficult task of playing spaciously but keeping up a momentum. In such tunes especially, rhythmic accuracy is important, with long notes given their proper length. (This applies just as much in simpler tunes, especially at the break in the middle. It is said that Victorian nannies used to consider the deadliest of all sins to be taking off shoes without undoing the laces! High on the organist's list of sins is to clip minims and dotted minims in the interests of keeping up the drive, thus tripping over the rhythm.) Each tune should be carefully examined to clarify its structure – for example, whether it is in two parts and if so where the second part begins, so as to judge if it would be helpful to lift the hands momentarily to help singers feel the shape. Sometimes one may have to add cues so that the rhythm is appreciated: for example, in *Finlandia* the pedal coming in a crochet beat early may make it more likely that people come in from the first note, and together.

Many other tunes by contemporary composers share these same challenges. They include *Highwood, Engelberg, Wolvercote, Lux Tremenda, Guiting Power* and *Coe Fen*. Characteristics they share are their extended nature; the adventurousness of their modulation; the reach required of the hands; constantly moving inner parts; the number of accidentals; their inherent drama. Sometimes we may want to echo Emperor Joseph II's criticism of Mozart's music: 'too many notes'! They are not easy to play and it may be politic sometimes to ask your priest or minister who wants to use any of these not to do so until you have had time to learn them. (We do sometimes have to help clerical colleagues to understand what it means for us to play effectively; this is particularly true when clergy fail to give players the hymn list until too near the time. 'They won't be too difficult.' Who says!?) It is better when preparing these tunes to master sections independently than to keep playing the tune through hoping it will get better. If the day is still further off when you feel you can play the tune sufficiently well, why not (taking *Engelberg* as an example) play the melody in unison, hands an octave apart, and only break into harmony at the third line, or even the Alleluia. The congregation might even appreciate being piloted through what is a tune with several leaps. Or use the simpler harmony setting, sometimes provided, for all the verses. The same approach could be used in *Guiting Power*, unison until the refrain. Note that in bar 3 the crotchet chords are stems down; hold the melody and bass Bb in the left hand and play the chords at a lower volume on a different manual.

## Other styles

It is being suggested that an understanding of the music makes for a more enriching experience for congregations as well as organists themselves. Examples have been taken from the hymn tune as it has developed through the centuries. The standard repertoire, however, contains many examples which are different in style. A few of these are now briefly sketched, with observations about accompaniment as appropriate.

As branches of the church share their traditions of worship, one feature which is increasing across the board is the *role of the cantor*. More often applied in the case of chant, some types of psalm setting, and service music,[7] a part for a solo voice now appears in some hymns. It is a practice which reminds us that singing together is not simply the blending of individual voices but the *interaction* of worshippers with each other as they share their faith, experience and gifts with each other – even when they are all singing the same tune at the same time. The voice of the cantor highlights this dynamic in the responsiveness of singers to each other. In the following examples, one can see the different roles that cantors were given. In 'Over my head, I hear music in the air', an African-American Spiritual, the cantor's insistent repetition draws out the people's response. In 'When Jesus the healer', the cantor or soloist recites the different healing narratives, stimulating the people's reiterated prayer. In 'He came down that we may have love', a song from the world church, the cantor's question 'Why did he come?' in between each verse releases another affirmation. Similar is 'Word of the Father' from the Iona Community where the cantor at the beginning of each verse declares a title or quality of Jesus Christ upon which the people offer a refrain-prayer. Bernadette Farrell's 'Unless a single grain' gives to the congregation a refrain from John chapter 12 while the cantor contributes a series of related texts. More ambitiously, the same author's *Eastertide Acclamation* calls potentially for three qualities of sound: a cantor declaiming characteristics of Christ, a choir (or it could be the whole congregation) exclaiming the words 'Jesus Christ' in climbing registers, and then all sing an Alleluia. Similar is 'All you works of God', where the refrain is sung by all, the call in the verses perhaps by a cantor, and the response, 'bless your Maker', by a choir or indeed by the whole congregation. For such songs, the accompanist has two aims in mind: to provide support for the different weights of sound, using perhaps different manuals, but also to preserve the flow and momentum as voices enter at different times.

Although Vaughan Williams had demonstrated the usefulness of *folk, traditional and carol melodies* in the first *English Hymnal* in 1906, it took some books, including Scottish collections, longer to recognise this. This has changed and now, for example, *Church Hymnary 4* has some 100 items from several nations and a similar balance can be found in other collections. They are often characterised by the gapped scale (the fourth and seventh missing), including those from Asia, their orally transmitted melodies direct and appealing. Some are dance-like and invite lighter playing, brighter registration, some use of staccato – a skip in their step; if they are in six-eight time, thinking two-in-the-bar captures it better. Others are lyrical, like *Kingsfold*, an English traditional tune which has both Scottish ('Gilderoy') and Irish ('Star of the County Down') cousins; in some books a lighter accompaniment is also offered, designed to draw attention to the fluency of the melody. Sometimes they call for more reflective treatment, like *O Waly Waly*, where the tune needs time to unfold and the expressive semiquavers given the space they need. Another example is *Bonnie George Campbell* which in its original Border-ballad form spoke of sorrow and loss. When set to Horatius Bonar's fine Ascension hymn 'Blessing and honour and glory and power', one may savour the way the melody rises to its highest note (penultimate bar) exactly on the word which is the crux of every final line: 'crown', 'song', 'tell', 'hymns', and finally 'rising to reign'. (This was a brilliant piece of match-making from the editors of *Church Hymnary 3*.) Its modal ancestry means that one should finish on the chord written (the dominant) and not 'finish it properly' with an additional tonic chord. (The same goes for *Galloway Tam*, or John Bell's 'Amen, Alleluia'.)

Another genre are the tunes (four-part with the tune

originally in the tenor) which come from the *Sacred Harp/ Shape Note* traditions, found in New England in the eighteenth and early nineteenth centuries, the heads of the notes by their shape indicating which note of the sol fa scale came next (at the beginning, four only: mi, fa, so, lah). They were related to revivalist movements and to the camp meetings which occurred on frontiers beyond established communities and churches. Traditionally unaccompanied, they generally have a very vigorous rhythm and a slightly raucous mode of performance, and call for a strong, rhythmic accompaniment. Some go best on the more percussive piano. This category includes such as *Nettleton*, *Holy Manna*, *Shout on* and *Beach Spring*. It would help the present-day accompanist to look at examples of this unique sound on YouTube.

*Central and South American* hymns are frequently in triple time, and with characteristic syncopation and sometimes crossrhythms. They suit a piano and/or instrumental group or praise band very well, especially with a variety of percussion instruments. They are generally exuberant and can add a warm note to worship. They are part of the interest in today's churches in what the rest of the world is singing, which not only potentially enriches our repertoire but opens awareness of the different kind of, very often intractable, issues that fellow Christians are facing. 'The Virgin Mary' calypso and 'Halle, halle' are already widely known.

Now more accepted in 'Western' worship, the *African-American Spiritual* owes a lot, in the settings we have, to nineteenth-century editing. The original African culture out of which the Spirituals were fashioned had been one where the events of life, interaction with the environment, and religious beliefs and rituals were captured in spontaneous and intricate musical rhythms (as well as movement), and these were translated into the new situation of slavery. They are varied in mood and call for different approaches to accompaniment, and some would lend themselves to jazz piano.

The adoption of song from the *world church*,[8] and its prevailing style of unaccompanied singing, has recently brought much refreshment to worship in the West. This has also brought back the possibility that unaccompanied singing is a form whose hour has come round again, not least in situations where accompanists may be in short supply. We should not assume, as organists, that because we *can* play we should *always* play. Some are call-and-response songs like 'Come let us seek our God's protection', where the nature of the tune calls only for a continuous drumbeat. A drum might also suit 'Come, let us eat for now the feast is spread', which is a call to the Communion table. It is a simple and effective song which is easy to perform because the congregation simply imitates the cantor. In some songs, harmony adds beauty and depth, as in 'Know that God is good'. Some of these are very easy to learn for people who don't read music, and there is a real sense of achievement when time is found to teach such songs. Nearer home, the earlier metrical psalm tunes sound glorious unaccompanied, led by a solo voice, but there are also songs like 'Lifted high on your cross', using a Gaelic folk tune, where the whole work of God in Christ is captured in three verses and a chorus. It has been given an accompaniment, but try it without: verses sung by solo, with all, ceilidh-style, coming in with the chorus.

However, there is one aspect of hymn playing that has not yet been explored, namely the words and the content and how to bring this alive. This is the subject of the next chapter.

## Notes

1 The Scottish Churches Organist Training Scheme, founded 1995.

2 Bell, John L., 2007, *The Singing Thing Too*, Glasgow: Wild Goose Publications, chapter 5.

3 Pronounced with the weight on the first syllable.

4 This is discussed more fully in Chapter 3, 'Psalms, Hymns and Spiritual Songs'.

5 This is the 'Hebrew' numbering. It is Psalm 120 in the Greek version, as used by Roman Catholics. Note the punctuation of these first two lines. The 'aid' does not come from the hills but from 'the Lord'.

6 When sung to 'Ye holy angels bright'.

7 See Chapter 4.

8 See Chapter 3.

# 14

# Playing the Words

No-one would be surprised that the organist is expected to play the music efficiently, but they might be a bit taken aback to learn that they also have to 'play the words'. Yet a hymn is nothing without its words. As with the music, there is information on the page that offers a starting point. We would first note in which sub-section of the book a particular hymn appears: 'Pentecost', 'in penitence', 'enlivening and renewing the church', 'justice and peace', 'our journey with God' etc., which can offer information about the general thrust of the hymn. To then read through the verses is to learn more about a particular hymn's nature – adoration, celebration, an expression of devotion, lament (especially some of the psalms), prayer, telling a story. We would also notice how the narrative of the hymn develops – for example, is the last verse a climax, to be played strongly, or does it end in a thoughtful or prayerful mood? Then, what feelings are engendered – joy, awe, compassion, conviction? Not least, we look for pictures and metaphors that help convey the meaning, and consider how they might be treated. A further piece of information not usually thought important by those who choose or sing hymns is the author and the period when the hymn was written, but this can sometimes be helpful. Some sources of background information are listed in the Appendix 2.

A congregation does not usually know the hymns in advance, although people can if they wish, and some do, look them up as they wait for the service to begin. Two aspects of modern practice add to the importance of approaching our task thoughtfully: first, it is much less common today for people to use the hymn book as a devotional resource, familiarising themselves with its content in more detail, and thus they are not ready with the hymn in their mind; second, in many congregations the words are fed verse by verse on to a screen and singers cannot look ahead to what comes next. Of course, many hymns are well known, but this does not always mean that the words have been reflected upon – the tune having been the component most enjoyed. The accompanist therefore has the task of opening up the hymn for worshippers and deepening their engagement in the hymn spontaneously as they sing, which leads to better engagement in the act of worship in general.

One way to assist, given that most people are used to reading prose rather than verse, is to clarify the grammar, thus making the meaning quicker to apprehend. Thus we may have to play through a line-break when a sentence continues. Again, a line may contain commas for grammatical reasons. While it is wrong to ignore these, at the same time it is not automatic that we observe them by lifting the hands off the keyboard every time. In 'How sweet the name of Jesus sounds', it would sound stilted if the words in the list in v. 4 ('Jesus, my Shepherd, Husband, Friend') were separated by pauses in between and would lead to the hymn losing momentum. Yet the cumulative nature of this succession of titles of Jesus increases the feeling of adoration and gratitude, both because of their number and wide embrace but also because each in its own right is important. This could be acknowledged, perhaps, by occasional tiny symbolic gaps at intervals – say after 'Shepherd, Priest' (line 2), 'Life' (line 3). Also, a lift-off after 'Dear name!' (v. 3) would be apt (the congregation would still be singing but they would get the point). Sometimes, therefore, one can acknowledge the punctuation without being too literal. If we were to note every dot and comma, we would be overbalancing in the direction of the text, while a hymn is also the music, which has its own shape and sense. However, there are times when the commas are part of a skilful hymn writer's arsenal and should be observed, as in the last line in v. 3 of 'And can it be': 'I rose, went forth, and followed thee', three separate acts in the drama of conversion. Again, in Bonar's 'Blessing and honour and glory and power', one might sing through the commas in 'ocean and mountain, stream, forest, and flower' but the last line of the hymn is a different matter: 'dying in weakness, but rising to reign' (and pulling back a little on the final phrase).

A second way in which the accompanist can assist the engagement of the singer is by following the sense of the words. When a hymn is studied as a whole, it can become clear that there is a progression, and that it is by no means automatic that it begins and ends loudly (although a fairly firm first verse is needed to get things going). It is often the case that one has to draw particular attention to a key verse which is neither at the beginning nor the end. It is v. 2 of 'On Jordan's bank' that is the key verse: 'then cleansed be every heart from sin', and the organist can help people see how this verse sums up the meaning of the coming of the Baptist, while subsequent verses, except for the triumphant last verse, unpacks the significance of this. In 'Thy Kingdom come!' it is v. 3 – 'the flags of dawn appear' – which requires the most colourful accompaniment, and the remaining verses are developments from that idea (as the use of the colon at the end of the verse makes clear). 'Come, let us to the Lord our God', one of the Scottish Paraphrases, is a penitential song with a focus at v. 3. In 'We have a gospel to proclaim', it is v. 4 to which our accompaniment will point – 'Tell of that glorious Easter morn'. Another Paraphrase, 'The Saviour died, but rose again', finds its heart in v. 3 where the writer captures St Paul's verses in a fine statement of Christian hope and resolve: 'through him all dangers we'll defy'. Similarly, 'God moves in a mysterious way' opens out in a rousing exhortation at the third verse.

Close reading is often needed to uncover what a hymn is saying. Contemporary American writer Carl Daw's 'Bright the cloud' reflects on a high point in the gospel narrative, the Transfiguration, but the hymn's main theme is to lament the darker changes in the world of today that meet our appalled gaze (v. 2), with the last verse not a climax or resolution but a plea. This is a suitable point at which to warn against the common practice of playing quietly whenever there is reference to death. Closer reading may reveal that it is saying something more affirmative or triumphant; in the last verse of 'O thou who camest from above', for example, death is seen as a culmination, a completion, of a life lived in faithful accord with the particular charism that God has granted to the writer and, by extension, to the singer.

We have spoken of two dimensions of hymn playing (to enable a good performance; to assist singing with understanding), but there is a third: namely, stimulating the imagination of the singers to bring home the inner meaning of the words. Hymns, because they are close to Scripture and are intended also to reflect human faith and experience, draw on the senses and are full of images, incidents, pictures. There are storms, peaceful green pastures, fire, doves, wind, light, song, taste, touch, strength, steep paths, places of safety, rocks, chains, toil, tribulation, darkness, dawn, chariots of wrath, breath, anger, peacefulness, love, sacrifice, serenity, hope. It is of course out of the question that the organist should give a detailed response to these stimuli. To do this would be akin to bullying, in that you are telling people how to feel. Singers lay hold of meaning from a combination of three things: your suggestion, their comprehension and their faith experience. This is a situation where less is more. While the cinema organ of yore, accompanying a silent film, would respond dramatically to every flutter of an eyelid, for us a touch here and there can open up a verse and help to transfer the sentiment or the idea from the writer to the singer. What should not happen is that the organist simply plays five verses in an identical way, without acknowledgement of the richness of language that brings a good hymn to life. On the other hand, variety should not be secured by having a standard procedure which is applied to every hymn – beginning firmly on the great manual, verse 2 a bit lighter on the swell, etc. There is no substitute for studying each hymn.

This third dimension (images) is greatly helped by the organist making time to explore the sound possibilities of the instrument. This is as true of the organ which seems to have little variety – such as the single manual and pedal instrument (like the one on which I first had to play for services) where you might have three or four 8ft stops with one, or two at the most, 4fts, and one single 16ft pedal. Even there one can cease to play the pedal, then bring it back for a key line or the next verse, having all the more effect from having been withheld; or, grouping alto and tenor in the left hand (with, of course, the bass on the pedals), play the melody an octave up; or choosing to thicken the harmonies in a line or a whole verse by adding notes; or to play all the parts an octave higher (filling in the chords in the left hand so that it doesn't sound too shrill) where the last verse calls for an outburst of sound (one should always have something in reserve); or use a staccato style to correct a congregation which is dragging or to bring out a rhythm more clearly.

With a larger instrument, it is easy to provide contrast in the middle of a hymn or indeed of a verse by switching from one manual to another or by the use of pistons and couplers. Try different combinations of stops, such as drawing an 8ft and a 2ft leaving out the 4fts in between, making for a brighter and lighter sound. On instruments without the freshness of upperwork (the high-pitched treble pipes that lend clarity and definition to the ensemble), and you only have 8ft and 4ft pipes available but also have a 16ft manual stop, try combining the latter with 8 and 4ft stops (or just the 4ft) and play it an octave higher. If you have mixtures (high-pitched stops where each key activates two or three pipes at different pitches), try them with various more basic sounds to find the best result. Thus you can build up a palette of colour that you know your organ can supply.

What cannot be done here is to say exactly how to achieve a particular effect, since this will vary from instrument to instrument, and player to player. It may help, however, to take a handful of hymns and note some possibilities within them.

'Lord, speak to me' offers a vivid picture (v. 3) of reaching out to 'wrestlers with the troubled sea' (the author, Frances Ridley Havergal, unusually for her time a mountaineer and an excellent swimmer, knew what she was talking about). You might add a 16ft stop on the manuals (if you have one – which applies to all the suggestions here) like a tug of an undercurrent, or the harsher sound of woodwind or brass suggesting the crash of a wave. Then in v. 4, perhaps a clearer and sharper sound for the 'winged words' – maybe adding 2ft tone for that couplet, then adding the pedal, which could have been silent during this verse, for the last line, suggesting (rather obviously but it might work) the 'depths' of the heart. In v. 5, the mixtures could 'kindle and glow'.

In 'Spirit divine, attend our prayers' the images of fire, dove and wind dominate successive verses, an opportunity to experiment with contrasting sounds. It would be doing the hymn an injustice to sing doggedly through without allowing the images freedom to draw out our song.

In 'O worship the King', Sir Robert Grant MP, whose constituencies included Inverness and Norwich and who was later Governor of Bombay, captures his experience of two dramatic countries and long sea voyages, creating a hymn which rings the changes between the limitless 'canopy' of a beautiful day and the storm and thunder cloud, from plentiful springs to the dust of parched ground. Just to point up some of these contrasts will call forth more from the singer, and call upon the whole range of your instrument, from deepest pedal to ethereal upperwork.

Or take 'Be still for the presence of the Lord', now a little hackneyed by overuse, but which could be refreshed by bringing out the glory, fire and splendour with mixtures and soaring upperwork in v. 2 and cancelling these in favour of a more foundational sound in v. 3. To do this is not to override the repeated command to 'Be still', but it may be that you want to remind your singers of the context by, in the last two lines of the final verse, pulling back the sound a little by partly closing the swell pedal.

## Other tricks of the trade

*Playing over and beginning to sing*: Unless a tune is not well known, it makes for better momentum if you only play over the first two lines. If the next two lines are identical (in a longer tune), it sounds odd when you simply repeat what you have already played. (If the purpose is to give people time to find the place and stand, allow a beat or two longer before starting the playover.) Mind you, this doesn't always work; if you only played the first two lines of *Michael* ('All my hope on God is founded') you will have left the congregation abandoned in harmonic outer darkness! It is not usually considered good practice only to play the last two lines as an introduction as it does not identify the tune nor give the singers a cue as to how they are to begin, but in some well-known hymns this can work well. The playover must be at the same tempo as that for the whole hymn. What is the right point for the congregation to stand? Some say as soon as the music starts, but this can make it difficult to find the place if books are used. Other congregations wait until the organist has finished before struggling to their feet, but this means that the momentum is interrupted. There should be the same gap between playover and first verse as between the rest of the verses. If it can be managed, and once it is recognised how much of a tune their organist usually plays, let people stand as you draw to a close; a slight rallentando on your part won't disturb the flow but can contain a signal. Don't hold on to the last chord; keep a sense of rhythm between verses.

*Choosing the speed*: To pick on the right speed in your head before the people have started to sing is a fine art. Some may make sure a hymn will not drag by starting on the fast side; this can degenerate into a fight with the congregation! However, this is not just the performance of a tune but a setting of words, and there has to be time to allow the words to speak to, and for, the singers. This doesn't mean slow, which courts the opposite danger of being pedestrian and can cause the hymn to feel too long. Some have suggested that the accompanist sings a verse through privately to try and arrive at a speed where the words are not garbled, but bearing in mind the difference between one person singing alone and the whole congregation together. One factor is the kind of language the hymn uses. Some hymn texts are more poetic (in fact some began life as actual poems), like Edmund Spenser's 'Most glorious Lord of life', or verses by John Donne or George Wither; or later poets like William Cowper ('God moves in a mysterious way') or Frances Ridley Havergal ('Lord, speak to me'). Another factor is the nature of the tune itself. Some tunes resist being rushed. The accompanist's own musical sense will be the best judge here, but examples might be *Abbot's Leigh*, *Blaenwern* and *The Flower o' the Quern*, especially the last, which goes more slowly than one might think. Considering that one must also balance the pull of the tune with the sense of the words, it can be seen how sensitive are the choices to be made. However, in addition to all these factors, there is the rather important one of the size and sonority of the building. In a cathedral or similar building, where there are more hard surfaces to confuse clarity and where the sound takes longer to travel, a slower tempo can better keep the connection between accompanist and congregation than in a more intimate space.

*The course of the hymn*: The gaps between verses should be consistent. One approach is to count two clear silent beats before beginning the next verse. Maintain the rhythmic drive, even if it means playing ever so slightly ahead of the singing. Even in a congregation with a tendency to drag, they will eventually sing to your beat.

*'Last verse in unison'*: There is an assumption that last verses should be loud, even triumphant, and there is a sense that a hymn, being a complete composition, does reach a climax which can be acknowledged by strong playing on the part of the organist. Some hymns, however, even though they are complete, do not end on a note of praise, such as 'God moves in a mysterious way'. However, last verses are often an opportunity for the organist to be creative and it may suit the sentiments of the verse to vary the harmony or add a descant. Even though a congregation may not notice that variation is taking place, they are affected by it. There is an uplift in being shown another way of supporting the melody. Most common is taking the tune on a journey through other keys. As we have seen, modulation is already a driving force in a hymn tune.

A more complex journey through keys leaves the singer on tenterhooks until resolution comes and this places the affirmation being made in the words against a deeper background and emerging to a more triumphant finish. Adding a descant (a counter-melody which conforms to the harmonic structure of the melody it accompanies) can cause the congregation to hold more strongly to their own melody line – in effect an invitation to push the boat out! A modest rallentando, marking the end of the hymn, also can have the effect of confirming what has been said by emphasising its completeness.

## Transposition

Pitch in modern hymn books is in general a semitone or two lower than in their predecessors. One reason is that the pattern of an assured four-part choir, made up of people who regularly exercise their singing voice, is far less prevalent today. Again, with generally smaller congregations, and where this means people are more spaced out, there is less support for the voice than where people are packed together. Another reason is that the range in which men's voices are comfortable is often said to be lower than that of women or trebles. Hymn books, however, have to compromise between enabling the best sound for a choir and an encouraging enough pitch for the average congregation. An accompanist may wish to transpose a tune down into a lower key (for example, if some men are heard singing the melody in their lower octave). Some will be able to do this by ear, hearing the same harmonic progression in the new key. Others will read each note down a semitone or tone as they play (a common test in an organ diploma), which takes a great deal of practice. Others still will write the whole tune out on manuscript paper, a note at a time. If you use a computer music package, it is easiest to copy out the tune as printed and then use the transpose key. Another reason for transposing is when you are handed a list of hymns all of which are in the same key.

## Easy arrangements

There is no shame about a slow build-up of one's hymn tune repertoire. With its sheer size, and the range of difficulty within it, organists or pianists who have recently begun playing for a congregation are going to be asked to play at short notice tunes which may not be known to them or which will require more preparation than there is time available. It is better to be able to lead the singing with confidence than attempt a setting which demands more than the organist at this stage can give it. Appendix 2 gives a link to a website where there has been stored a bank of simple arrangements, some in only two parts, which can be freely downloaded.

# 15

# Leading and Accompanying Worship Songs

Part and parcel of the worship song experience is the accompanying instrumentation, and there will be many churches which will be well equipped with musicians and the technology to go with it. This section has in mind congregations who are less well resourced and who have to work with what they've got. It also explores how the organ can support worship song, both when it (or a piano) is the only instrument available but also how it can enhance and partner a band. What is true of praise bands is also true, of course, for other instrumental ensembles on which many congregations call. Like the west-gallery musicians of the eighteenth century, such bands and groups can be a motley crew. A colleague reports having to arrange the music for Sunday to be accompanied by a group comprising bassoon, descant recorder and djembe drum. She reports that the resulting sound had a distinctly medieval flavour which worked really well for 'Jesus Christ is waiting' but stumbled a bit over Graham Kendrick![1]

For a song like 'How great is our God' or '10,000 reasons', the holy grail may be a line-up of guitars, keyboards, bass and percussion (whether electrified or not), and of course singer(s), but a band can be built up from simple beginnings. If you have a competent pianist or guitarist you are well placed – whatever else is there – as these instruments act as a kind of sonic glue that can hold quite diverse tones together. The addition of recorders, flute, clarinet, strings will give a lift to the song, also enabling the adding of parts. If you have a number of melody instruments there is no harm in having several people playing the tune, as a unison melody sounds good with different timbres of sound such as clarinet, violin and flute. As long as you have a pianist or guitarist providing some harmony and rhythmic drive this works well. Simple percussion could enhance the sound.

Many songs – for example, 'In Christ alone', 'There is a Redeemer', 'Be still for the presence' – have conventional harmonies and can be enriched by instruments playing the parts. This needs considerable preparation by a music director or band leader, who will have to write the parts out. This requires knowledge, of the needs of 'transposing instruments', which sound in a different key from one that plays at concert pitch. Clarinets and saxophone, for example, come in several sizes and therefore keys, but the player uses the same fingering. A Bb clarinet or soprano sax plays a written C one tone lower, at Bb, as does the trumpet – therefore the music is written one tone higher. The Eb clarinet or alto sax sees C and plays the Eb below, so its part is written a major sixth higher. Similarly, the horn (in F) is written a fifth higher. There are also some conventions about clefs. Instruments whose range straddles the treble and bass clefs are usually written with one of the clefs in between (alto and tenor) to save too many accidentals above or below a stave. Thus the viola is written with an alto clef. Happily, charts and lists may easily be found online to facilitate this task.

Although skilled players are a great blessing, it should be remembered that everyone who has taken up an instrument can play *something* and can add to the sound. Music directors and band leaders will often have to provide simpler parts that move more slowly and perhaps involve many rests. If notes are rationed in this way, the skilled orchestrator will pay some attention to the lyrics and save the sounds for particular climaxes or emphases. In writing these parts, bear in mind that players of wind and brass instruments tend to begin their education with the flat keys, but string players with the sharp keys.

These observations apply to songs with fairly basic harmonies, and would apply equally well to hymns. However, hymns may look straightforward but tend to change harmony frequently, sometimes from chord to chord. This can immediately be a problem to the average guitar player, who reads chord symbols rather than written-out music, and who would be daunted by a score where the chords call for identical harmonies to the keyboard. Either one has to drop the guitar for that hymn to save uncomfortable clashes of harmony, or to reharmonise the hymn. On some websites, helpful guitar charts can often be found.

A church band may be called upon to accompany a variety of songs or hymns and it goes without saying that one does not always throw the whole band into the mix. For gentler songs the guitarist should use a more sustained tone and the drummer should drop the driving beats and substitute soft beaters on one cymbal, or switch to hand percussion. Sometimes a simple instrument and voice will be the best lead, like in the case of a contemplative chant. On the other hand, bearing in mind that the worship song has historical links with jazz, and that worship song scores are frequently there to capture the basic idea of the song and not for exact performance, there is room for improvisation in a church band, which can lift a song out of the ordinary. Sometimes a player might be asked – say, when a firmer rhythm is required – to take up a percussive instrument instead. Bear in mind that a band doesn't need to play for every item, but may give way to the organ or electric piano, or a single solo instrument, or percussion with otherwise unaccompanied voices.

Other practical points: always rehearse what the introduction to the song will be, and make sure you are giving a lead into the song that the congregation will hear clearly; make sure the instruments are balanced in volume – this may require use of amplification if you have quiet and loud instruments together, such as clarsach (harp) and trumpet.

## Recruiting musicians

Ask the band. Musicians often know other musicians. If you are looking for players of all ages in your own congregation, it is not always enough to put a note in the parish magazine. People need to be approached directly, and to find those to approach often means a good deal of asking around. Younger people are easier to find. If someone on your ministerial team is chaplain to a local school, they will be able to alert staff to the opportunity. Instrumental teachers, whether in school or working privately, might identify students who would benefit from live playing experience. Who knows? They might be interested themselves, to play or to assist. Are there other music groups in your community, such as folk singers or a fiddle orchestra, from whom you might borrow?

Music teachers frequently find themselves asked by their students to help them with music they have to play for their church bands, which can mean writing out the parts in a suitable way. Sometimes music has to be altered to suit the child's ability, or to suit their particular instrument better. It is important that the part is not out of reach for the child, as this means their experience in the band may not be enjoyable. While it is to be hoped that most children would have chances to play in ensembles within the school system, a group outside school gives them a different experience: it can be something unique to them among their peers, giving them a sense of individuality and confidence; it is a chance to play with a mixture of adults and younger people, sometimes even with parents or other family members; and it is a chance to be an active and valued member of a community.[2]

It is here that the question of commitment is often raised. We often make the assumption that other people's spiritual journey is similar to our own, that if someone's involvement is tangential or irregular it can't be serious. Yet to offer your time and your talents in this way is saying something very positive. Musicians are often surprisingly open to offering their gifts if they are treated with warmth and respect, and welcomed regardless of where their spiritual journey has led them. You could think of it as a subtle form of outreach that also reaches back into our churches with benefits for all. One should not be discouraged when some musicians cannot commit to regular attendance. Often time is in short supply. Behind the appearance of a musician is practice and preparation, and this extra demand is coupled with the fact that good musicians can be balancing a number of playing commitments which require careful management to avoid clashes. It may be that in your situation a basic pattern is adopted where a simple core group – piano or guitar, voice(s), say – can call on a pool of players who can come if they are able or for special festivals and occasions.

## Managing the band

Keith Richards of the Rolling Stones once remarked: 'The only things Mick [Jagger] and I disagree about are the band, the music and what we do.' Bands need management, which may come from the church's director of music or someone with responsibility only for the band (who may be one of the players). Bands do not just have musical issues but can also have issues of personality, punctuality or lack of preparation. They may also need help to blend with each other. The title of the autobiography of the (piano) accompanist Gerald Moore was *Am I too Loud?* There are also matters of beginnings and endings, and decisions to be made during playing, like whether to repeat a chorus. A main task is to ensure that the congregation are not left on their own to keep with the band as best they can. The band leader might be the one to decide whether to teach or demonstrate a song to the congregation before the service begins.

Of course, the manager of the band may also be the worship leader. At their most comprehensive, a worship leader is in control of a section of worship which is based on song, being the front person of the band, announcing, leading the song with their own voice (and very likely guitar), perhaps adding other material such as prayer, biblical references, shaping the course of worship with songs moving through different moods. The worship leader will usually be partnered by the minister of the congregation, both in planning and guiding the worship. Worship leaders ideally should have imagination, a wide knowledge of repertoire, and should understand the nature of worship and how it is led.

## Visiting or joining with other churches

It is important that a band doesn't fall into a rut of playing the same repertoire in the same old way week by week. Continued refreshment of material will help the members feel they are developing. One way of freshening the band is to join with another similar group on occasion, going to the other's church for a service or evening praise gathering and having a return match sometime later. Let each band propose, say, four songs to do together on that occasion. The first surprise could be that the two repertoires have significant differences from which each can learn. The other surprise could be the totally different line-up of the other band, meaning that the result of playing together will be something else again. One account[3] showed one band as comprising amplified guitars, electric keyboards and a smattering of strings and brass, the other with lots of clarinets, several flutes, saxes and recorders, a couple of classical guitars, one piano and a drum kit. It is probably a good precaution, though, to survey the line-ups in advance; a dozen electric guitars and a euphonium may not delight! Practising at home then meeting on, say, the Sunday afternoon, will usually allow enough time to prepare. For the two bands on whose experience these remarks are based, praise evenings became a regular fixture.

## The siting of the band

The place where worship takes place, unless it is in a public hall, is not simply a location. Generally, it will have been designed for worship, and, in its overall shape or orientation and in the detail of its furnishings and decoration, contributes to the quality of worship that takes place within it. Where the eighteenth-century west-gallery band had a place of its own, from which it could be well heard without being seen, usually the praise band finds itself in full view of the congregation, perhaps sharing a raised platform which also houses pulpit, table and lectern, and standing between the congregation and any visual focus – window, altar or communion table, or reredos – that is part of the worship environment. Even if members of a band moved offstage in between, the complex electric environment of the band cannot be quickly dismantled and moved, restoring the sight lines of the congregation and preventing the unsettling untidiness that can disturb concentration. One solution would be to site the band to the left or right, with the worship leader moving to the centre to lead the song, but given the great variety of interiors this may not work. Each church will seek the best solution for its own circumstances. There will be occasions, however, perhaps not a main service, when a band fully facing the worshippers is part of the vibe.

## Using the organ

This section explores the situation where there is no band and the only instrument available is the organ. The first impression the organist may have is that the music looks more complex than that of a hymn. One reason for this is that worship songs are very often composed by the writer/singer working with guitar or chords on a keyboard. This is the reason why some songs are shown to be arranged by a different person from the one who wrote it; in other words, it was written down from performance. In that sense the score that you are looking at is an approximation, an impression, and has to be further adapted. Of course, you can work up a reasonable performance of the notes before you and that will carry you through, but there are some things an organist can do to enhance everyone's experience of the song.

Before looking at some of the more common characteristics of the genre and discussing how they may be tackled, it is worth spending time listening, for example to a song on YouTube, if a good performance is available, to help not just in bringing it to life in your situation but in understanding its musical character or genre. For as well as skill, the musical intelligence is a key component in approaching this task. What kind of music is this? What makes this work? It is an important question since there is considerable variety across this one category. Worship songs have evolved over half a century; does this one derive from early choruses, or from the folk-song revival, from popular ballad, or rock, or from dance or jazz streams? Recognising the style of the music gives one a place to start. This probably explains why two of the most memorable and idiomatic renderings of a worship song that I have heard accompanied by the organ were from first-class musicians, respectively in a cathedral and an abbey.

One characteristic of many worship songs is that they can be more closely allied to a solo voice and are commonly led by a singer. The melody is prioritised, unlike the hymn tune where the progress of the harmony is an equal feature. What the band is doing (that is, what you are supplying on the organ) is backing the singer by improvising round the chord symbols provided. You don't usually see a music stand on stage. Organist Tom Bell, commenting that 'organs are surely the greatest ever one-man band', suggests[4] a general approach in which the melody is prominently played solo on one manual, the left hand filling in the chords on the other – possibly derived from the guitar symbols on the score – while the pedals play the bass. He notes that a lot of printed arrangements of worship songs are reworkings of a piano improvisation. A piano score often has the bass moving in arpeggios, to keep the momentum and suggest a freer idiom, but this is not characteristic of an organ, which can better signal momentum playing sustained chords punctuated by a rhythmic pedal. Bell comments favourably on the four-part arrangements in *Singing the Faith* (the Methodist hymn book) and sees them as one model. These are more choral-friendly and sound idiomatic on the organ. Another point is that the music can often be simplified by leaving things out, especially if there are elaborate, pianistic inner parts in the arrangement.

Another difference between the worship song and the standard hymn is that the latter continues line upon line while in the former there are many gaps or silences when the instruments keep things going until it is time for the next vocal entry. It can be difficult for a congregation to know when to come in, or at least to come in with confidence, since often the momentum in the written keyboard accompaniment dies away. Continuing the rhythm in some way, bass notes, chords or improvised melodic passages, can better signal the point at which people come in again. An example would be 'He came to earth' (John Pantry) where the expected next line is delayed by a bar's rest; what is provided is a Bb arpeggio which does not include within it the pitch on which the voice comes in; a new melodic phrase, continuing on the dominant from the previous bar and ending on the tonic at the beginning of the next bar, in which the voice re-enters on an up-beat, would be more comfortable for the singer. Something similar occurs at the entry to the refrain.

Sometimes the arrangement fills in the gaps itself, as in 'He is exalted' (Twila Paris), where v. two is launched with an improvisatory uprushing scale (small notes). This song contains some tricky rhythms, as at the end of the first line when 'I will praise him' enters with two semiquavers on the sixth pulse of the bar and then breaks the flow with a hemiola (effective word-painting for what is an exuberant shout). In a hymn tune, the rhythm is within and around the melody; in worship songs the rhythm is an underlying pulse against which the melody pushes. Tom Bell suggests that one priority should be to make sure the rhythm is accurately and firmly played, especially if syncopated, for once a congregation has picked it up wrongly it is very difficult to correct. Its accuracy will be better heard if a solid pulse is maintained, maybe from the bass line. (The organ has the advantage that it can emphasise the bass.) In shorter, chorus-like songs, as in the case of the song just mentioned, the practice is often to repeat the whole, sometimes several times; in this case the organist may slip in a two-bar flourish in place of the tied dotted minims in the last bars to prepare for the repeat. Another example, of many, would be 'Salvation belongs to our God' (Howard and Turner). It could be argued that this syncopated kind of rhythm, where the entry is anticipated by as short a note value as a semiquaver, is an attempt to capture an improvised rendering, and that other rhythms might suffice; it is just that with everyone singing at once, it may be desirable that they be in agreement with each other, and with you also.

While hymns usually begin with a hearing of the tune, or part thereof, so that the congregation is readied to take part, a worship song typically has a shortish keyboard introduction. This is often quite bland (listen to a Hillsong on YouTube and notice how the opening music is more a deliberately random series of sounds which settle the audience and gradually rouse performers and people towards the song). The organist may wish to replace this introduction with an improvisation of similar length or longer, but with more musical interest, to anticipate the song and encourage a firm beginning. Also, it can be difficult for people to hear the rhythmic pattern of the verse from a short introduction.

Another point where a transition has to be managed is often a chorus which can work like a climax, a peak in the drama, and this is quite often expressed by the fact that it begins at a suddenly higher pitch, as in 'Salvation belongs to our God' (Howard and Turner) or, famously, in 'Lord, the light of your love' ('Shine, Jesus, shine'). While it is not difficult for the soloist to hit that high C sharp, it is more so for a congregation. Where a band would perhaps use percussion to sharpen the attention or an instrumental flourish to anticipate the new pitch, the organist can assist by, say, an upward-moving melodic phrase. (The same gambit may be used in the middle of the chorus, on the G minor chord.) In more recent performances of 'Shine', it seems common to replace the B of the last note of the verse with an E, reducing the interval from a ninth to a sixth. In many scores, there is no introduction given, and it is not always appropriate to play over a verse. In such cases ('Make me a channel of your peace', for example) an introduction may be added, which at its simplest might use the last line of the verse, perhaps adding a melodic tail that carries over on to the first beat of the bar in which the verse comes in on an offbeat. This last song, where pitch and rhythm do not change much and monotony is a danger, is helped by a strengthened rhythm in the accompaniment.

## Playing along with the band

There is also the opportunity for the organist to play *with* a band. Too often there is a standoff between the organ/choir establishment and the praise-band contribution, with the attitude that 'never the twain shall meet'. There can, on the contrary, be opportunities for the organ and the regular singers to help enhance the sound and the experience. Graham Kendrick speaks of memorable events where the organ joined in for a last verse of one of his songs, 'taking it to another level'.[5] In other circumstances, as in many local situations, there are missing timbres or parts in the band (often, it is a good bass that is absent) and these the organ can supply, especially the latter.

Tom Bell notes that if the band is a small one, the organist can, at the very least, provide a bass line, creating a richness of texture that would otherwise not be there. With backing chords as well, skilful use of registration can also help the dynamic range and simulate the effect of a bigger band. This can make a world of difference as to how the band sounds and how well the congregation sings. Sometimes, where there is already sufficient instrumentation, even a single bass note can transform a moment. As well as playing skills and enriched sound, a band should not underestimate the assistance that its church's music director can offer, both in the preparation and arrangement of the music and in management of musical forces.

### Notes

1 I am grateful for a comprehensive series of articles in the former magazine *Different Voices* by Suzanne Butler, on whose insights and experience I draw in the first half of this chapter.

2 Petrie, Joanna, 2009, 'Does Anyone Here Play Anything?', *Different Voices*, No. 5, Martinmas, pp. 33f.

3 Hill, Robin, 2008, 'Two's Company', *Different Voices*, No. 2, Martinmas, pp. 2f.

4 Interview with Tom Bell, 2019, 'Playing Worship Songs on the Organ', *Church Music Quarterly*, June, pp. 38f.

5 Perona-Wright, Leah, 2004, 'The Future is Eclectic!', interview with Graham Kendrick, *Church Music Quarterly*, March, pp. 33f.

# Related Issues

# 16

# Technodoxology

## *New Technologies in Worship and Music*

Each of you is to set aside a contribution to the LORD. ...
Let all the skilful among you come
and make everything the LORD has commanded: ...
fasteners, ... bars, posts, and sockets, ...
the curtain of the screen, ... the lampstand for the light,
its fittings, lamps, and the lamp oil, ...
the stitched vestments for ministering in the Holy Place.
(Exod. 35:5–19 *selected verses*, REB)[1]

When we talk of technology in relation to the church, its worship and its music, we tend to dwell on the digital and the electronic. Our attention is gripped by the potential of the internet to share resources, to widen choices, indeed to reach beyond the walls of the church building to make known the message of the gospel. We hope it will attract more people to worship and a physical involvement in the church. As regards music, there are the state-of-the-art sound desks, electric instruments, amplification, and the forms of music that this brings with it. There are also the websites and online videos that promote a ready-made repertoire and with it styles of musical performance and of related worship.

However, we should remember that these new communications media are merely the newest expression of our ability to create new tools and discover new techniques. Behind this last word is the Greek *techne*, which means not merely a craft but the wisdom that belongs with a craft – a knowledge that is broader than just enough to practise your skill. The creative people in the Exodus passage directed their skills towards the tabernacle, the holy place where God was to be met. Their knowledge was knowledge of God and God's relationship with the people of God, a way of understanding the world and their place in it. Their successors have continued to wield their tools and practise their techniques in the church through the centuries. Their work affected the developing nature of the buildings in which the church gathered, but it also brought about change and innovation in what people did when they worshipped and how they experienced worship.

New building techniques made possible the construction of high towers; mechanical methods of sawing timber, as well as the use of slate rather than stone slabs, made larger roofs practicable and affordable; the use of cast-iron columns to support roofs and galleries gave better sight lines; improved oil lamps, gas and finally electric lighting made it possible to hold services when natural light was inadequate; central heating allowed worship in the worst of weathers.[2] New tools and techniques also left their mark on the way people worshipped. Bells called the people together, and marked the high point of the mass; rosary beads and statuary encouraged devotion; embroidered stoles focused attention on the presiding clergy and their actions; coloured pigments combined on the icon drew people into the communion of saints and aided their prayers; lit candles placed in holders completed a prayer or marked the commemoration of a loved one; metal communion tokens confirmed people's qualification to meet with God in the sacrament; printing and books gave people access to Scripture and the words of the liturgy.

More recent innovations have made their own changes in the style of worship, such as the photocopier which provided orders of service to enable better engagement in worship, the pulpit sounding board which in its ability to throw the voice further enabled the development of worship where the focus was on the closely argued sermon listened to by large congregations. Later, the microphone was to improve on this but it also opened the door to other stylistic changes, enabling, for example, a greater informality as a minister moved to address particular groups (e.g. children) and use more conversational tones and vocabulary.[3] Informality was also a result of the practice of making the worship environment more welcoming, with chairs and carpeting. Some newer technologies (along with attitude change) have assisted people for whom access to worship was a challenge: seats for the elderly or those with impaired mobility; pew cushions and kneelers to alleviate discomfort; ramps for those using wheelchairs; loop systems for the hard of hearing.

As regards *music*, as larger buildings came into use, chant would enable the words of prayer and Scripture to carry through the space, giving rise to the plainchant repertoire which continues today. Again, as layouts became established, people facing each other across the area known as the choir engendered antiphonal singing. The construction of galleries in the eighteenth century enabled, in Scotland, multiple lofts for voice parts, which contributed to the spread of singing in harmony, and in England enabled the west-gallery bands. All of these not only enabled the making of music but affected the kind of music that was made. Organs[4] had been blown by hand, but the invention of hydraulic motors allowed very large organs to be built. In the late nineteenth century, electric motors displaced them, and electric and electropneumatic actions further increased both the power and flexibility of organs. Mass-produced reed organs – harmoniums and American organs (often confused; in the former the wind is forced through the reeds, in the latter the sound is caused by suction) – were not only widely used in such churches as might not have space or could not afford a pipe organ but also provided a bridge into the home and the singing of hymns in domestic situations.

## Detrimental effects

In spite of very real advantages, new tools and techniques did not always bring blessings. Sometimes indeed their practitioners were branded as heretics, seen as challenging not only the accepted norms for worship and belief but also the existing power structures, whether of church or nation. It could happen that new abilities concealed dangers or disadvantages not seen at first, as circumstances changed, or as they became outdated. The rood screen (the beautifully crafted wooden or stone partition between nave and chancel which carried a representation of the rood, the cross, at its apex) spoke of the mysteries that took place beyond but was subsequently ordered at the Counter-Reformation to be removed as creating an unhelpful division between the ordinary worshipper and the altar. The sounding board, in a sense, could be seen as creating a similar division, where the people became passive listeners instead of full participants, while preachers remained 'six feet above contradiction' in their high pulpits. It is suggested also that it contributed to creating the artificial 'pulpit voice' as preachers, striving to reach every corner of the church, sensed that, in their resonant buildings, the vowel sounds travelled least well and had to be exaggerated.

Again, some find the vestments of the clergy, often decked with meaningful symbol, a distancing between clergy and people, or worse, between people and God, instead of being symbol of the people's oneness with the Holy Trinity – the root meaning of hierarchy as we saw in the first chapter. Many would see the dangers of another example of division in what seemed the brilliant innovation at the time of the hygienic individual cups now used at Communion by many congregations, together with the bread diced into small pieces, as emphasising individualism over against the common cup and broken loaf which symbolised the church's oneness with Christ as his body.[5] Even the organ had its negative side, the pipes so often sited, for want of better, full in the face of the congregation (and the console half-sunk into the floor just in front of the communion table) so that, it was often said, people now worshipped the organ pipes. Some also regret the displacement of the style of unaccompanied song which very quickly followed its adoption. Enemy of the organ is central heating which, when not used with care, dries out the moving leather parts of the mechanism. Carpeting dulls the acoustic, both for music and speech.

It is clear that we should approach the matter of technical innovation with care, and that we should arm ourselves with principles from which to critique them as they become available or as we use them. At a study day on handling new technologies in worship,[6] main speaker Graham Maule[7] brought the work of some contemporary thinkers to bear on some of today's favourite technological innovations. The people present used these to reflect on their own experience with technology, and some of what follows incorporates their insights. Six factors were isolated.

## 1 Is technology in worship our golden calf?[8]

French sociologist Jacques Ellul (d. 1994) noted that virtually everything in our natural and cultural environment had been affected by technology. In former times we used to have sacred wells; are we in danger of investing sacredness (unquestioning acceptance) in technology? The cleverer our tools the more we are enslaved by them and by the experts who provide and operate them. We make the assumption that if we can do it it must be worth doing. We may persuade ourselves that to use the most up-to-date techniques will result in reaching contemporary people, but it may be the case that for some it is the ritual and the mystery, the *difference* from the rackety everyday backcloth to life, that potentially attracts them to the church. As we adopt new openings, we should ensure that they are going to deepen rather than dominate. Without careful scrutiny, we risk merely following the market, turning congregations into consumers.

## 2 Is our technology 'convivial'?

The danger of becoming mere consumers also features in the thinking of Austrian philosopher Ivan Illich (d. 2002). The more like *consumers* we become, the more reduced is the ability to think for ourselves, to be free *agents*. Our tools must be convivial, meaning sociable. Otherwise we are in danger of losing previous skills on which we relied (think of memory, or mental arithmetic – or even unaccompanied singing). Might new tools be shaping our worship in a wrong direction, and without our even noticing?

### 3 Does our technology cause us to run before we can walk?

Another French cultural critic, Paul Virilio (d. 2018), is remembered for his metaphor of the shipwreck (the inevitable outcome of inventing ships). New technology usually speeds things up compared with the old. Is installing the latest technology automatically a step forward? The faster you go the further ahead you need to look to avoid collision. Concentrating on the demands of our forward movement, we can lose our lateral vision. That is, we are diverted from working out sufficiently well what our goals are or noticing the new context we are passing through. For example, the motive in embracing modern technologies is often given as reaching young people. A problem with that can be that we are more out of date than the young people we want to reach. There was also the consideration that all new systems rapidly become obsolete, a factor we need to be more aware of.

### 4 Is our technology human-scaled, nourishing the soul, enriching community?

Scottish writer, ecologist and land reformer Alastair McIntosh (b. 1955) asks if we are sure that our tools and technologies serve the interests of community, that they are human in scale. Too often, our investment in technological equipment can be a vanity project so that a church can say, 'We are on message, in the vanguard'. Do we sometimes turn to technology to bring the life we feel we lack? There is something missing, but we are not sure what it is, so we rush into a cure. What in fact may be missing is a quality of interaction, or a lack of love, an absence of spiritual depth, a weariness; the church community may not be as inclusive as we think ('but we are all nice people'), or congregational life is distanced from the real world. There will surely be tools that will help, but let us make sure it is these we develop.

### 5 Is our technology merely a tool or one of the 'vocabularies' of worship?

A tool is used to achieve something apart from itself. Should our aim be rather that a new technology takes its place *as part of* the experience of worship and doesn't stand out as a feature? In the Exodus passage at the head of this chapter, there were many new things created, and they had a practical purpose – but in the end they would fade into the greater experience of being part of the holiness of the holy place. Philosopher Marshal McLuhan (d. 1980) – famous for the slogan, 'the medium is the message' – remarked that a light bulb will open up a space, but it is as yet empty space. A new idea or ritual which in some way opens up the reach of worship will cause that technique to become one of the vocabularies of worship, just as a language or a song, the lectern that is a symbol of the Word, the stained glass window that captures the ministry of Jesus, or the cup that vividly brings to mind the sacrifice of Christ. Light itself can become a new vocabulary as imaginative designs or uses can bring out the new in an old space.

Albert Bogle, a pioneer minister of the Church of Scotland, has come to the same conclusion through his work in developing a worshipping community whose life together is entirely online:

> Technology is neither good nor bad. It is a tool in many ways to be used in both corporate and private worship but in such a way that it enables truthful worship. Like all tools we need to ensure that it doesn't obscure the passion and the intention of the heart and mind to worship God. However, it will not be technology that renews the church ... All forms of

our technology, be it architecture or music or the fruits of the digital revolution, need eventually to submit to the place of silence in worship ... Prayer and imagination and vision often operate at best in silence. I have come to see the significance of silence and how it can be woven around a holy place or space, be it on the ground or the internet.

For Bogle, it is not the externals, the images, the music, that make for worship. Rather, 'it is the preparation and practice of the heart before worship that transforms a performance into more truthful worship and shapes our community worship and practice'.[9]

Graham Maule himself offered an example of a technique becoming a vocabulary that related to the congregation he was part of.[10] Although a very media-savvy establishment, the attraction was not that in itself. A controversy had raged on social media over an invitation to a Muslim to read from the Koran, related to ongoing local dialogues between Christians and Muslims. The congregation had experienced a 15–20% growth in the last year or so due to the inclusiveness expressed in the pastoral relationships there, of which this was a part. The furore, which was UK-wide, led people to realise that here was a place of hospitality, justice and love. A technology had become part of that pastoral reach.

## 6 It is not enough to use new ways, they have to be used well

Where new technologies disturb or dominate worship, this can be because they are of poor quality. Churches can over-reach themselves by installing cutting-edge systems but without developing the expertise, as well as a necessary discernment, to use them. How many times have there been microphones which don't work, or people not sure how to use them! There are times when the sun is too bright for screens to be seen clearly (unfortunately, at 11am in northern latitudes light can come in at an angle). Slides and illustrations on screen can be poorly chosen, opportunities lost. Excerpts from film can be badly edited. The musicians' volume can be disturbingly high. Another factor is when the equipment dominates the space, blocking sight lines, disturbing concentration, detracting from the balance of the building and a gracious interior.

A lot depends on the operators. Some suggest that a developed use of communications technologies requires a team of people (up to six persons perhaps) so that people do not find themselves constantly at the delivery end and unable to take part fully in worship. There are also maintenance tasks to be carried out, accessing updates, keeping the equipment in good condition (e.g. batteries in microphones). However, those who operate equipment for worship need more than just technical know-how; they need to know what worship is and how it is planned. Indeed, there are some long-established techniques which continue to require trained people, such as teaching new hymns, and of course leading and co-ordinating worship.

## A case study: projection screens

Almost a symbol of the use of technology in churches today is the projection screen. To explore its uses would be a good test of these theories. It would seem that the greatest use of the screen today is for projecting the words of hymns and songs, one advantage being that a wider range of songs can be used than may be found in the hymn book most in use in that place – and which may have been published a decade or more ago. Those who advocate the projection of the words of hymns and songs legitimately argue that the holding up of heads greatly enhances the enthusiasm and the corporateness of the singing. Screens can improve its quality – the posture means people can breathe better. The screen is most useful when worship songs and choruses are sung, where frequently verses can stand alone and do not rely on adjacent verses for their sense.

Hymns are different in structure and many would argue that the hymn is a continuous document where there is a progression towards a climax, an argument or spiritual reflection which has an outcome. It can help greatly to see where we are going in such a structure, to be able to make connections between verses as we sing. It is more likely in a hymn that we want to check ahead and be putting together in our mind the whole message of the hymn as we make connections between one verse and the next, or the previous. One hymn, for example, has a colon in an earlier verse that grammatically refers to the next three verses. Helpful too is looking ahead to the period from which the hymn comes – is this a contemporary writer speaking to people with similar concerns and experiences, or is it perhaps a classic hymn of the church from a writer we know and trust? (Too often such information is left off the screen.) When we sing, we are dwelling in the hymns rather than reacting to lines of text, with no opportunity in advance to know what one is about to sing and invest in it mentally, spiritually, emotionally. Thus, it is felt, our relationship with the hymn has changed; we are no longer dwelling within it but being fed it verse by verse.

If, however, people had a choice, and books were provided, they could use either the screen or the book, or both, with the additional information on the page that sometimes can help one's singing, not least the melody. Indeed, the hymn book is not a single-use tool but a resource for spiritual and reflective material which you can browse in before and during the service or at home. For some, the screen is a barrier to worship; you sing between yourself and the screen, which can feel like a cul-de-sac, a short circuit, when your aim is to sing into the worship space and beyond that space. A screen, therefore, in itself neutral, can become a single point of power and authority. Like the chancel screen of old, a projection screen can hide as well as reveal.

Do we make sufficient use of the screen? The most common use is probably *text*, whereas perhaps its chief advantage is that it enables the employment of *images*, just as stained glass did for our predecessors and still does for us today. As embodied persons, we bring more resources to worship from within ourselves than our hearing and understanding of words. Perhaps to use screens well we need to devote attention to researching images and matching these to the course of the worship – indeed bringing back the power of the visual that our ancestors would have known. In one church, where a new Christmas event involving adults and children was being planned, the mums asked that the complete Christmas story should be read. The minister felt children would lose focus during this and prepared a PowerPoint of clip-art slides to match the progress of the readings and projected them on to the wall beside the pulpit. The children were fascinated – and the move also involved a husband who was not a churchgoer but whose expertise was given a place.

At baptisms in another church, where often there were many in the congregation who rarely attended church, the words spoken by minister and parents were placed on the screen. The minister noted with interest how some, particularly the younger adults, followed the course of the liturgy intently and commented that, without the words on the screen, the chances were that their minds would have been miles away. Of course, to use a screen to show the progress of a liturgy is not always the best thing to do. Another minister reports that one Sunday the whole of the Communion section was placed on screen by a zealous operator. She noticed, from behind the table, that there was no eye following the eloquent signs and rituals of the sacrament but all looked at the screen over to the right.

## Alternative worship

Projection is also much used in what has come to be called alternative worship. A major difference is that the congregation is not static, but invited to move within a prepared space. One example was when five or six projectors threw psalms on to the walls, the roof, the floor, through archways in different parts of the space. People moved between them in their own time, experiencing a freedom from following an order of worship, yet enabled to worship in ways they themselves chose. In these experiences, the screens may not be projection screens but computer monitors at which tasks of various kinds might be offered. In this style it is common for the ancient and the modern to come together, digital technology with traditional liturgical procedures, the former not serving or losing itself in the latter but rather, in their juxtaposition, potentially creating a depth of engagement, a bodily involvement, a religious experience that is not tied to speech or doctrine.

A growing component, in which Graham Maule himself was involved through Iona Community Wild Goose worship events, is the use of art installations in creating the worship space. The artist Carol Marples, who through her organisation, the Soul Marks Trust, works with congregations to create environments for, and experiences of, worship and prayer, has made a study of this phenomenon, which she calls 'liturgical installation'.[11] She traces a link between this, which she predicts could become a much more widespread phenomenon, and earlier developments in the secular art world of multimedia installations which created an environment rather than offered an exhibition to look at. David Stancliffe sees performance and installation art as offering the potential for a new and collaborative way of working towards authentic liturgy: 'It is my conviction that we are on the threshold of a new relationship between the Church and the arts ... We are beginning to understand that the arts and their practitioners are co-celebrants with us in this process of celebrating life.'[12]

## The streaming of services

The last few years have seen some congregations live-streaming their Sunday services in a bid to extend their reach into their communities, and sometimes beyond.[13] This increased during the pandemic of 2020–21 when it was also for a time the only way regular churchgoers could join in worship.[14] Many have had misgivings. Is this merely the result of a fascination with modern digital technology? Is there a missed opportunity in simply pointing a camera at a big space in which a service is taking place when the small screen requires a different kind of imaginative presentation? Can a virtual congregation correspond to the physically gathered people of God for Sunday worship, not least when there is a lapse of time before it may be watched – for example on the congregation's YouTube channel? English Baptist theologian Paul Fiddes addresses the latter issue, suggesting that God willingly enters into and inhabits all worlds, including digital and virtual:

> The combination of the doctrines of the incarnation and the resurrection of Jesus encourages us to think that God is present in a virtual world in a way that is suitable for its inhabitants ... Taking a trinitarian perspective, we may say that the whole universe lives within the interweaving relations of the triune God, and through Christ God deepens God's own reciprocal living in us. One ought not to assume that cyberspace is a disembodied world. The net is composed of a form of energy, just as is the familiar 'physical' world in which we operate every day.[15]

In a webinar sponsored by Hymns A & M on worship during the Covid-19-related lockdown 2020–21, Anglican priest Fr Simon Rundell also took up the matter of authenticity. He argued that what we were seeing was not 'the church online' (which people watched) but genuine 'online church' (in which they were participating). We connect with God on two levels, externally and internally. The *external* is through worship and its contents and the space in which it takes place. But we also connect with God in 'spiritual communion', an *interior monologue* – prayer and meditation, reading Scripture, revelation by the Holy Spirit. However, we can experience the external not only in (what he calls) the analogue church but also the digital. In both contexts, our souls reach out to God in prayer and worship. Yet there has to be also, between the external and internal, a point of contact, where the externals of worship and the internal dialogue with God enliven and connect with each other. He calls this 'a liminal intersection – a thin place – between the external and the internal which is where ritual and sacrament inhabit both domains'. Fr Simon speaks sacramentally but this surely applies also to Services of the Word, the threshold point where a phrase of sermon or hymn rises from the page to connect with our souls, and where simultaneously our inner spiritual core opens in readiness to hear the divine voice. He sums up:

> Thus technology and digital space is not an end in itself, but an enabler. In the same way, a non-digital church, from a mighty basilica to an intimate country chapel, is not an end in itself but a medium through which the interface between our interior dialogue and God's mystical presence is enabled.

In spite of his affirmation of the authenticity of the digital church, Fr Simon does not go as far as to say that there can therefore be virtual Communion: 'I am cautious to regard a piece of bread and a cup of wine placed before the laptop as capable of being consecrated remotely by a priest … (W)e can only receive digital sacraments fully immersed in digital space … I believe that this makes Remote Communion impossible … At present, we are in a hybrid context: a merger of digital and analogue worlds.'[16]

The statistics suggest that through the streaming of a service of worship contact can be made with rather more people than come to church. The use of the internet to reach beyond the walls of the church may be understood not just in terms of missionary outreach but also in the context of a new discussion among those who study the church's worship. This debate draws attention to the importance of recognising the opportunities of 'public liturgy' or 'liturgy in the public square'.[17] It recognises this as a time of change in patterns of churchgoing when, although there are fewer 'hearers' in church Sunday by Sunday, these are balanced and complemented by many more 'overhearers' who are by no means closed to the church and even its rituals. What may be included in public liturgy are memorial rituals after attacks or disasters, ecumenical Holy Week processions, *Songs of Praise* programmes, spiritually themed exhibitions and events in museums, church-driven voluntary work and cultural initiatives, or the growing pilgrimage movement (at base a leisure pursuit but with strong overtones from the, invariably, historic Christian routes that are followed).[18] One might add the concert works with religious themes such as oratorios, or works by Sir James MacMillan where gospel incident, traditional chant and sometimes political themes rub shoulders.

The continuing conversation about public liturgy received new encouragement from Pope Francis's 2014 encyclical *The Joy of the Gospel: Evangelii Gaudium* with its call for 'new Areopagi'.[19] One might see the more 'public' liturgies (weddings, funerals – and we can now add streamed acts of worship), which drew in the unaffiliated and the tangential believer, as potentially Areopagi in the sense that at these points something of the faith and the purpose of the church gets out. The weight of opportunity in the streaming of worship is such that care must be taken to design such events with these more informal audiences in mind.

## Social media

You might say that social media is the new church notice board, or the bell that calls people to come. Maule gives the example of the day a school made a visit to the cathedral. 'The pupils heard the organ and wouldn't leave. We should use such media to arouse curiosity about the church. We are counter-cultural, we are different; we have insights that no-one else does; we have worship and ritual. We can use social media to make people curious, to tickle their fancy.'[20] Sometimes social media can do more than invite, but even assemble the congregation. A Borders minister told of how:

> prior to Christmas, I heard that the young mums were very keen to be involved in the Christmas Eve Family Service, and in fact plan something themselves. In the past couple of years, I could never ascertain how many children would be there – to do a Nativity play or anything. However, this year, one of the mums sent Facebook messages round them all, rallied them all to dress the children up as the various

characters (and the costumes were excellent, having been done at home), choose a song for them to sing – and that's all they actually did: walked in, sang the song, sat down while someone read a poem, and glow-sticks were handed out at the end. All quite spontaneous![21]

From this emerged a second use of social media, as a mode of pastoral care. One of the networking mums was ultimately ordained an elder and her 'district'[22] was not geographical but the existing network of young mums. Thus a new pastoral tool was created, reaching back into the core of the local church.

## Attitudes to change

New technologies, like other changes in local church life, can bring controversy and complaint. This should not always be dismissed by the more adventurous as lack of vision or clinging to the past. There are many reasons for resistance: emotion, history, theology, how people understand and experience worship, all different but all needing to be unpacked. When change is proposed, seeing what others have done is helpful, as is engaging in conversation with them as to what they have learned.[23] It is also important to generate discussion within the congregation, when different views might surface. It may well be that the discussion extends beyond the immediate proposal and opens up useful discussion about worship in general as practised in that congregation.

## Conclusion

One week, a Tree of Life was laid out on the floor of a central Edinburgh church which people could walk through. Although many 'tools' were used in physical layout and in interpretation, a user commented that it was 'great to be in a space which was technology-free'.

## Notes

1 REB has 'skilled craftsmen', NRSV 'All who are skilful among you'.

2 Hume, John R., 2007–08, 'New Technologies, New Ways', Church Service Society *Record*, Vol. 43, pp. 15–24.

3 Hume, 'New Technologies, New Ways'.

4 Hume, 'New Technologies, New Ways'.

5 In one of the pre-union presbyterian churches in Scotland, a device was invented which clipped on to pews and which contained an individual 'helping' of bread and wine; the bread was under a cap in a container which could then be flipped up and a glass of wine lifted out.

6 This took place in March 2018 under the title 'Technodoxology' and was convened by the Church Service Society.

7 Dr Graham Maule, himself an artist and well known also as a hymn writer, now deceased, was a member of the Wild Goose Resource Group of the Iona Community and was involved in innovative alternative worship projects.

8 Exodus 32.

9 Contribution *in absentia* of the Very Revd Albert Bogle to the Church Service Study Day at Lanark, March 2018.

10 St Mary's (Episcopal) Cathedral in Glasgow.

11 Marples, Carol, 2018, *Contrasting examples of liturgical installation art in Christian worship in England and Scotland from the 1980s to the present day*, PhD thesis, University of St Andrews.

12 Stancliffe, David, 2010, 'Liturgy as art', *Art and Christianity*, No. 63, Autumn, p. 2.

13 The parish church in Luss on Loch Lomond, during the ministry of the Revd Dr Dane Sherrard, came to be known as a venue for international wedding ceremonies, for a time at a rate of 140 per annum involving couples from some 70 countries. These were streamed to their home countries, and resulted in a congregation of 25,000 watching the live streaming of worship each Sunday.

14 In a bid to control the virus, governments banned gatherings in public places, including churches.

15 Fiddes, Paul S., 2018, 'Sacraments in a virtual world? A further contribution', paper delivered at the Centre for Digital Theology Symposium, Durham, pp. 6, 10.

16 www.frsimon.uk.

17 The latter was the theme of the biennial congress in Palermo in 2007 of Societas Liturgica, a body made up of liturgiologists and those who write and prepare forms of worship in different branches of the church.

18 Post, Paul, 2011, 'Profiles of pilgrimage: on identities of religion and ritual in the European public domain', *Studia Liturgica*, Vol. 41, No. 2, pp. 129–55.

19 A reference to Acts 17:16–34, when Paul at the Areopagus in Athens noticed an altar 'to an unknown god' and took this as a cue to preach about the God whose Son was Jesus Christ.

20 Church Service Society study day on 'Technodoxology'; see note 6 above.

21 The Revd Marion Dodd at Church Service Society study day on 'Technodoxology'; see note 6 above.

22 Church of Scotland elders usually are responsible for a geographical district, and keep in touch with church members who live there.

23 The host church in which the study day was held had recently begun to feature digital technologies in its work. In a short period they had had seven visits from other congregations who were at different stages in their thinking and experimenting.

# 17

# Making Music Safely

The report in 2020 of the Independent Inquiry into Child Sexual Abuse (IICSA)[1] is a reminder of the high importance of safeguarding in the church. Safeguarding highlights one of the church's core characteristics, that it is a place of safety, a welcoming space, a haven of hospitality. In earlier centuries the church offered sanctuary for the persecuted. Safeguarding is not one of the functions of the church but a dimension of its very nature. Marty Haugen's hymn captures this:

> Let us build a house where love can dwell
> and all can safely live,
> a place where saints and children tell
> how hearts learn to forgive;
> built of hopes and dreams and visions,
> rock of faith and vault of grace;
> here the love of Christ shall end divisions:
> *All are welcome,*
> *all are welcome,*
> *all are welcome in this place.*

Hospitality is much more than a good habit or moral duty, the giving of a friendly welcome to any strangers who come to our church, important though this is. Dutch Catholic priest, theologian and spiritual writer, Henri Nouwen, suggests that hospitality is no less than a fundamental attitude towards our fellow human beings, something we have to grow towards, a 'conversion' which we have to develop from within. It means inviting the stranger, the Other (this refers also to people we may have known for many years), into our world on their terms, not on ours. We do not seek to change people 'but offer a space where change can take place ... a friendly empty space where we can reach out to our fellow human beings and invite them to a new relationship'. Nouwen warns that this task is far from easy, likening it to the police officer trying to create some space in the middle of a crowd of panic-driven people for an ambulance to reach the centre of an accident.[2]

This more positive approach to safeguarding, that the church by nature and calling is a safe place, a hospitable space, is becoming more common. One core document (to cite the example of one denomination on behalf of many) states:

> The witness of Scripture recognises and affirms God's love for all members of the human family and the priority given in Jesus' ministry to children and the vulnerable of society. His ministry was one of welcome for all. To be free to worship and participate in the life of the Church, people need to feel safe and included. Good safeguarding practice helps to ensure that everyone is welcome in a church community. Good safeguarding practice is part of how we value people, and treat them with respect.[3]

Outlining the principles that undergird this aim, the variety of types of ministry exercised in a congregation by both clergy and church workers, paid and voluntary, is acknowledged. These ministries are to be pursued in the best interests of those to whom they are offered. We tend to assume that people are grateful for our ministry, but a recipient may not see it that way. A hymn by Brian Wren reminds us that being ministered to is not always welcome, particularly when offered from a position of strength:

> Spirit of Jesus, if I love my neighbour
> out of my knowledge, leisure, power, or wealth,
> help me to understand the shame and anger
> of helplessness that hates my power to help.

And if, when I have answered need with kindness,
my neighbour rises, wakened from despair,
keep me from flinching when the cry for justice
requires of me the changes that I fear.

Children and vulnerable adults are recognised as vulnerable
in specific ways and are protected in law accordingly, but all
people can be vulnerable in different ways and at different
times in their lives. The principles outlined translate into five
commitments, commitments which are expressed in differing
ways in other Churches' policies and practices. Behind them all
is acceptance of the fact that, although a local church studies to
mirror the Kingdom of God, this is often seen 'through a glass,
darkly'.[4] The pursuit of a 'culture of safety' is not only so that
individual hurt or abuse is avoided but so that the character of
a congregation's life is developed towards a situation where all
people are safe and valued. 'People in the church are to work
together to prevent abuse, seek justice when it has occurred,
and care for those affected by abuse.'[5]

Churches typically commit themselves to further this aim by
the following:

- Education and training through presbyteries, provinces, dio-
  ceses or districts, depending on denomination.
- Taking action to filter out the risk to the vulnerable by
  assessing the suitability of those who are called to positions
  of trust, including compliance with legal requirements for
  criminal record checks.
- Setting standards for employees and volunteers to help correct
  any imbalance that could come from power (deriving from
  knowledge, expertise, spiritual authority) wrongly exercised.
- Responding fully and appropriately to allegations of abuse,
  including supporting the complainant and the congregation
  in the process, while also assessing the suitability for continuing ministry of the employee or worker about whom the
  complaint is made, whether the abuse was unconscious or
  intentional.

• Providing support for the abused and all associated in any way, ensuring they will not be silenced by pressures on the part of the church or the abuser, listening without judgement, responding with compassion and maintaining confidentiality.

One thing is emphasised, a lesson hard-learned from historical abuses, that persons who have suffered abuse must never be pressured to forgive their abuser; this can cause further hurt and confusion when people come to believe they are 'not being Christian' if they are not willing or able to forgive. Christian doctrine teaches that forgiveness is not one-sided but is costly both for the one who offers and the one who seeks, requiring from the latter – to borrow liturgical language – true repentance and amendment of life. The impact of abuse can be lifelong, and the perpetrator, and even the church as an institution, may similarly have a long journey to undertake.

These policies and practices, then, if they address specific ministries and tasks, also simultaneously embrace the membership of the church as a whole, as it gathers for worship and as it meets in groups and guilds and in outreach and service. This understanding of safeguarding when applied to the church's music takes it beyond the choir room and into all the places where music is made and the various groups that select, prepare and make it. First, however, it should be understood by all that there is no place in the church's ministry for people who use their position of authority and trust (whether clergy, musician or other church worker) to perpetrate abuse.

In moving into this wider territory, there are two aspects in particular that bring this dimension of church life close to the door of the music-makers. One arises from the compelling nature of music-making. Particularly in preparing choral music, there are pressures and imperatives which drive the process. There is a desire to honour composers by doing justice to their creativity, vision and insight. There is pressure to aim for a performance that is accurate, which communicates the feelings captured in the music and which is a worthy offering in the context of worship. This necessary single-mindedness, on the part of director and singers, could be in danger of obscuring the fact that one is dealing with human resources. Ways need to be found of acknowledging the individuality and, indeed, the vulnerability of singers and players. A pastoral ear, not necessarily that of the choir director, can enable anxieties or hurts to find expression, but it is also of high importance that all involved in preparation and training know and treat the musicians as people.

Another consideration is that in one sense musicians are conspicuous in possessing a particular area of knowledge and have developed an expertise that others do not have, and which many see as a particular blessing and talent. Yet to be highly valued and consistently visible is also to provide an easier target for criticism, and sometimes a focus for more general discontent. Sometimes what we want to offer is not comprehended by people generally, whether in performance or in the economics of developing and delivering our music. There can be complaints – tunes that are not known, styles people do not appreciate, demands for more resources a ruling body does not understand the need of. It is somewhere in this territory that belong the, thankfully occasional, high-profile disputes between musical and clerical staff. What can cause this to arise is the fact that usually ministers or incumbents have overall authority over the worship of which the music is an integral part, and it may be that the necessary processes of consultation have not been established or have not been successful. There is ample opportunity here for forms of bullying, subtle or not – or even quite unaware – to emerge out of fear or desperation, as well as experiences of being set aside and diminished.

A quite different but common situation is where a local church has embraced styles of worship and song that, say, are believed to be more attractive to younger people or relevant to the times we are in, but which others feel are unsuitable. These issues are discussed elsewhere; here it is just acknowledged that, rightly or wrongly, there can be resentment Sunday by Sunday when people are made to feel they are ungracious or blame-worthy for refusing to embrace change but there is no way of working this through. The safe church will be one which gives opportunities which allow people to put issues on the table so as to reach understanding, although not necessarily agreement. For there is another aspect of the hospitable space which is relevant when considering difficult issues. Nouwen goes on to say that our openness to the stranger, our creating space to receive them on their own terms, doesn't require that we allow the Other to dictate to us. Receptivity is only one side of hospitality. The other side, equally important, is what he calls confrontation, by which he means the importance of preserving one's own integrity, both for ourselves and for the sake of the stranger. He writes:

> Real receptivity asks for confrontation because space can only be a welcoming space when there are clear boundaries, and boundaries are limits between which we define our position ... Confrontation results from the articulate presence, the presence within boundaries, of the host to the guest by which he offers himself (*sic*) as a point of orientation and a frame of reference. We are not hospitable when we leave our house to strangers and let them use it any way they want. An empty house is not a hospitable house.[6]

Safety may also be threatened in that some may feel marginalised or diminished by language, including the language set to music. Language which is sensitively inclusive, whether related to gender, disability or self-esteem, can avoid the shock of someone finding they are on the wrong side of a divide. We are most aware today of how many women *and* men are angered or disturbed at the overuse of male imagery and language in prayers and in hymns – thus the, often unwelcome, changes in the wording of well-known hymns. But there are other less obvious stumbling blocks, such as the hymns and songs which emphasise sinfulness or seem to prioritise a faith where there is no room for doubt, which can plant in people the seed that they consistently fall short and do not belong in the fellowship of the church.

Marty Haugen's hymn ends:

Let us build a house where hands will reach
beyond the wood and stone
to heal and strengthen, serve and teach,
and live the Word they've known.
Here the outcast and the stranger
bear the image of God's face;
let us bring an end to fear and danger:
*All are welcome,*
*all are welcome,*
*all are welcome in this place.*

## Notes

1 Independent Inquiry into Child Sexual Abuse, *The Anglican Church: Safeguarding in the Church of England and the Church in Wales*, Investigation Report, October 2020.

2 Nouwen, Henri J. M., 1976, *Reaching Out*, London: Collins, pp. 68–9, 73.

3 Scottish Episcopal Church, *Principles and Commitments*. This document makes reference to the (worldwide) Anglican Communion's *Safe Church Charter*.

4 1 Corinthians 13:12, KJV.

5 Scottish Episcopal Church, *Principles and Commitments*.

6 Nouwen, *Reaching Out*, p. 91.

# 18

# A New Dimension in the World of Sound

## *Making Musical Judgements*

In the early 1990s, as a visiting lecturer in a theological college in Adelaide, South Australia, I was seconded to a group of linked congregations for a month to partner them in reviewing and developing their worship. During an incognito (I thought) reconnaissance visit the Sunday before, I was spotted by the lay preacher, who gave me a rather guarded welcome, while reassuring the congregation, with a meaningful glance in my direction: 'The Lord doesn't look for quality in worship; He looks for effort'!

The idea of *quality* in music can trigger anxieties for many. Will this be out of my league? Difficult to listen to, to sing? Will this take away from my enjoyment in participating in worship through singing together what we know and love? It helps to realise that the Latin original has the more general meaning of 'nature', 'property' or 'characteristic', whereas we tend automatically to add a silent adjective, '*good* quality'. To ask: 'What characteristics does music need to have to awaken us to the mystery at the heart of worship?' is a different question. Furthermore, it asks the question not just of music but also of worship, of the people who worship, and of the church which calls different voices together into one.

It should not be overlooked, however, that we are dealing here not only with theory or aesthetics or theology but also with pain, hurt and alienation. The church's worship has throughout history been sensitive to each new tremor in cul-

tural movements and socio-political change in wider society
– and typically it has been the music that has borne the brunt.
Each change or development is accompanied by controversy,
and innovations have often been attacked as bringing about a
lowering of standards, not just in musical or liturgical terms
but in their effect on the spiritual and moral life. One of the
reasons why so much pain and upset can be engendered is that
music is part of our inner as well as our outer worlds, intimate and personal, producing intense feeling. Millennials and
Generation Z put together their own playlists – songs and
compositions which interpret individuals to themselves and
how they relate to the world. A *Guardian* columnist writes
of how fans of the late David Bowie 'could measure out their
memories in his songs: where they were, how they felt, who
they loved'.[1] This could apply to the music of the church.
Indeed, a website devoted to *Church Hymnary 4* includes a
facility for people to put together their own hymn playlists.[2]
People enjoy and are nourished by particular hymns and styles
of music. Conflict is aroused when a local incumbent removes
or sidelines the choir, or there is a wholesale change in idiom
(in the cause of relevance or wider appeal), or the old hymn
book is banished in favour of another, or a choir doesn't feel
valued because so many of the newer hymns are in unison, or
a projection screen is erected in the chancel. It is often at these
points that the cry 'quality' goes up, although frequently other
issues are involved.

These are matters that are raised in every generation. In the
Church of England there have been within the last hundred
years no fewer than three substantial reports on church music
– in 1922, 1951 and 1992. Each has tackled the issue of what
makes music fitting for use in worship. The most recent, *In
Tune with Heaven*, recognised that the criterion 'only the best
is good enough for God' raised more difficulties than it solved.
The report introduces an important qualifier, suggesting that
the key question should be: 'Within the style which is suitable, comprehensible and helpful to my congregation, is this of
the best quality I can find?'[3] At the report's launch, a *Church
Times* editorial summed up:

People know what they like. The commission finds that they are entitled, within certain limits, to hear it in church ... What it asks is that critical faculties should not be suspended, that worshippers should recognise that within any style there are more or less objective standards of composition and perform-ance to be aimed for, and that congregations, musicians, and clergy should show mutual respect and tolerance.[4]

The report widens the parameters of the discussion, but again (the best) quality is the ultimate goal. There may, however, be an alternative way to approach this criterion – namely that, with all the other factors defined in the report having been taken into consideration, we should seek music that is *well made*. In the 1640s there was a move to make a new version of the metrical psalter that would be used north and south of the Border. The Scots commissioners, although supportive of the unifying potential of the project, proved the most difficult, with the Revd Robert Baillie urging: 'These lines are likely to go up to God from millions of tongues for many generations; it were a pity but all possible diligence were used to have them framed so well as might be.'[5] Even when the joint committee had officially finished their work, what is now known as the 1650 psalter, which has never been superseded, was revised several more times before the General Assembly agreed to accept it.

John Harper has suggested that an important characteristic of the music we seek today may find its models in the world of crafts rather than art, quoting Eric Gill: 'Things must be right in themselves, and good for use.'[6] The composer makes some-thing as well as he or she can and if it is beautiful it is a bonus. The true artist or craft worker will testify to the struggle to reach full expression, and the journey will be experienced and appreciated by those who see (or sing) the finished work. The typeface designer and sculptor Richard Kindersley, who created the stone in Dunblane Cathedral in commemoration of the tragic shooting in 1996 in the local primary school, said in an interview:

Craft can't be machine made. The 'craft' bit is the human intervention in the making process, which has all sorts of other qualities: when you make something you might be relaxed, or you might be tense, or you might be happy, or you might be upset – and all this background vibrato goes into the making. If you show people a bit of very nice craft making, the first thing they want to do is touch it, and I'm sure they're getting some sort of feedback from the maker in doing that. *The more quality there is in the making* [my italics], the more people want to touch it, pick it up, feel it or whatever; so I think that's really important.[7]

There is nothing elitist in this. The thing well made attracts, and people are drawn to touch as the artist touched and laboured. They are in their way sharing in this act of creation, or making. Yet there remains the fact that not everyone reaches out to touch, and, when they do, the threshold is not necessarily at the same point. When do we recognise that something is well made?

Historic criticism has tended to focus on two areas in particular, one being that the music should not obscure the words that are set. This warning was in circulation well before the Reformation, and was particularly levelled as polyphony developed. It was famously expressed by Archbishop Cranmer in a letter to King Henry VIII: 'In my opinion, the song that should be made thereunto would not be full of notes, but, as near as may be, for every syllable a note, so that it may be sung distinctly and devoutly.' It is not unlikely that at different times this seemingly sensible criterion was driven by other factors: to keep musicians under ecclesiastical control, perhaps, or a puritan suspicion of glorying too much in music, or a feeling that music could become too elitist and beyond the comprehension of the ordinary worshipper.

The other critique was the warning that to admit styles of music which originated with the popular song or the theatre not only endangers the soul but taints the purity of worship by association. Here is John of Salisbury (d. 1180): 'Bad taste has ... degraded even religious worship, bringing into the presence of God, into the recesses of the sanctuary, kinds of luxurious and lascivious singing, full of ostentations ... more fitted to excite lust than devotion.'[8] Did he have in mind, perhaps the exuberant and popular round, 'Sumer is icumen in', found in a mid-thirteenth-century manuscript in Reading Abbey, where under the sprightly lyric there has been added an alternative set of words beginning 'Perspice Christicola', a song of the crucifixion of Christ? Or perhaps the *contrafacta*, alternative texts to existing secular songs,[9] or the popular devotional songs that accompanied Christian feasts as people took to the streets after worship,[10] or the songs which grew up round the mystery plays?

Centuries later, the anxiety remained. John Calvin, whose convictions owed a great deal to the early patristic writers of the church, wrote in his introduction to the Genevan Psalter of 1543: 'It should always be seen to that the song should not be light or frivolous, but that it have weight and majesty ... (for) there is a great difference between the music that is employed for enjoyment at table and in the home and the psalms sung in the church in the presence of God and the angels.'

Yet the truth is that church music forever looks over its shoulder at the wider culture to the secular forms whose language it shares, at ease in either company. Over centuries, notwithstanding pronouncements by clerics or councils, the music which has accompanied the life of the world has also made the liturgies of the church resound. One example among many: as polyphony became established, composers were as likely to borrow from popular secular melodies as they were from plainchant to provide a firm foundation (*cantus firmus*) for complex fifteenth- and sixteenth-century mass settings. These not only served to inspire the composer but also identified the setting with the title of the original chant. A perennial favourite was 'L'homme armé'; another was the love song 'Westron wynde', used by John Taverner (d. 1545) and two other English Renaissance composers, possibly a much earlier song. Leading writer on early music Gustave Reese remarks that composers seemed to have intended listeners to recognise the melodies they had adopted, placing them in the most prominent voice, the tenor, setting it in long note values, and perhaps also doubling the voices with a slide trumpet.[11] Surely recognising the song would contribute to earthing a eucharistic celebration in the life of the world and the experience of the people:

> Westron wynde, when wilt thou blow,
> the small raine down can raine.
> Cryst, if my love were in my armes
> and I in my bedde again!

Luther famously took his melodies (those he didn't himself compose) from a variety of sources, from the plainsong office hymns and the sequences of the medieval church to the popular song of the guilds of musicians and poets who, starting with the Troubadours, flourished from the tenth century onwards. He wrote:

> When natural music is sharpened and polished by art, then one begins to see with amazement the great and perfect wisdom of God in his wonderful work of music, where one voice takes a simple part and around it sing three, four or five other voices, leaping, springing round about, marvellously gracing the simple part, like a square dance in heaven with friendly bows, embracings, and hearty swingings of partners.[12]

The two historical criteria we have discussed have not gone away. Yet the most effective critic of all has been time itself. The music of any period has included both its wheat and its tares, growing together.[13] As time goes on, the tunes which have particularly connected remain to enrich the repertoire but others are forgotten. This natural process has, however, been paralleled and assisted by criteria applied by editors and other influencers.

To take the eighteenth and nineteenth centuries as an example, Methodism captured the attention with music which drew on the styles of the day (popular theatre, public concert, domestic song). This did not always have the blessing of the Wesleys, especially when found in a more extreme form as Primitive

Methodist preachers, sometime known as Ranters, sought out those in the lowliest occupations whom the church had not reached and led them in enthusiastic open-air song which drew more on the world of ballad and street songs, drinking songs, colliers' rants and costermongers' cries.[14] This movement overlapped with what is known as the west-gallery style, which evolved in congregations of the Established Church that did not rise to organs and singers, a style lively, rhythmic, simple and appealing. Some were repeater tunes (lines or parts of lines reiterated, postponing and therefore making for a more dramatic climax); others were fuguing tunes (voices entering in sequence in imitation of the towering fugal choruses of Handel). Examples are with us still in such tunes as *Lydia*, *Cranbrook*, *Sagina*, *Lyngham* (or *Desert*, aka 'The Presbyterian Cat'), *Diadem*, *Orlington*. It was to tunes in these styles that prefaces to psalm collections referred when they claimed they had excluded compositions 'of questionable character' or the 'grosser instances of the florid and repeating' tunes.[15] In this long tradition of borrowing from secular music, the church has frequently returned the compliment, as in Thomas Clark's psalm tune *Cranbrook*, now better known to the words 'On Ilkley Moor baht 'at'.

## The conversation renewed

A new energy has come to the debate following the Second Vatican Council, which brought many insights towards renewal in a number of different areas, including the liturgy of the church, as set out in the key document *Sacrosanctum Concilium* and in later explanatory documents, a primary concern being 'the full, conscious and active participation of the faithful'.[16] In spite of the fact that this and other documents highlighted the continuing importance of traditional practices – plainchant, polyphony, the use of the organ and the central contribution of the choir (*schola*) – the new notes which had been struck regarding the admission of the vernacular (local languages as opposed to Latin) and the place allowed for local cultural practices sounded more loudly at first. This, combined with the coincidence at that time of a widespread folk-music revival in the English-speaking West, resulted in a growing repertoire of popular settings of the mass and other congregational song which threatened to engulf the tradition. This has heralded a period of sometimes anguished debate, which continues to rage,[17] resourced by several documents and reports which, both from the perceptiveness of the material and the passion behind them, has greatly assisted the conversation in other branches of the church.

Much of the discussion has centred round the triple criteria first proposed by the (American) Bishops' Committee on the Liturgy (1972), intended to help gauge what was suitable for worship: a composition or setting must be *musically good, liturgically appropriate* and *pastorally sound*.[18] This contributed to the debate but did not close it: how were these three criteria to be balanced? What constituted musical goodness? And who would be the judge? Significant among the many other documents and reports that followed was the *Snowbird* statement from an international group of musicians (1995), which prioritised the need for quality. It dismissed the claim that popular idioms were exempt from judgement, since many cultural musical idioms in use in the church are 'dialects of the same larger musical language'. Not only must more objective standards be brought to bear but the 'Catholic ethos' of church music (which is at odds with current 'personalized, introverted or privatized' styles) should be recovered.[19]

It was another, albeit unofficial report that seemed to offer a way ahead, the work of a group called Universa Laus, which first met in Switzerland in 1966, a Catholic initiative but of ecumenical composition. Among its founders was Fr Joseph Gelineau, known for his innovative psalm settings which many denominations had adopted. The group's manifesto has an unusual and readable format: a relatively brief statement, a longer but commendably succinct commentary, and a glossary which is composed not just of words but ideas and a wide range of background information on the components of worship – Catholic and Reformed – and music in all its guises.

Seeking criteria with which to assess music for worship, the group found two different approaches being taken. One is expressed in terms such as *dignity, beauty, appropriateness, good taste, quality, art* – you might say, the more objective aesthetic qualities. The other approach looks for music that can express *holiness*, music that is *prayerful, sacred*. This last approach captures what people invest in their music, their point of connection with it, and is preferred by the group as the best way into the discussion. In the first approach (the report avers), people's judgements can depend on their cultural habits – what they are accustomed to, what the schools teach, what music groups tend to perform, and the fashions imposed by the media. In the second (holiness) approach, church traditions approach this in their characteristic ways – Calvinistic, Ignatian, Charismatic etc. There is therefore no one set of objective criteria which will stand up for everybody. What must happen, concludes the report, is a 'patient and persistent programme' of listening to each other – not to find some kind of average or lowest common denominator, a levelling out of differences (even the most extreme views should be taken into account), but to ascertain, at a given moment with a particular place and people, what is valued and where growth might take place. A 'working space' is to be sought which strikes a balance between the music 'that is capable of drawing forth or supporting the radical conversion demanded of every believer' and the degree of receptivity of the believers gathered together.[20]

## Local discussion

What is being suggested by Universa Laus, and implied in the Church of England report, is that explorations need to take place on a local level. It may be felt that in a particular congregation there is no issue – for example where a music team has already engaged effectively with the matter, with the result being music that is clearly suitable for its situation. In another, however, there may be an awareness that there are people who might be disturbed by the style of the music and feel less able to join freely in worship. It may also be felt that there are categories of people who are open to involvement, and who would feel more welcomed by an adjustment in the musical provision (no assumption is made here about which direction this might be in). These situations are all the more urgent when (as in a village setting) there is no alternative on offer.

That this should be suggested as a way towards finding the most fitting music for worship may be alarming to many, especially to those who believe that objective, aesthetic assessment is an essential part of the process. Yet, as Erik Routley remarks, church music 'stands ... under the discipline associated with its being used to further the aim of worship. It is always used in a context where the performers are not exclusively, and the hearers are not even primarily, concerned with music in itself.'[21] He goes on to say that modesty is one of the qualities necessary for a good composer of church music, and writes: 'The best church musicians have always been the best listeners.' They 'listen to the conversation already going on before joining in it' and are the more likely to 'compose church music which ... will mean something to the unmusical while commanding the respect of the musical ... It will fittingly take its place in an activity whose chief object is not musical.'[22] Although one might be reticent about naming people as musical and unmusical (Routley in fact always used the terms as if they bore invisible quotation marks round them), the opportunity for reflecting on the music of worship can enhance anyone's appreciation and perhaps may deepen involvement.

Rather than approach the matter as an issue which needs resolution, it would be more productive to help people in such conversations reflect on how they themselves relate to music – what they like and dislike – and to listen to other people with different approaches and experiences. They may also be unaware why another should prefer a style of music which they themselves do not like. The aim would be to reach a point of mutual respect, and a sense that we are ministering to each other. Jock Stein calls this 'loving others in their choice of hymns'.[23]

To avoid the danger of simply having merely a free-for-all

sharing of likes and dislikes, a structure is required, one that starts further back than immediate opinions.

One such framework is provided in *Inspiring Music in Worship*,[24] described as 'a short course of guided conversations for churches'. This is far from being just a series of five discussion starters but a continuous experience, each session ending with tasks to be continued in one's own time and then, before the group next meets, each new conversation is primed by participants following guided reflection on the theme to be explored. Each conversation takes a wide sweep through a particular characteristic of the worshipping church back to its implication for music: namely, what it means to be a worshipping person, discovering skills and releasing gifts, how music reaches out to people whether within or beyond the church, starting from where we are in our church at the moment, setting a new vision for worship and music, and the steps we need to take. It is buttressed by background information and uses a variety of approaches within each session.[25] The final pages offer Scripture-derived theological themes and observations, suggesting that sooner or later we need to establish criteria, or goals, beyond the point we ourselves might have reached, to help us travel further in understanding and appreciation of all that music can bring to worship.

## Two approaches to the development of criteria

### An approach from the study of worship and liturgy

One proposal for a starting point for church music criticism comes from Societas Liturgica, the international body for liturgical scholars and those who prepare liturgies and orders of worship in the various denominations. The gathering at Turku in Finland in 1997 was given over entirely to the matter of music in worship. In her presidential address, Professor Irmgard Pahl, a Roman Catholic from Germany, proposed seven 'critical criteria of a qualitative nature' based on how we understand the nature of worship, arguing that the music that accompanies worship should bear the self-same qualities:[26]

1 *Music as expression of the proclamation character of the liturgy*
   Does music interpret the message in a suitable manner? Does it express the whole truth, or does it level down the truth by, for example, the elimination of tensions? Do we hear in it the faith of the church in its entirety becoming audible?

2 *Music as expression of the doxological character of the liturgy*
   Worship gives glory to God in psalm, in prayer of adoration, in the great thanksgiving of the eucharist. Does our music enable us to bring to more worthy expression the whole-heartedness of this utterance?

3 *Music as expression of the dialogical character of the liturgy*
   Worship is dialogue with God, in psalm, hymn, prayer, ritual, silence. The community recalls, in singing, God's saving activity, and it responds in acclamation and thanks. The music must both symbolise and actualise this dialogue.

4 *Music as expression of the incarnational character of the liturgy*
   The Logos, Christ himself, takes on bodily form in sermon and sacrament and therefore human beings are valued in their creatureliness. This implies diversity characterised by different cultures and their variety of musical styles and forms, but all based ultimately on the mystery of the incarnation. Worship and its music must constantly make new room for the incarnation of the Word. It lives in the tension of accepting cultural variety but also the capability of new creation within these forms and styles.

5 *Music as expression of the* communio-*character of the liturgy*
   Worship is made by the whole community together. This means that the musical components, cantors, choirs, instrumentalists, and congregation together make the music, with no part disengaged, and all given a voice.

6 *Music as expression of the festive character of the liturgy*
Festival is a concentration of life at its most intense and thus
there is demand on the music to find its highest expression.
This must not depend on trained choirs but all must be
drawn in.

7 *Music as integrating component of worship as a whole work
of art*
Music is one dimension among many that interact within
the liturgy, yet music particularly is an integrating component. This asks more of it, both in artistic quality and
spiritual content.

These considerations, as Professor Pahl expressed it in her
conclusion, require a 'striving towards the highest possible per-
fection of form and of input on the part of people who are ready
to give their best'. Even the simplest song in one voice, 'if it is
but permeated with self-giving veneration, can be a radiantly
powerful work of art. In essence, what it is all about is that
the work be authentic, that is, an adequate expression of inner
movement and feeling and of a deeply anchored sense of faith.'

## An approach through biblical theology

The possibility that the music of worship should be regulated
by the Word of God in Scripture as it is read, prayed and studied in the church was proposed by that prolific commentator
on church music, Erik Routley (1917–82).[27] While developing
several criteria, drawing on both Old and New Testaments,
one in particular stands out, namely the imperative that
Christians grow towards maturity in Christ. 'Where church
music inhibits the growth of the Christian society to maturity
it is to be censured ... We contend that this is the heart of
Christian criticism of church music.'[28] The question to be put
is whether the music enables growth, onward movement and
maturation, or whether it merely anchors people at the point
they have reached – offering a diet of milk instead of meat
(Heb. 5:11–14).

An expression of gratitude usually follows a service rendered. For St Paul, whose letters invariably begin by giving thanks for the faith and life of the people who will receive them, that is never enough, and he goes on to instance even greater things he longs to be able to give thanks for: a work has been started that is to be brought to completion, as love grows richer in knowledge and insight (Phil. 1:6, 9); to share in the sufferings of Christ means also to share in the hope this engenders (1 Cor. 1:7). Why are gifts given but 'for building up the body of Christ, until all of us come to the unity of the faith and of the knowledge of the Son of God, to maturity, to the measure of the full stature of Christ' (Eph. 4:9–16)? This is a growth that begins at baptism and continues all one's life and which, unlike other kinds of growing which come to a peak and deteriorate, continues through and beyond the decline of other abilities. Baptism is the beginning of a journey measured not in miles or years but in a deepening ability to love God and neighbour. Christ has invited us to find life for ourselves in the life he has already led in obedience to God.

One characteristic of music Routley identifies which inhibits such growth is where rhetoric suppresses reason, where the composer makes large gestures without backing them up with good sense (his example is the hymn tune where the melody compels the attention but the musical hinterland is weak). Such music 'combines a large and impressive size with cheap materials',[29] and with an implied contempt for crafting skills. An example is the eighteenth-century desire to capture for worship something of the marvellous inbuilt drama of Handel's oratorios. This in lesser hands has led to musical sensationalism, where a composer has copied others but without the same ingenuity as the originators. The result is no more successful than when Peter in imitation of Jesus tried to walk on water. It is a striving after an effect that somebody else has achieved 'without the need for prayer and fasting' (or without the struggle to communicate a fresh idea).[30]

Particularly susceptible to this was the music of the Romantic era, which dominated the song of the nineteenth-century church. In less competent hands, its tendency towards 'expressiveness'[31] could force-feed religious feelings without leaving space for the journey, set-backs and all, that textured genuine devotion. What this means is that a good song or prayer has to open us to new listening. If it is too immediately appealing, grabbing our attention, it may not be able to do that, because then we say: 'That was great; I feel satisfied – and don't need to search anymore.' Some of the music we choose, especially that which is easy to listen to, may not be providing handholds for the level of engagement that discipleship requires.

What draws us on is a desire or a challenge to engage with what is to come next, in musical terms the turn of melody, the unexpected juxtaposition of harmonies, *difference*. 'One of the important questions to ask ... is: What in this is new?'[32] An Old Testament scholar, Routley claims that in practice the Law always contained an irrigation of generosity and that this prepared it for the gospel, which did not dismiss but fulfil. Music is to be judged not by its correctness in keeping to musical laws but by whether it has creative energy. This is not the clean sweep of old ideas, a striving for newness or novelty, but a freshness that flowers out of the familiar. 'A good hymn tune is about 10% original and 90% traditional. It cannot succeed if it says nothing new.'[33] Good songs and settings always have within them what is recognisable but also something unheard of, something that suggests there is much still to find. This is readily confirmed in our own experience. It is the new element which so often turns a congregation away from singing what they do not know, but which, when it becomes known, draws them back time and again.

Jeremy Begbie speaks of music teaching the patience of waiting in eager longing (Rom. 8:19ff), a patience in which '*something new* is *learned* of incalculable *value*, which cannot be learned in any other way' (Begbie's italics). Church music should reflect the belief that salvation is a learning process 'in which we are led towards goals by paths that are not easy, straightforward or expected'.[34] The assumption by some in the aftermath of the Second Vatican Council that music for the congregation must be easy to sing (to satisfy the requirement, for example, that people be enabled to participate actively)[35] is by this called in question. When we are required to make an effort to appreciate a composition or setting, something in us grows to meet it. The subtle and varied vocabulary of music is well equipped to foster growth, to take listener and performer on a journey, to prefigure what is still to be known, to communicate what cannot be captured in words. Mode and modulation, metre that spans a phrase or a whole movement, the interplay of strands and voices, repetition and contrast, shape and structure, all carry the listener forward not just to the end of the piece but beyond.

## Taking the next step

If it should be felt that to seek the most suitable music for worship by interrogating our own tastes and setting them against the likes and dislikes of others, rather than accept the dictates of history or the judgement of the professional, will result in the lowest common denominator, perhaps we should hear St Paul, who gives thanks for what we have become but who believes we have much more to give. Taste, in people, paperbacks or pastimes, is a very personal thing. It is an intimate part of our identity, and may be thought difficult to change. Yet perhaps tastes are more flexible than we think, and such pejorative descriptions as highbrow or lowbrow are an imperfect assessment of where someone's tastes reside. Might we rather say that what we prefer – what 'tastes good' to us – are the things that hold our attention and keep us guessing. They are the novels where you can't predict how the characters will react, the musical track that is not just a rehash of the same old sounds, the politician who doesn't speak in clichés, the preacher without platitudes. In church, there are the stained glass windows which compel you to look again, the furnishings that you want to touch and admire and not just put things down upon, the words of prayer that stir more prayer, the flowers not just stuck in a vase but arranged to suggest the greater mystery by which nature arranges its beauty. You might say that taste has to do with how interesting something is, or how far it answers all we bring to it, not just particular talents but the life we live and all we have experienced. It is true that we are not all at the same place, nor have we had the same level of experience. What's more, people's taste may be developed in some areas and not in others. The person with an ear for speech may have eyes that notice little.

Yet think of what corporately we already have come to value. Take the psalms, searching the heart, touching the complexities of life and the mysteries of belief in God. Take the stories of Jesus, artful, compelling, with hidden meaning. Take our places of worship, built to last, enfolding us in hope. Take the tradition of good preaching, true to life and to the gospel. Take the hymns of a Wesley or a Bonar, words carefully chosen, rich in scriptural reference. All well made, holding the interest, demanding our full attention. When we come to savour, sift and select the song that most fully expresses our faith and carries our praise, we are *already* growing, changing. Frank Burch Brown breaks taste down into three aspects: perceiving, enjoying, judging (the latter as you ask yourself, Do I like this? Why? or Why not?). He sees that all of these component parts, far from being static, 'have to do with stretching and learning'.[36]

The suggestion that there is already enough in our own experience and the long growth of the church as the body of Christ to renew and regulate music for worship has a bearing on the question Irmgard Pahl left with us. In speaking of the incarnational characteristic of liturgy which embraces humanity in all its cultural diversity (including its song), she also suggests that such an acceptance carries a new demand, rather like those of St Paul, that in that context they must make, within their popular and cultural expressions, 'new room for the incarnation of the Word'. Even as they take their place, at the same time they seek the 'new creation' that is the goal of all liturgical music.

This is a version of the question already posed: 'What in this is new?' How can cultural music be made new but still retain its characteristic sounds? Gordon Lathrop proposes that, whether music, images, stories or persons remembered for their notable witness, the 'local' should be juxtaposed with the 'more-than-local'. That is, the specificity must be tempered, strengthened or completed by the experience and witness of the church across the globe and down through time.[37] Virgil Funk, founder of the National Association of Pastoral Musicians in the USA, makes a parallel approach through 'codes'.[38] His suggestion is to 'mask' and 'mix' codes, with the result that a composition can unite contemporary style and religious tradition, citing as an example J. S. Bach's transformation of the secular tunes used as chorale melodies. He cites a number of contemporary composers as examples, such as Joncas and Haugen in the USA, and Rimaud and Berthier (Taizé) in France. The Iona Community might provide other examples, while James MacMillan's popular mass settings show how idiomatic styles can sit within music of a longer tradition.[39] Another example of mix and mask could be the arrangements of worship songs in publications from the RSCM, where harmonies, the way the music is set out between voices, and styles of accompaniment are altered in such a way as to acknowledge the wider norms in liturgical writing – 'more-than-local'.[40]


## Growing into the music

Discussion so far has focused on creating or finding the right music, the music which is suitable for worship. There is, however, another aspect: how we ourselves approach the music and allow it to reveal its full meaning. What is it that enables us to find 'a new dimension in the world of sound'?[41] We may appreciate or 'enjoy' the music in an act of worship but have we allowed it to draw us to the presence at the heart of worship? In seeking a process by which we can grow in our hearing, United Methodist liturgical scholar Don Saliers makes his starting point the centrality of the senses to the spiritual life. To hear in its fullness music that has a potentially numinous quality, we have to school our senses,[42] since one does not simply gain access to the transcendent. What is happening as we respond positively to certain music or types of music is that in them we are recognising our own experience of the 'melody and rhythm of life', and this reciprocity of sound on the one hand and life on the other can deepen through time. But for this to happen, work must be done. We have, he says, to bring as much of our life as possible to bear on our experience of music in worship (elsewhere[43] he suggests that we are prone in worship to filter out the more disturbing feelings and emotions) and we have also to work on the depth and reach of our sense perceptions. He makes an interesting comparison. A deeper hearing of music could be likened to the way some traditions come to appreciate icons. Viewing an icon requires a trained mind and sensibility to see it in such a way that the person feels 'gazed upon' by the image. Thus the eyes of the heart are rendered open to receiving divine communication.

Saliers is reminding us that growth to maturity in Christ is not just about prayer, meditation and the study of Scripture, a compartment of our life, but how we live our lives in the body. Those who have been on directed retreats – for example, an Ignatian 'retreat in daily life' – know how in the process one feels a clarity and a grace, a sharpening of the senses and a self-awareness that illuminate tasks and relationships, worship, the perception of the natural world, and how, conversely, the encounters of the day play upon one's reading of Scripture and times of prayer. There is a physicality about growth 'to the measure of the full stature of Christ', not only because we are part of his physical body but in that we follow in the steps of the fully human person who took the form of a slave and who 'humbled himself and became obedient to the point of death' (Phil. 2:8). The Church and its members share in this servanthood, seeking the humility which keeps us right-sized[44] in our relationships with God and other people, a readiness to share the suffering of others, to confront evil, to speak for the marginalised, to care for creation, to keep alive hope in the heart of humanity.[45]

Within this we rejoice, but the Easter joy of which the church sings is a joy that arises from the dark places, a joy that discovers God even in the depths, 'the joy which seekest us through pain'.[46] One of the most telling criticisms that Routley brings to bear is on music in which there is an unwillingness to encounter tension, music which 'bypasses the way of the cross'.[47] In his hymn, 'In praise of God meet duty and delight', there is this verse:

No skill of ours, no music made on earth,
no mortal song could scale the height of heaven;
yet stands the cross, through grace ineffable
an instrument of praise to sinners given.

Earlier in the chapter we heard the artist and craft worker speak of the struggle to create a work with which they could be satisfied – a new creation. There is evidence of such a journey in musical compositions which have been laboured over, which have been made with cost, perhaps laid aside at a time of difficulty and then returned to, mirroring the life experience – perhaps the Christian life – of the composer. It is there too in the way performers put themselves into the rendering of a work, or where a choir labours at perfecting a strand of the music, or the congregation struggles with a challenging melody that in time will bring a new note to their praise. Maybe the lay preacher with whom this chapter began was not so far wrong!

The long-standing study group Universa Laus, which has guided the discussion at several points in these pages, concludes its earlier report with its own summing-up of the unique nature of the music of the church:

The ultimate goal of this music ... is to make manifest and make real a new humanity in the risen Jesus Christ. Its truth, worth, and grace are not only measured by its capacity to arouse active participation, nor by its aesthetic cultural value, nor its long history of acceptance in the church, nor by its popular success, but because it allows believers

to cry out the *Kyrie eleisons* of the oppressed,
to sing the *Alleluias* of those restored to life,
and to uphold the *Maranatha* of the faithful
in the hope of the coming of the Kingdom.[48]

## Notes

1 Freedland, Jonathan, 2020, 'When our idols die, we mourn for our own loved ones too', *Guardian* Journal, 19 December.

2 https://music.churchofscotland.org.uk.

3 *In Tune with Heaven*, 1992, Report of the Archbishops' Commission on Church Music, London: Church House Publishing and Hodder & Stoughton, para. 167.

4 *Church Times* editorial, 8 May 1992.

5 Patrick, Millar, 1949, *Four Centuries of Scottish Psalmody*, Oxford: Oxford University Press, pp. 91f.

6 Harper, John, 2005, 'Throughout all generations', *Church Music Quarterly*, December, p. 7.

7 www.fontsmith.com/, blog, 2-18/08/15. Behind-the-scenes-tools-of-the-trade-with-richard-kindersley.

8 https://en.wikipedia.org/wiki/Notre-Dame_School, contemporary accounts.

9 See also the references to early metrical psalms and the *Red Book of Ossory* in Chapter 3.

10 The closely researched novel by James Meek, *To Calais, in Ordinary Time* (2020, Edinburgh: Canongate), set in south-west England in 1348, contains a description of such an event, including what would typically have been sung.

11 Reese, Gustave, 1954, *Music in the Renaissance*, London: Dent, pp. 66f, 779.

12 Bainton, Roland H., 1950, *Here I stand: A life of Martin Luther*, New York: Abingdon-Cokesbury Press, p. 69.

13 Matthew 13:24–30 (Authorized Version); modern versions contrast the wheat with 'weeds' or 'darnel'.

14 Clarke, Martin V., 2018, *British Methodist Hymnody: Theology, Heritage, and Experience*, Abingdon: Routledge, pp. 116f.

15 Prefaces of: *Church of Scotland Psalm and Hymn Tune Book*, 1870, Edinburgh: Thomas Nelson & Sons; *The Scottish Psalmody*, new and enlarged edition, 1866, Edinburgh: Thomas Nelson & Sons.

16 www.vatican.va/archive/hist_councils/ii_vatican_council/documents/vat-ii_const_19631204_sacrosanctum-concilium_en.html, chapter 6, 'Sacred Music' (accessed 17.5.21).

17 Ferguson, Michael, 2015, *Understanding the tensions in liturgical musicmaking in the Roman Catholic Church in contemporary Scotland*, PhD thesis, University of Edinburgh.

18 Bishops' Committee on the Liturgy, 1972, *Music in Catholic Worship*.

19 Snowbird Report, 1995, www.canticanova.com/articles/liturgy/art901.htm (accessed 17.5.21).

20 Duchesneau, Claude and Michel Veuthey, trans. Paul Inwood, 1992, *Music and Liturgy: The Universa Laus Document and Commentary*, Washington: The Pastoral Press, pp. 103–4.

21 Routley, Erik, 1980, *Church Music and the Christian Faith*, London: Collins Liturgical Publications, p. 65.

22 Routley, *Church Music and the Christian Faith*, pp. 89f.

23 Stein, Jock, 1988, *Singing a New Song: Fresh Resources for Christian Praise*, Edinburgh: The Handsel Press, p. 7.

24 Bent, Helen, 2017, *Inspiring Music in Worship: A Short Course of Guided Conversations for Churches*, Salisbury: Royal School of Church Music, in partnership with Praxis.

25 See also Bent, H. and L. Tipple, 2013–14, *Worship 4 Today: A Course for Worship Leaders and Musicians*, London: Church House Publishing.

26 Pahl, Irmgard, 1998, 'Music and the liturgical celebration', *Studia Liturgica*, Vol. 28, No. 1, pp. 1–13, translated from the German by Robert J. Daly, SJ.

27 Leaver, Robin A. and James H. Litton (eds), 1985, *Duty and Delight: Routley Remembered*, Norwich: Canterbury Press.

28 Routley, *Church Music and the Christian Faith*, pp. 20, 76.

29 Routley, *Church Music and the Christian Faith*, pp. 32, 71.

30 Routley, *Church Music and the Christian Faith*, pp. 74, 76, 94.

31 Routley, *Church Music and the Christian Faith*, p. 42.

32 Routley, *Church Music and the Christian Faith*, p. 35.

33 Routley, *Church Music and the Christian Faith*, p. 91.

34 Begbie, Jeremy S., 2000, *Theology, Music and Time*, Cambridge: Cambridge University Press, p. 106.

35 Ferguson, *Understanding the tensions*.

36 Burch Brown, Frank, 2000, *Good Taste, Bad Taste and Christian Taste: Aesthetics in Religious Life*, Oxford: Oxford University Press, p. 23.

37 Lathrop, Gordon W., 1999, *Holy People: A Liturgical Ecclesiology*, Minneapolis, MN: Fortress Press, pp. 129–30.

38 Funk, Virgil C., 1998, 'Secular music in the liturgy? Are there any rules?', *Studia Liturgica*, Vol. 28, No. 2, pp. 185f.

39 The *St Anne* and *Galloway* Masses. Individual movements can be found in hymn books listed in Appendix 1.

40 For example: *Water of Life: A Festival Service for Young Voices*, 1992, Croydon: Royal School of Church Music.

41 From the hymn 'When, in our music, God is glorified' by Fred Pratt Green.

42 Saliers, Don E., 2007, *Music and Theology*, Nashville, TN: Abingdon Press, pp. 67f.

43 Saliers, Don E., 1981, 'The integrity of sung prayer', *Worship*, Vol. 55, No. 4, p. 294.

44 Mitchell, Nathan D., 2004, 'The amen corner', *Worship*, January 2004, 78, No. 1, pp. 67–72.

45 Best, Thomas F. and Günter Gassmann (eds), 1994, *On the Way to Fuller Koinonia*, Faith and Order Paper No. 166, Geneva: WCC Publications, p. 275.

46 From the hymn by George Matheson, 'O Love that wilt not let me go'.

47 Routley, *Church Music and the Christian Faith*, p. 67.

48 Duchesneau et al., *Music and Liturgy*, Section 10.1, p. 26.

# Appendixes

# Appendix 1

# Table of Hymns and
# Tunes Referred to

A&M – *Ancient and Modern* (2013)
StF – *Singing the Faith* (2011)
CH4 – *Church Hymnary 4* (2005)
(also published as *Hymns of Glory, Songs of Praise*)
Lau – *Laudate* (2000, latest edition 2009)

## Hymns

|  | A&M | StF | CH4 | Lau |
|---|---|---|---|---|
| Abide with me | 10 | 141 | 580 | 907 |
| All creatures of my God and King | 532 | 99 | 147 | 694 |
| All glory, laud, and honour | 159 | 262 | 364 | 229 |
| All my hope on God is founded | 584 | 455 | 192 | 959 |
| All things bright and beautiful | 533 | 100 | 137 | 685 |
| All you works of God | x | x | 151 | · x |
| Alleluia (Word of the Father) | x | x | 428 | x |
| Alleluia *other versions* | | *See indexes* | | |
| Amen, Alleluia | 830 | x | 822 | x |
| And can it be | 588 | 345 | 396 | 790 |
| Angel voices ever singing | 589 | 39 | 498 | 724 |
| Be still for the presence of the Lord | 358 | 20 | 189 | 720 |
| Be thou my vision | 595 | 545 | 465 | 970 |
| Blessing and honour and glory and power | x | x | 441 | x |
| Bright the cloud | x | x | 353 | x |
| Brother, sister, let me serve you | 604 | 611 | 694 | 924 |
| Calm me, Lord | 832 | 624 | x | x |
| Christ, of God unseen the image | x | x | 453 | x |

| | A&M | StF | CH4 | Lau |
|---|---|---|---|---|
| Christ, whose glory fills the skies | 2 | 134 | 578 | 670 |
| Come, all you people | 361 | 22 | 757 | x |
| Come, Holy Ghost, our souls inspire | 241 | 373 | 586 | x |
| Come, let us eat for now the feast is spread | x | x | 660 | x |
| Come let us seek our God's protection | x | x | 487 | x |
| Come, let us to the Lord our God | 117 | x | 482 | x |
| Eastertide Acclamation | x | x | 428 | x |
| Eat this bread | 442 | 583 | 661 | 633 |
| Eternal Father, strong to save | 623 | 517 | 260 | 963 |
| For all the saints | 296 | 745 | 740 | 371 |
| Glory to God (Peru) | 416 | 753 | 762 | x |
| God bless to us our bread | x | x | 763 | x |
| God moves in a mysterious way | 647 | 104 | 158 | x |
| God, we praise you | 402 | x | 120 | x |
| Goodness is stronger than evil | 835 | x | x | x |
| Halle, halle | 836 | x | 345 | 178 |
| He came down that we may have love | x | x | 359 | x |
| He came to earth | x | 445 | 394 | x |
| He is exalted | x | 52 | 437 | x |
| He is Lord | x | 348 | 443 | 761 |
| Here am I, Lord (Northumbria) | x | 552 | x | x |
| How deep the Father's love | 144 | x | 549 | x |
| How shall I sing that majesty? | 663 | 53 | 128 | x |
| How sweet the name of Jesus sounds | 664 | 322 | 461 | x |
| I heard the voice | 669 | 248 | 540 | 795 |
| I, the Lord of sea and sky | 494 | 663 | 251 | 865 |
| I to the hills will lift mine eyes | x | x | 81 | x |
| In Christ alone | 678 | 351 | x | x |
| Jesus, name above all names | x | x | 774 | x |
| Jesus shall reign where'er the sun | 691 | 328 | 470 | 322 |
| Jesu tawa pano | x | 27 | 773 | x |
| Just as I am | 451 | 556 | 553 | x |
| Know that God is good | x | x | 788 | x |
| Kyrie eleison (Ukraine) | 372 | 750 | 776 | 519 |
| Lamb of God | | See indexes | | |
| Let us build a house where love can dwell | 365 | 409 | 198 | 458 |
| Lifted high on your cross | x | x | 386 | x |

| | A&M | StF | CH4 | Lau |
|---|---|---|---|---|
| Like the murmur of the dove's song | 252 | 389 | 592 | x |
| Listen now for the Gospel (Alleluia) | x | x | 779 | x |
| Longing for light | 42 | 706 | 543 | 883 |
| Lord, have mercy | | *See indexes* | | |
| Lord, hear our cry | 404 | x | x | x |
| Lord Jesus, think on me | 127 | x | 491 | 204 |
| Lord of all being | x | x | 125 | x |
| Lord, speak to me | 718 | x | 542 | x |
| Lord, teach us how to pray aright | 129 | x | 545 | x |
| Lord, the light (Shine, Jesus, shine) | 719 | 59 | 448 | 770 |
| Love divine, all loves excelling | 721 | 503 | 519 | 801 |
| Make me a channel of your peace | 725 | 707 | 528 | 898 |
| Mayenziwe (Your will be done) | 412 | 760 | 805 | x |
| May the God of peace go with us | x | x | 786 | x |
| May the Lord, mighty God | x | x | 787 | x |
| Most glorious Lord of life | 210 | x | 215 | x |
| My hope is built on nothing less | x | x | x | x |
| Night has fallen | x | 145 | 222 | x |
| Now go in peace | x | x | 789 | x |
| Now let us from this table rise | 456 | 596 | 675 | 647 |
| O for a thousand tongues | 742 | 364 | 352 | x |
| O God of Bethel | 744 | 475 | 268 | x |
| O laughing Light | x | x | 135 | x |
| O Lord, listen to my prayer | 406 | x | x | x |
| O Lord my God! when I in awesome | 546 | 82 | 154 | 721 |
| O Lord, the clouds are gathering | x | x | 708 | x |
| O thou who camest from above | 258 | 564 | 625 | x |
| O worship the King | 754 | 113 | 127 | 683 |
| One bread, one body | 461 | x | 665 | 832 |
| On Jordan's bank | 46 | 182 | 334 | 94 |
| Over my head, I hear music in the air | x | x | 575 | x |
| Praise my soul | 766 | 83 | 160 | 807 |
| Prayer is the soul's sincere desire | 767 | 529 | 546 | x |
| Salvation belongs to our God | x | x | 131 | x |
| Santo | x | 779 | 769 | 723 |
| Seek ye first | 775 | 254 | 641 | 820 |
| Send me, Lord (Thuma mina) | 481 | 782 | 800 | x |

| | A&M | StF | CH4 | Lau |
|---|---|---|---|---|
| Sent by the Lord | 482 | 239 | 250 | 855 |
| Singing, we gladly worship | x | x | 257 | x |
| Source and Sovereign, Rock and Cloud | x | x | 133 | x |
| Spirit divine, attend our prayers | 260 | x | 583 | x |
| Spirit of Jesus, if I love my neighbour | x | x | 621 | x |
| Spirit of the living God | 263 | 395 | 619 | 306 |
| Stay with me | 172 | 780 | 793 | 249 |
| Take, O take me as I am | 336 | 781 | 795 | x |
| Tell out my soul | 394 | 186 | 286 | 880 |
| The peace of the earth be with you | 845 | 774 | 798 | 901 |
| There is a Redeemer | 805 | 338 | 559 | x |
| There's a Spirit in the air | 265 | 398 | 616 | x |
| The Saviour died and rose again | x | x | 425 | x |
| The spacious firmament on high | 550 | x | 148 | x |
| The Virgin Mary | x | x | 300 | x |
| This is my will, my new command | x | x | 357 | 921 |
| This is the body of Christ | 469 | x | 799 | x |
| Thuma mina (Send me, Lord) | 481 | 782 | 800 | x |
| Thy Kingdom come! | 815 | x | 473 | x |
| To God be the glory | 818 | 94 | 512 | 719 |
| Unless a (single) grain of wheat | 155 | x | 347 | 748 |
| We believe in God the Father (TDS) | 403 | 764 | x | x |
| We have a gospel to proclaim | 507 | 418 | 363 | 852 |
| We need each other's voice to sing | 508 | x | x | x |
| We will walk with God | 846 | 484 | 803 | x |
| When, in our music, God is glorified | 821 | 731 | 203 | 729 |
| When I survey the wondrous Cross | 157 | 287 | 392 | 756 |
| When Jesus the healer | x | x | 350 | x |
| Word of the Father (JLB) | x | x | 480 | 740 |
| Ye gates, lift up your heads (Ps. 24) | x | x | 19 | x |
| Ye holy angels bright | 826 | 69 | 179 | x |
| Your will be done (Mayenziwe) | 412 | 760 | 805 | x |

## Tunes

| | A&M | StF | CH4 | Lau |
|---|---|---|---|---|
| Abbot's Leigh | 315 | 410 | 615 | 344 |
| All for Jesus | 246 | 341 | 187 | x |
| Beach Spring | x | x | 252 | 828 |
| Bishopthorpe | 7 | x | 22 | x |
| Blaenwern | 337 | 503 | 468 | 328 |
| Bon Accord | x | x | 59 | x |
| Bonnie George Campbell | x | x | 165 | x |
| Church Triumphant | 93 | x | 129 | x |
| Coe Fen | 663 | 667 | 128 | 431 |
| Crimond | 799 | 480 | 14 | 806 |
| Croft's 136$^{th}$ | 278 | 16 | 92 | x |
| Cwm Rhondda | 652 | 465 | 113 | 960 |
| Desert (Lyngham) | 742 | 364 | 352 | x |
| Diadem | x | 342 | 457 | x |
| Down Ampney | 238 | 372 | 489 | 303 |
| Dunfermline | 657 | 9 | 70 | x |
| Ein' Feste Burg | 759 | 623 | 454 | 826 |
| Elgin | x | x | x | x |
| Engelberg | 491 | 731 | 203 | 729 |
| Finlandia | 524 | 419 | 691 | x |
| French (Dundee) | 52 | 549 | 81 | 168 |
| Galloway Tam | x | x | 284 | x |
| Guiting Power | 612 | 319 | 436 | 763 |
| Hereford | 258 | 564 | 625 | x |
| Highwood | 37 | 3 | 246 | 415 |
| Holy Manna | 504 | x | 655 | 285 |
| Hyfrydol | 422 | 103 | 39 | 421 |
| Invocation | x | x | 35 | x |
| Kelvingrove | 510 | 339 | 533 | 877 |
| Kingsfold | 204 | 231 | 291 | 180 |
| Lauds | 265 | 398 | 616 | x |
| Lobe den Herren | 310 | 88 | 124 | 601 |
| London New | 647 | 111 | 28 | x |
| Love Unknown | 147 | 277 | 238 | 752 |
| Lux Tremenda | x | x | 120 | x |

| | A&M | StF | CH4 | Lau |
|---|---|---|---|---|
| Lydia | x | 357 | x | x |
| Lyngham (Desert) | 742 | 364 | 352 | x |
| Martyrs | x | x | 34 | x |
| Nettleton | 618 | 494 | 339 | 836 |
| Old Hundredth | 357 | 1 | 63 | 466 |
| Orlington | x | x | 15 | x |
| O Waly Waly | 165 | 287 | 234 | 165 |
| Prabhoo Lay Lay | x | x | 571 | x |
| Richmond | 613 | 155 | 352 | x |
| Sagina | 588 | 345 | 396 | 790 |
| Salzburg | 198 | 475 | 268 | 269 |
| Sheffield | x | x | 46 | x |
| Shout on | x | x | 423 | x |
| Sine nomine | 296 | 745 | 736 | 371 |
| Somos Pueblo | x | x | 262 | x |
| Song 24 | 133 | x | 40 | x |
| St Botolph | 313 | 588 | 1 | 331 |
| St George's Edinburgh | x | x | 19 | x |
| St John/Havergal | x | 208 | 104 | x |
| Stroudwater | x | x | 6 | x |
| The Flower o' the Quern | x | x | 552 | x |
| The Rowan Tree | x | x | 540 | x |
| Vox dilecti | x | 248 | 408 | x |
| Vulpius | 203 | 755 | 412 | 259 |
| Westminster Abbey | 291 | 207 | 200 | 250 |
| Wolvercote | 748 | 563 | 644 | 875 |
| Woodlands | 394 | 186 | 286 | 108 |
| York | x | x | 79 | x |

# Appendix 2

# Planning Worship: Resources

### Sunday by Sunday
Lists hymns and songs from 14 collections; anthems and vocal music; Iona, world songs and shorter songs and chants; psalms; organ music (graded for difficulty); music for children and all-age worship, for each Sunday in the Christian Year, based on the Revised Common Lectionary, the *Common Worship* Sunday Lectionary and the Roman Lectionary. There are also special articles and features, reviews and orders of service for festivals. Available to individual members and affiliated congregations of the Royal School of Church Music (RSCM): email, membership@rscm.com.

### Hymn books
Many hymn books have thematic, biblical and other indexes. *Ancient & Modern* (2013) and *Laudate* also have selections from their contents for every Sunday and feast day in the Christian Calendar across the three-year cycle.

## Online resources

### The Canterbury Dictionary of Hymnology
https://hymnology.hymnsam.co.uk
This is the successor to the iconic Julian's Dictionary of Hymnology first published in 1892. Ecumenical and international, it has over 5,600 individual entries on hymns, authors, hymnals, organisations, themes, tunes and composers. It is regularly updated. There is an annual subscription (subscribe online).

## Singing the Faith Plus website

www.methodist.org.uk/our-faith/worship/singing-the-faith-plus
Suggestions for hymns and shorter songs and chants from the
Methodist hymn book *Singing the Faith* (2011) in accord with
the Revised Common Lectionary. The website supports and
complements the printed hymn book with: information about
the contents of the book, indexes, news, features, articles (for
example, help in leading worship), and new, unpublished
hymns and songs.

## Church of Scotland websites

www.churchofscotland.org.uk/worship
Suggests material for all aspects of worship, including music
and preaching, based on the Revised Common Lectionary. The
tunes of all hymns in *Church Hymnary 4* sung by a variety of
local choirs as well as background notes on the writers and
the circumstances of writing can be found on https://music.
churchofscotland.org.uk.

## Hymn Quest

https://hymnquest.com
This is a hymn and worship song database set up by the Pratt
Green Trust and published in software form by Stainer & Bell
Ltd. It is edited by Andrew Pratt and Don Pickard. A very
comprehensive list of hymns is offered, searchable for themes,
sources, tunes, authors and composers etc. There is a free
online version where only public-domain hymns can be seen
and searched, and versions requiring an annual subscription,
one of which allows the export of all public-domain texts and
another which gives copyright cover via a One Licence or CCLI
licence. These last are only available, for copyright reasons, to
residents in the UK and Ireland.

# Sources of music

## Music from the Taizé Community
www.taizé.fr/en > Community > The Brothers' Work > Download recordings and printable music. There is also an online shop for books and printed scores and information about getting permission.

## The Wild Goose Resource Group (Iona Community)
www.wildgoose.scot
'Liturgy and worship, music and song, prayer and politics, diversity and devotion, participation and perception, curiosity and creativity.' The aim is to help congregations and clergy shape and create new forms of contextual and relevant, participative worship. The site has an online shop. Email: wildgoose@wildgoose.scot

## RSCM Music Direct
www.rscmshop.com
Music for choirs and organ in a wide variety of idioms. There is a comprehensive body of service music, both RSCM's own publications and some from other publishers.

## Kevin Mayhew
www.kevinmayhew.com
Collections of organ music, easy-to-play-hymns, the Hymns Old and New series, mass settings, choral music etc.

## Song and Hymn Writers Foundation
www.jubilate.co.uk
A long-standing focus for authors and composers, now some 60 in number, with new congregational songs in a variety of styles. It has an online shop. 'Resound' (below) is associated.

## Worship song sites
https://resoundworship.org
Resound Worship is a collective of British worship songwriters, established in 2006, 'seeking to resource the church with songs

that engage heart, mind and soul'. The songs are birthed in the local church and then refined by a process of collaboration and peer critique through songwriting groups, before they are shared more widely on the website. A recent album is *Doxecology* (13 new songs on the themes of creation, ecology and Christian hope, with an accompanying study guide).

www.theportersgate.com is an American site which is a forum for 'justice songs' and 'lament songs'.

www.wendellk.com (USA) and www.thepsalmproject.nl (Netherlands) set out to combine the psalms with a worship-song format, the latter specifically making some use of Reformation forms.

www.satelliteworship.com is a collective of songwriters from churches across Scotland.

*Several of the writers mentioned in the book have their own websites, where new work is made known.*

## Playing and accompanying

### Simple hymn arrangements
www.churchservicesociety.org – Simple hymn arrangements
This is a growing bank of simpler arrangements of hymn tunes to assist those in the earlier stages of learning to play piano or organ. They are in two parts or three. Free to download.

### An introductory course on improvisation
www.churchservicesociety.org – Learning to improvise
Brigitte Harris's three-part course is intended for novices in improvisation. No prior experience of improvisation is needed. It begins with simple melodies, then moves on to two-part playing, the addition of chordal patterns and the use of rhythm. Free to download.

# Bodies that support church music

## Royal School of Church Music

www.rscm.org.uk, www.rscmshop.com

The RSCM provides a wide range of resources and training, particularly through its education and publishing departments. These include: *Voice for Life* – a comprehensive scheme to support and promote singing in church and school; *Church Music Skills* – training programmes for organists, cantors and music leaders; *Lift up your voice* – a scheme for churches with few or no musical resources; *Music for Mission and Ministry* – for worship leaders, ordained and lay, and musicians. It publishes *Church Music Quarterly* and *Sunday by Sunday* (see above). Individual membership and congregational affiliation.

## The Hymn Society of Great Britain and Ireland

https://hymnsocietygbi.org.uk

The Society encourages study and research in hymnody, promotes good standards of hymn singing, encourages the discerning use of hymns and songs in worship, publishes a quarterly bulletin. There is a useful (free) online series of short guides on many aspects of music in worship, including hymn suggestions for particular events such as baptisms and funerals, or situations such as those where people with dementia are present. There is an annual subscription, which also gives free access to the online *Canterbury Dictionary of Hymnology.*

## Scottish Churches Organist Training Scheme

www.scotsorgan.org.uk

SCOTS exists to find and encourage emerging organists as well as to assist those already in posts who wish to develop their skills. The focus is not so much on achieving technical brilliance as on developing the gifts, skills and understanding to contribute to a more satisfying experience of worship for the whole congregation. Participants work at their own pace towards three successive certificates but with occasional meetings with an Adviser who is an experienced organist and church musician. They follow the SCOTS syllabus, which lists organ pieces and hymn/psalm tunes, chants and settings suitable for each stage. There are regular Local Organ Workshops in different parts of Scotland. SCOTS is a partnership between the Scottish Federation of Organists, the RSCM in Scotland, the Royal College of Organists, and the Scottish Churches.

## Praxis

www.praxisworship.org.uk

Praxis works with RSCM to support ministerial training across the church. It is sponsored by the Liturgical Commission of the Church of England, the Alcuin Club, and the Group for Renewal of Worship. It provides opportunities in which different worshipping traditions of the church can meet and engage creatively with one another. It publishes the quarterly magazine *Praxis News of Worship*. Back numbers are archived on www.praxisworship.org.uk/praxis_news_of_worship.html

# Appendix 3

# Further Reading

## *Liturgy and worship*

Baker, Jonny, 2010, *Curating Worship*, London: SPCK.

Berger, Teresa (ed.), 2019, *Full of Your Glory: Liturgy, Cosmos, Creation*, Collegeville, MN: Liturgical Press Academic.

Bradshaw, Paul F. (ed.), 2002, *The New SCM Dictionary of Liturgy and Worship*, London: SCM Press.

Bradshaw, Paul and Peter Moger, 2008, *Worship Changes Lives: How it Works, Why it Matters*, London: Church House Publishing.

Cherry, Constance M., 2010, *The Worship Architect: A Blueprint for Designing Culturally Relevant and Biblically Faithful Services*, Grand Rapids, MI: Baker Academic.

Clifton-Soderstrom, Michelle A. and David D. Bjorlin, 2014, *Incorporating Children in Worship*, Eugene, OR: Cascade Books.

Evdokimov, Paul, trans. Steven Bigham, 1990, *The Art of the Icon*, Redondo Beach, CA: Oakwood Publications.

Getty, Keith and Kristyn, 2017, *Sing! How Worship Transforms your Life, Family and Church*, Nashville, TN: B&H Publishing Group.

Grainger, Roger, 2009, *The Drama of the Rite: Worship, Liturgy and Theatre Performance*, Brighton: Sussex Academic Press.

Harper, Sally, P. S. Barnwell and Magnus Williamson (eds), *Late Medieval Liturgies Enacted: The Experience of Worship in Cathedral and Parish Church*, Farnham: Ashgate.

Holmes, Stephen Mark, 2015, *Sacred Signs in Reformation Scotland: Interpreting Worship, 1488–1590*, Oxford: Oxford University Press.

Hunter, Graham, 2017, *Discipline and Desire: Embracing Charismatic Liturgical Worship*, W233, Cambridge: Grove Books.

Lathrop, Gordon W., 1999, *Holy People: A Liturgical Ecclesiology*, Minneapolis, MN: Fortress Press.

Moger, Peter, 2009, *Crafting Common Worship: A Practical, Creative Guide to What's Possible*, London: Church House Publishing.

Papadopulos, Nicholas (ed.), 2011, *God's Transforming Work*, London: SPCK.

Spinks, Bryan D., 2010, *The Worship Mall: Contemporary Responses to Contemporary Culture*, London: SPCK.

Spinks, Bryan D., 2020, *Scottish Presbyterian Worship: Proposals for Organic Change, 1843 to the Present Day*, Edinburgh: St Andrew Press.

Stancliffe, David, 2003, *God's Pattern: Shaping our Worship, Ministry and Life*, London: SPCK.

Steven, James H. S., 2002, *Worship in the Spirit: Charismatic Worship in the Church of England*, Milton Keynes: Paternoster Press.

Witvliet, John D., 2003, *Worship Seeking Understanding: Windows into Christian Practice*, Grand Rapids, MI: Baker Academic.

## Music in worship

Darlington, Stephen and Alan Kreider, 2003, *Composing Music for Worship*, Norwich: Canterbury Press.

Documents of the Second Vatican Council, 1963, *Sacrosanctum Concilium*, chapter 6, 'Sacred Music'.

Ingalls, Monique M., 2018, *Singing the Congregation: How Contemporary Worship Music Forms Evangelical Community*, Oxford: Oxford University Press.

Joncas, Jan Michael, 1997, *From Sacred Song to Ritual Music: Twentieth-Century Understandings of Roman Catholic Worship Music*, Collegeville, MN: The Liturgical Press.

Kroeker, Charlotte (ed.), 2003, *Music in Christian Worship* (Collegeville, MN: The Liturgical Press).

Ward, Pete, 2005, *Selling Worship: How What We Sing Has Changed the Church*, Milton Keynes: Paternoster Press.

Westermeyer, Paul, 1998, *Te Deum: The Church and Music*, Minneapolis, MN: Fortress Press.

## Church music in practice

Bell, John L., 2000, *The Singing Thing*, Glasgow: Wild Goose Publications.

Bell, John L., 2007, *The Singing Thing Too*, Glasgow: Wild Goose Publications.

Bent, Helen, 2017, *Inspiring Music in Worship: A Short Course of Guided Conversations for Churches*, Salisbury: Royal School of Church Music, with Praxis.

Earey, Mark, 2009, *How to Choose Songs and Hymns for Worship*, W201, Cambridge: Grove Books.

Harrison, Anne, 2003, *Sing It Again: The Place of Short Songs in Worship*, W176, Cambridge: Grove Books.

Harrison, Anne, 2009, *Recovering the Lord's Song: Getting Sung Scripture Back into Worship*, W198, Cambridge: Grove Books.

Jones, Kate, 2000, *Keeping Your Nerve: Confidence-Boosting Strategies for Musicians and Performers*, London: Faber Music.

Thomas, Andy, 2020, *Resounding Body: Building Church Communities Through Music*, Durham: Sacristy Press.

## Hymns

Bradley, Ian, 1997, *Abide with Me: The World of Victorian Hymns*, London: SCM Press *and other titles*.

Brown, Rosalind, 2001, *How Hymns Shape our Lives*, S78, Cambridge: Grove Books (e-book).

Routley, Erik, 1957, *The Music of Christian Hymnody*, London: Independent Press.

Routley, Erik, 1968, *Words, Music, and the Church*, London: Herbert Jenkins *and other titles*.

Watson, J. R., 1999, *The English Hymn: A Critical and Historical Study*, Oxford: Oxford University Press.

Wootton, Janet (ed.), 2010, *This is Our Song: Women's Hymn-Writing*, London: Epworth.

Wren, Brian, 2000, *Praying Twice: The Music and Words of Congregational Song*, Louisville, KY: Westminster John Knox Press.

## Church music history

Clarke, Martin V., 2018, *British Methodist Hymnody: Theology, Heritage and Experience*, London: Routledge.

Dowley, Tim, 2018, *Christian Music: A Global History*, London: SPCK.

Duguid, Timothy, 2014, *Metrical Psalmody in Print and Practice*, Farnham: Ashgate.

Foley, Edward, 1992, *Foundations of Christian Music: The Music of Pre-Constantinian Christianity*, Alcuin/GROW Liturgical Study 22–23, Nottingham: Grove Books.

Forrester, Duncan B. and Douglas M. Murray, 1996 (second edition), *Studies in the History of Worship in Scotland*, Edinburgh: T & T Clark.

Gant, Andrew, 2016, *O Sing unto the Lord: A History of English Church Music*, London: Profile Books.

Patrick, Millar, 1949, *Four Centuries of Scottish Psalmody*, Oxford: Oxford University Press.

Routley, Erik, 1977, *A Short History of English Church Music*, Oxford: A. R. Mowbray Ltd.

## Church music and theology

Begbie, Jeremy, 2000, *Theology, Music and Time*, Cambridge: Cambridge University Press *and other titles.*
Drake, Nick, 2015, *A Deeper Note: The 'Informal' Theology of Contemporary Sung Worship*, W218, Cambridge: Grove Books.
Duchesnau, Claude and Michel Veuthey, trans. Paul Inwood, 1992, *Music and Liturgy: The Universa Laus Document and Commentary*, Washington: The Pastoral Press.
Foley, Edward, 1984, *Music in Ritual: A Pre-Theological Investigation*, Washington: The Pastoral Press.
McGann, Mary E., 2002, *Exploring Music as Worship and Theology: Research in Liturgical Practice*, Collegeville, MN: The Liturgical Press.
Routley, Erik, 1980, *Church Music and the Christian Faith*, London: Collins Liturgical Publications.
Saliers, Don, 2007, *Music and Theology*, Nashville, TN: Abingdon Press.

## Leading worship

Hovda, Robert W., 1976, *Strong, Loving, and Wise: Presiding in Liturgy*, Collegeville, MN: The Liturgical Press.
Long, Kimberley Bracken, 2009, *The Worshiping Body: The Art of Leading Worship*, Louisville, KY: Westminster John Knox Press.
Reynolds, Simon, 2014, *Table Manners: Liturgical Leadership for the Mission of the Church*, London: SCM Press.

## General

Aisthorpe, Steve, 2016, *The Invisible Church: Learning from the Experience of Churchless Christians*, Edinburgh: St Andrew Press.
Buchan, Alan and David A. Stewart, 2018, rev. 2020, *Organs in Scotland*, Edinburgh: Edinburgh Society of Organists.
Robinson, Edward, 1987, *The Language of Mystery*, London: SCM Press.

# Appendix 4

# A Prayer for the Music and Musicians of the Church

Creator God,
who made order out of chaos,
released truth from the midst of confusion,
and brought beauty to birth,
we give you thanks
that you have given to us
not only great reason for praise
but the forms in which to express it,
with songs which refresh our souls
and sonorities which move us to new faith,
so that with mirth and melody
we may declare your glory.

We pray for the church at worship
as it feels for the cadences of our time,
that it may both be renewed by its traditions
and recalled to old truths through new sounds.

We pray for those who exercise a ministry of music
– choir and congregation,
clergy, musicians, administrators –
that each may value the gifts of the other
and seek to build each other up in skill and in love.

We pray for congregations where resources are few
but the desire to praise is great.
Make eloquent what struggles to be heard

and magnify the gifts that are least
that all may feel they sing with the angel choir.

Now we who lift our voices
remember those who are cast down;
we who have ample cause to praise
remember those on whose lips the song has died;
we who sing with confidence
remember those who have to whisper in the shadows.
Save us and all people
from pursuing joy without justice,
from continuing in celebration
while others lack the means to live.

In all the music we make
may we and all believers be enabled
to cry out the Kyrie eleisons of the oppressed,
to sing the Alleluias of those restored to life,
and to uphold the Maranatha of the faithful
in the hope of the coming of the Kingdom.

*Written by the author for the Royal School of Church
Music's Celebration Day in Glasgow Cathedral (St Mungo's),
18 September 1999*

# Index of Biblical References

# Index of Names and Subjects